RETHINKING THE BLACK FREEDOM MOVEMENT

Yohuru Williams

Routledge
Taylor & Francis Group
NEW YORK AND LONDON

First published 2016
by Routledge
711 Third Avenue, New York, NY 10017

And by Routledge
2 Park Square, Milton Park, Abingdon, Oxon OX14 4RN

Routledge is an imprint of the Taylor & Francis Group, an informa business

Library of Congress Cataloging in Publication Data
Names: Williams, Yohuru R., author.Title: Rethinking the black freedom movement / Yohuru Williams.Description: New York : Routledge, 2015. | Series: American social and poltical movements of the twentieth century | Includes bibliographical references.Identifiers: LCCN 2015019620Subjects: LCSH: African Americans—Civil rights—History—20th century. | Civil rights movements—United States—History—20th century. | Black power—United States—History—20th century.Classification: LCC E185.61 .W7377 2015 | DDC 323.1196/0730904—dc23LC record available at http://lccn.loc.gov/2015019620

ISBN: 978-0-415-82612-9 (hbk)
ISBN: 978-0-415-82614-3 (pbk)
ISBN: 978-0-203-43186-3 (ebk)

Typeset in Bembo
by Keystroke, Station Road, Codsall, Wolverhampton

RETHINKING THE BLACK FREEDOM MOVEMENT

The African American struggle for civil rights in the twentieth century is one of the most important stories in American history. With all the information available, however, it is easy for even the most enthusiastic reader to be overwhelmed. In *Rethinking the Black Freedom Movement*, Yohuru Williams has synthesized the complex history of this period into a clear and compelling narrative. Considering both the Civil Rights and Black Power Movements as distinct but overlapping elements of the Black Freedom Struggle, Williams looks at the impact of the struggle for Black Civil Rights on housing, transportation, education, labor, voting rights, culture, and more, and places the activism of the 1950s and 1960s within the context of a much longer tradition reaching from Reconstruction to the present day.

Exploring the different strands within the movement, key figures and leaders, and its ongoing legacy, *Rethinking the Black Freedom Movement* is the perfect introduction for anyone seeking to understand the struggle for Black Civil Rights in America.

Yohuru Williams is Professor of History and Dean of the College of Arts and Sciences at Fairfield University.

American Social and Political Movements of the Twentieth Century

Series Editor: Heather Ann Thompson, University of Michigan

Rethinking the American Anti-War Movement
By Simon Hall

Rethinking the Asian American Movement
By Daryl J. Maeda

Rethinking the Welfare Rights Movement
By Premilla Nadasen

Rethinking the Gay and Lesbian Movement
By Marc Stein

Rethinking American Women's Activism
By Annelise Orleck

Rethinking the Chicano Movement
By Marc Simon Rodriguez

Rethinking the Black Freedom Movement
By Yohuru Williams

CONTENTS

Editor's Series Introduction   *vii*
Preface: Under Our Own Power: Rethinking Black
Freedom Struggles   *ix*

1 "A Continuing Evolving Process": The Predecessors and
   Origins of the Civil Rights and Black Power Movements   1

2 America's Second Civil War   18

3 Power to the People: Black Power   49

4 The Art of War: The Cultural Productions of the 1950s
   and 1960s Era Black Freedom Struggles   87

5 "A Larger Freedom": The Strengths, Weaknesses, and
   Legacies of the Civil Rights and Black Power Movements   108

Bibliography   *123*
Index   *137*

EDITOR'S SERIES INTRODUCTION

Welcome to the *American Social and Political Movements of the Twentieth Century* series at Routledge. This collection of works by top historians from around the nation and world introduces students to the myriad movements that came together in the United States during the twentieth century to expand democracy, to reshape the political economy, and to increase social justice.

Each book in this series explores a particular movement's origins, its central goals, its leading as well as grassroots figures, its actions as well as ideas, and its most important accomplishments as well as serious missteps.

With this series of concise yet synthetic overviews and reassessments, students not only will gain a richer understanding of the many human rights and civil liberties that they take for granted today, but they will also newly appreciate how recent, how deeply contested, and thus how inherently fragile, are these same elements of American citizenship.

Heather Ann Thompson
University of Michigan

PREFACE

Under Our Own Power: Rethinking Black Freedom Struggles

> This is a national, not a southern, phenomenon. And it is largely unrelated to whether a particular State had or did not have segregative school laws.
>
> Justice Lewis F. Powell, *Keyes* v. *School District No. 1* (1973)[1]

On the afternoon of April 24, 1942, thousands of African American protestors convened on the state capitol at Annapolis, Maryland. The demonstrators came to protest the killing of an unarmed soldier named Thomas Broadus who was shot by Baltimore police officer Edward Bender. Broadus was one of 10 Black persons killed by police in Baltimore since Robert Stanton had become Commissioner of Police in that city in 1939. When local protests to remove Stanton and bring Broadus' killer to justice produced no results, the organizers turned their attention to the Governor. Lillie Jackson, the President of the Baltimore National Association for the Advancement of Colored People (NAACP) and the *Baltimore Afro-American* newspaper editor Carl Murphy had teamed up to mobilize more than 150 organizations and approximately 2,000 people under the aegis of a group called the Citizens' Committee for Justice. Lillie Jackson set the tone for the demonstration, reminding Governor Thomas O'Connor "this meeting is the direct result of your refusal to answer the letters of the National Association for the Advancement of Colored People asking for a conference in police killings in Baltimore."[2] While the protestors presumably came to ask for redress in the Broadus case, their demands covered what Carl Murphy described as five planks representing Black Baltimoreans' grievances including concerns over police brutality, high incarceration rates, employment discrimination, and greater representation on state boards. Prominent among the speakers that day were several Black women who, like Jackson, were key organizers of the march.

While the Annapolis protest focused on a local killing, it attracted national attention. The night before the march, New York Congressman Adam Clayton Powell, Jr., then one of only two African American representatives serving in Congress, arrived in Baltimore to address an overflow crowd gathered at a local church. "This year," Powell defiantly told those in attendance, "the future of the Black man is being written for the next 100 years." He continued: "It is up to the colored people now to save democracy in America, for it seems there is no one left in America who knows what democracy is." With "Nazism fascism on one hand and pseudo democracy on the other," Powell warned of the challenges ahead. We "have twelve million colored Americans without great leaders – misguided, misled, divided." Nevertheless, he remained hopeful. "It is up to us to move or die," Powell strenuously asserted. "We must move now under our own power or be exterminated."[3]

The 1942 Annapolis march was by no means an anomaly. In 1941 labor and Civil Rights leader A. Philip Randolph organized a campaign aimed at compelling President Franklin D. Roosevelt to end discrimination in the nation's defense industries. The President narrowly averted a mass march on Washington, the central feature of the campaign, by issuing Executive Order 8802 outlawing such discrimination. One of Randolph's chief lieutenants was Benjamin F. McLaurin, a longtime labor leader who had helped to organize sleeping-car porters in the 1920s and 1930s and who Baltimore activists called upon in April of 1942 to help organize the Annapolis march. NAACP activists such as Lillie Jackson were critical to local and national desegregation efforts. For instance, the NAACP legal campaign against segregation helped secure important Supreme Court decisions in interstate transportation, voting rights, and education. Unrest nevertheless punctuated the period. Serious race riots in Detroit and New York in 1943 preceded postwar violence against African Americans, especially in the South where loose efforts at attacking segregation and inequality took shape.

As in Baltimore, in the years during and after World War II, African Americans and their allies confronted racial segregation in six key areas: housing, education, labor practices, access to places of public accommodation, voting rights, and Jim Crow Justice. At the 1942 Annapolis March, for instance, Mrs. Virgie Waters, president of the Master Beauticians used the occasion to challenge exclusion by demanding representation on the State Board of Beauty Culturists and Hairdressers for the "1,100 of the 2,340 beauticians in the State of Maryland" of color and the 400 shops "operated by colored beauticians."[4]

As should be clear, this story of police brutality in Baltimore and the subsequent Annapolis march is not a discursive digression into antiquarian protests of a bygone era. It is an affirmation of the relevance, as well as the need to consider a much longer view of the Civil Rights and Black Power Movements of the 1950s and 1960s—characterized in this volume as the Black Freedom Struggles of the 1950s and 1960s. As the historian Rhonda Y. Williams has observed, the ideas that informed Black Freedom Struggles, such as the Black Power Movement, "were not only firmly grounded in the experiences that punctuated black lives and freedom struggles for many decades, but also produced the particular child of the post–World War II era." "Providing a longer narrative arc," she continues in *Concrete Demands*, "exposes not just the activists and organizations, but also Black Power's coming of age process with stages of development, contingencies, ruptures and continuities, and historical markers that help to expose a rich and nuanced story—not necessarily a lengthier story without distinctions."[5]

Reimaging Black Freedom Struggles

In the opening to every volume of the Harlan Davidson American History book series, historians John Hope Franklin and Abraham Eisenstadt write that, "Every generation writes its own history, for the reason that it sees the past in the foreshortened perspective of its own experience."[6] As the nation pauses to remember the 50th anniversary of the passage of the Voting Rights Act of 1965 in 2015, there is perhaps more interest in Black Freedom Struggles than at any time in the nation's history, even as much of what those struggles fought to accomplish seems to be in jeopardy.

Alongside the victories accomplished by the Black Freedom Struggles are the challenges of the contemporary moment, including staggering Black unemployment rates, widespread police brutality, and unprecedented mass incarceration. A boom in the number of studies dedicated to Black Freedom Struggles over the last two decades has resulted in an enriched historiography of the Civil Rights and Black Power Movements—one that has not only documented the past and sought to make sense of the present, but also raised substantive questions about how we understand the history and legacies of both.

Periodization and Parameters

Much of the new scholarship has displaced an older narrative that viewed the Civil Rights Movement, in particular, as the product of distinct forces inspired largely by the U.S. Supreme Court's 1954 decision in *Brown* v. *Board of Education* and coalescing in the early 1950s. The dominant 1954 to 1968 paradigm that bracketed the Civil Rights Movement between the *Brown* decision and the assassination of the Reverend Dr. Martin Luther King, Jr. has given way, at least in academic circles, to a much broader view. More recently published historical works have pushed the temporal boundaries of the movement to the World War II era where much of the groundwork and antecedents for both the Civil Rights and Black Power Movements can be found.

Periodization of the movement, nevertheless, remains a cause of disagreement. While the *Brown* decision still looms large in most accounts of 1950s and

1960s Black Freedom Struggles, scholars have recognized the limitations of any periodization that does not take into account the histories and activism of various persons and groups who contributed to lesser-known precedents. The *Brown* case was the culmination of more than 30 years of legal wrangling and hard won legal precedents established by the NAACP as it sought to undermine "separate but equal" as established by the U.S. Supreme Court in *Plessy* v. *Ferguson* (1896).

Several historians, including Jacqueline Dowd Hall, Robin D.G. Kelley, Thomas Sugrue, and Nikhil Singh, have suggested pushing the temporal boundaries of the Civil Rights Movement beyond the standard 1954 to 1968 paradigm to stress important antecedents that help lay the groundwork for the Civil Rights Movement. Expanding the time frame of the movement has allowed for important events—such as the passage of Federal Employment Practices Commission, the desegregation of the military, the integration of baseball, and the 1947 Freedom Rides—to be included in the narrative of the movement.[7] This "long" Civil Rights Movement thesis also has created room for some historians to highlight what they consider important organizational ties between Civil Rights groups and organized labor that coalesced around the New Deal and World War II, as well as crucial intersections between Black activism, Third World anticolonial struggles, and the often overlooked peace and pacifist movement.[8] Labor historians Nelson Lichtenstein and Robert Korstad, for example, situate the origins of the Civil Rights Movement (not without some debate) in radical labor activism in the 1940s, "when the social structure of black America took an increasingly urban proletarian character."[9] In his book *A New Deal for Blacks*, Harvard Sitkoff likewise traces the emergence of Civil Rights as a national concern to the Depression decade—a time period that saw an incredible increase of the national NAACP's membership from 50,000 to 450,000 members.[10]

While the birth of some organizations and the expansion of others was an important step in the growth of Civil Rights struggles, historian Robert Norell also asked readers to pay attention to local differences. He insisted that the Civil Rights Movement had a "different experience in each place." In other words, he maintains that, unlike in the 1950s and 1960s, there was no centralized national movement in the earlier decades. In the 1930s and 1940s, the South witnessed "not just a few tantalizing moments of protest but a widespread, if not yet mature, struggle to overthrow segregation and institutionalized racism."[11] There is certainly abundant evidence to support this argument and to serve as a reminder that in rethinking the Black Freedom Struggles, one must pay attention to not only the existence of similar struggles, but also how they might be dissimilarly expressed.

While the notion of a long Civil Rights Movement or long Civil Rights era extending back to the 1930s has gained currency, unsurprisingly there are dissenters from this view. Historians Sundiata Cha Jua and Clarence Lang, for instance, have argued most vociferously that a lack of distinctiveness in the way that scholars approach the movement denies the unique elements of particular Black Freedom Movements and problematically reduces Civil Rights and Black Power to one continuous struggle. While this argument has merits, the linking of Civil Rights and Black Power Movements under the banner of Black Freedom Struggles does not have to diminish their uniqueness, but also can serve to highlight the similarities and continuities as historical actors traversed familiar issues of social, economic, and political inequality, not to mention cultural identity, over the course of the 20th century.[12]

For the purposes of this volume, therefore, I have adopted the notion of a Long Black Freedom Movement as an umbrella for any number of distinct local, national, and international Black Freedom Movements that have taken place that have been geared toward addressing issues of Black inequality. In the United States these issues have coalesced around what Hasan Jefferies has aptly described as "Freedom Rights" or "Freedom Politics" and what I like to call the "Six Degrees of Segregation." These include campaigns for decent housing, quality education, the right to vote, equal access to transportation and places of public accommodation, fair labor practices, and freedom from both legal and extralegal forms of Jim Crow Justice.[13]

While the Six Degrees of Segregation simply represents an easy way to identify certain core issues around which activists organized and or mobilized, Jeffries' notion of Freedom Politics includes an assessment of how activists sought to combat these issues. "Freedom rights," Jeffries argues, encompasses essential civil and human rights, including "the franchise, quality education, and the chance to earn a decent living," which African Americans in Lowndes County, Alabama, the subject of his scholarship, had fought to secure since their emancipation that first allowed for a "local organizing infrastructure."[14] While Jeffries effectively charts local Black people's various victories over many years, his study *Bloody Lowndes* also points to the ways in which other communities organized around related issues within their own local organizing infrastructures. How communities responded depended on a host of factors. In his comprehensive study of Black Freedom Struggles in the North, historian Thomas Sugrue, for instance, explores how efforts to secure open housing and create opportunities for economic development in the Black community were essentially different, conditioned by the needs of the community and the activists who spearheaded them.

Our ability to recognize activists organizing around freedom politics in early movements, such as a campaign in 1900 to end segregation on trolley cars, is one way of seeing the connective tissue that binds without suggesting one continuous movement. In this way, persons in Montgomery, Alabama in 1955 could act to end segregation on local buses completely unaware of the campaigns at the turn of the century, but organizing roughly around the same principles and with the same purpose to live without the humiliating sting of Jim Crow accommodations on public carriers.[15] Thus, while acknowledging Rosa Parks as a catalyst for the Montgomery Bus Boycott, the Reverend Dr. Martin Luther King nevertheless could proclaim that the situation with Montgomery buses was "not at all new." "The problem," he told those in attendance at a mass meeting to call for a boycott of the city's buses, "has existed over endless years."[16] The problem was obviously not confined to southern buses. As studies such as Jeff Wiltse, *Contested Waters: A Social History of Swimming Pools in America* (2007) and Stephen Grant Meyer, *As Long As They Don't Move Next Door: Segregation and Racial Conflict in American Neighborhoods* (2000) illustrate, protests emerged around a variety of issues easily mapped to the Six Degrees of Segregation. The other side of this, as Andrew W. Kahrl demonstrates in his book, *"The Land Was Ours": African American Beaches from Jim Crow to the Sunbelt South* (2010), was the autonomy and freedom from Jim Crow African Americans could enjoy on their own separate beaches—what he called "Black Privatopias," its own form of Black Power.[17]

Personalities and Organizations

Popular studies of the 1950s and 1960s Black Freedom Struggles have generally focused on key leaders and organizations. A slew of autobiographical accounts by movement participants complement these accounts. David Garrow's *Bearing the Cross*, Harvard Sitkoff's *King: Pilgrimage to the Mountaintop*, and Taylor Branch's trilogy of works of books on American in the King years have focused their gaze on the activism of Martin Luther King and the campaigns that intersected with his work beginning in Montgomery in 1955 and culminating with his assassination in Memphis in 1968. These works have tremendous value as scholarly resources on the movement but tend to privilege the work of King over other activists and organizations. While distinct in depth and scope, they all position King as a central force behind the mainstream movement. Although clearly not working in a vacuum, they credit King's charismatic leadership as the driving force behind the national movement that helped to transform law and social custom in the South and fortify voting rights for African Americans.[18] While the authors of these works readily acknowledge King's debt to scores of individuals and groups who helped to achieve these victories, they argue that King's national leadership was indispensable to major legislative victories including the Civil Rights Act of 1964 and the Voting Rights Act of 1965.

Recent studies have explored the lives of advisors who facilitated and in many cases preceded King in this work. These include studies of the lives of Ella Baker, Bayard Rustin, and James Farmer at the national level. In addition, local studies that seek to recover the stories of local leaders such as Gloria Richardson in Cambridge, Maryland, Catholic Priest James Groppi in Milwaukee, Wisconsin, James and Grace Lee Boggs in Detroit, Michigan, and Raymond Pace Alexander in Philadelphia, Pennsylvania to name a few have been instructive in demonstrating the contours of the movement at the local level.

New scholarship has also sought to frame the lives of proponents of Black Power. Political scientist Manning Marable's 2010 book *Malcolm X: A Life of Reinvention* surprisingly was the first major scholarly excavation of the fiery Muslim minister. For years, scholars and the public relied on Alex Haley's auto-biography of Malcolm published shortly after his death as the major source on Malcolm's life. While challenging elements of the autobiography for its re-creation of Malcolm, Marable's own work has come under fire demonstrat-ing the challenges of presenting the life of iconic figures. Peniel Joseph's 2014 biography *Stokely: A Life* has also sought to recover one of the most controver-sial figures associated with the Black Freedom Struggles of the 1960s.

Unquestionably, however, more work is needed on key figures to flesh out the philosophical and personal motivations that compelled individuals to dedicate themselves to making social change.

Critical to moving beyond a focus on marquee, charismatic, or individual leaders who grace the national stage is paying attention to the engagement of local leaders and organizations. Two of the most important studies on the significance of local activists, John Dittmer's *Local People* and Charles Payne's *I've Got the Light of Freedom*, focus their scholarly attention on the state of Mississippi. Despite being widely regarded as one of the primary citadels of white supremacy, and the site of some of the bloodiest showdowns with segre-gationists, Mississippi is often overlooked in popular accounts of the movement because it ultimately did not serve as one of the key battlegrounds in the King-led national movement. Numerous other cities and the local struggles that took place there suffer the same fate. Interestingly enough, activists, early on, had actually identified Mississippi as a key battle state, thereby illustrating one of the central points advanced by Dittmer and Payne—that the Civil Rights Movement at its core emerged from the numerous local revolts against Jim Crow that swept the nation in the 1950s and 1960s.[19] As Dittmer explains, "there would have been no organization, no movement, no victories" without the local people.[20] Local studies have thus provided a rich portrait of the move-ment beyond the national story.

Part of the rethinking of the movement, therefore, involves looking beyond those individuals and organizations most associated with the standard narrative. Traditionally the story of the Black Freedom Struggle has been told through the Civil Rights lens of the charismatic leadership of the "Big Six" leaders and their organizations. This includes Dr. King and the Southern Christian Leadership Conference (SCLC), the NAACP, the Congress of Racial Equality (CORE), the Student Nonviolent Coordinating Committee (SNCC, pronounced 'snick'), the National Urban League (NUL), and A. Phillip Randolph and the Brotherhood of Sleeping Car Porters.[21]

In this regard Glenda Gilmore's 2009 book *Defying Dixie: The Radical Roots of Civil Rights, 1919–1950* was exemplary. Set in the 30-year period before the traditional date given for the start of the movement, Gilmore explores the work of numerous important, if altogether forgotten, including socialists and Communists whom, she argues, helped pave the way for the likes of more well known historical actors like Rosa Parks and the Reverend Dr. Martin Luther King. In the process Gilmore illustrates the paradox of activists who would have been considered un-American and the role they played in strengthening American democracy.[22] Brenda Gayle Plummer's *In Search of Black Power: African Americans in the Era of Decolonization* (2013) and Minkah Makalani's *In the Cause of Freedom Radical Black Internationalism from Harlem to London, 1917–1939* (2011) are two works that explore the work of comparable groups and individuals for Black Power. Rod Bush's *We Are Not What We Seem: Black Nationalism and Class Struggle in the American Century* (1999) is also notable for its broad view of Black Power.[23]

Drawing on the examples and rich research of others like Gilmore, Jeffries, and Williams, this volume will share the experiences of a range of actors beyond the most familiar and well known who played a variety of roles in challenging racial oppression on the path to seeking justice.

Women, Gender, and Sexuality

Other studies that consider the importance of gender have also been helpful in helping historians and social scientists rethink the history and legacy of Black Freedom Struggles. These have included notable biographies of prominent women within the movement such as Barbara Ransby's *Ella Baker & the Black Freedom Movement: A Radical Democratic Vision* and Jeanne Theoharis' *The Rebellious Life of Mrs. Rosa Parks*.[24] Studies have also explored the significant grassroots organizing and leadership Black women displayed in shepherding both national and local protest movements and organizations.

Danielle Maguire's *At the Dark End of the Street* meticulously documents the rampant sexual violence and abuse visited on Black women by white men under segregation and how resistance to such violence played a key role in setting the context for 1950s and 1960s Black Freedom Struggles. The sadistic gang rape of 24-year-old sharecropper Recy Taylor in 1944 is the backdrop for Maguire's work. A group of seven armed white men brandishing knives and shotguns assaulted the respected wife and mother as she was returning from a prayer meeting at the Rock Hill Holiness Church in Abbeville, Alabama. The president of the local branch assigned one of his surest organizers, Rosa Parks, to the case in an effort to win justice for Mrs. Taylor.[25]

This was just one of many actions that Parks had been involved in to challenge Jim Crow Segregation before and after Montgomery—which has led her biographer Jeanne Theoharis to lament the "southernization" of her story.

In the decades after Montgomery, Parks moved to Detroit where she involved herself in various campaigns for Civil Rights and open housing in that city. Years before her courageous refusal to yield her seat on a Montgomery bus that would launch the Montgomery Bus Boycott, Parks was already deeply involved in protest activities. A short time before her arrest in Montgomery in 1955, Parks had participated in a two-week retreat entitled "Racial Desegregation: Implementing the Supreme Court Decision" at the Highlander Folk School where she befriended two other female activists, Ella Baker and Septima Clark. The women would develop lasting friendships based in part on their activism and shared experience in battling racial inequality. Each in their own way showed the long trajectory of the movement.

Ella Baker's activism exceeded four decades. Her biographer Barbra Ransby details how Baker tackled important issues of social justice including poverty, Civil Rights, women's rights, and labor. In the 1930s, Baker worked to establish buying clubs and consumer cooperatives to help relieve the painful impact of the Great Depression for African Americans. In the 1940s, she accepted a position with the NAACP where she honed her skills as an organizer. In the 1950s, she was a central figure in the formation of the SCLC. In the 1960s, she was one of the primary motivating forces behind the creation of SNCC. As the national movement drew to a close in the 1970s, Baker remained heavily involved in Third World Liberation Struggles, lending her considerable talents to the Puerto Rican independence movement.

The lives of lesser known Black women activists and rank and file organizers continue to be fleshed out by scholars like Rhonda Y. Williams, Cynthia Griggs Fleming, Robyn C. Spencer, Ruth Feldstein, Erik McDuffie, and Dayo Gore.[26]

Historian John D'Emilio's insightful 2003 biography *Lost Prophet: The Life and Times of Bayard Rustin* documents much of the opposition Rustin faced from both allies and enemies. His sexuality became an issue on numerous occasions. For instance, plans for a march on Washington in 1960 stalled after Congressman Adam Clayton Powell threatened to tell the press that King and Rustin were paramours—a lie, which nevertheless had the desired effect of driving a wedge between King and Rustin. When plans for the march began afresh in 1963 organizers remained concerned. Despite his enormous contribution to organizing the logistics for the march, Rustin was denied a more visible role out of fear that his sexual preference might endanger support. As NAACP head Roy Wilkins conceptualized the problem, "This march is of such importance that we must not put a person of his liabilities at the head."[27]

Whiteness

The impact of the movement on white Americans and conceptions of whiteness has also been a topic of interest. As Jason Sokol writes:

> During the civil rights movement, epic battles for justice were fought in the streets, at lunch counters, and in the classrooms of the American South. Just as many battles were waged, however, in the hearts and minds of ordinary white southerners *whose world became* unrecognizable to them.[28]

Responses by whites to this significant change took many forms that have occupied the attention of scholars. Violence and intimidation ran rampant in Southern states. The White Citizens' Council, the Ku Klux Klan, and various State Sovereignty Commissions work to maintain the system of racial separateness. Even in large southern cities like Atlanta, obstruction proved the watchword.

In southern cities whites adopted strategies to confront the crisis of Black integration. When whites began deserting northern cities in droves in the late 1960s and early 1970s, historian Kevin Kruse observed, they were merely continuing a practice they had refined decades before, in cities like Atlanta, to stave off integration. While southern politicians campaigned on platforms of massive resistance pledging to fight school integration in the decades of the 1950s and 1960s, Atlanta's white population found white flight an effective strategy. When civil rights activists succeeded in forcing the desegregation of public transportation, for instance, whites increased their use of private automobiles. Similarly, when confronted with the integration of schools, whites elected to send their children to private schools. After two decades of successfully evading integration in this manner Kruse notes that Atlanta's white residents were convinced that this was "the most successful segregationist response to the moral demands of the civil rights movement and the legal authority of the courts."[29]

"Freedom" North

The white flight documented by Kruse in Atlanta would come later to northern cities where the number of Blacks remained relatively low. While the well-documented history of the fight to end segregation in the South remains central in most accounts of 1950s and 1960s Black Freedom Struggles, studies exploring the nature of racial inequality outside the South have grown steadily. Like Leon Litwack's classic *North of Slavery* that sought to document the influence of the "Peculiar Institution" outside the South, studies of freedom struggles in the North and West have greatly expanded our knowledge and understanding of both movements in all of their dimensions. Since the publication of my own study on the Civil Rights and Black Power Movements in New Haven, Connecticut in 2000, numerous scholars, most notably Heather Ann Thompson, Martha Biondi, Matthew Countryman, Patrick Jones, and Thomas Sugrue, have examined Civil Rights struggles in notable communities north of the Mason

Dixon line. In the process of interrogating the existence of de facto segregation their works have also explored the new forms of segregation that accompanied white suburban flight and the massive unemployment brought on by job discrimination and deindustrialization.[30]

African Americans outside of the South also battled the Six Degrees of Segregation made more insidious by the reputation of the North as a refuge from more overt forms of Southern Apartheid. To be sure in the North and West, African Americans and other racial minorities encountered discrimination in housing, education, and employment as well as feeling the bitter sting of Jim Crow Justice. These problems were most acute in the arena of the search for fair and open housing. The steady increase in Black migration that accompanied World War II accelerated the process of suburbanization and deindustrialization. As a result, Black people, who were largely relegated to the lowest paying and most disposal types of labor including domestic and janitorial services, if they had work, faced a precarious financial existence. This, too, alongside housing discrimination before *and* after successful legal cases and non-discrimination ordinances in some states, impacted where and how they lived. This is why it is important to consider these issues when thinking about the history of Black Freedom Struggles. Glimpses are weaved throughout this volume because they are critical to the narrative and how we must rethink it.

The World Stage

Recent historical scholarship on Black Freedom Struggles also highlights the links between other global movements for human rights and the struggle for Black equality in the United States. Studies by historians such as Kevin Gaines, Carol Anderson, Mary Dudziak, and Brenda Gayle Plummer, for instance, have explored the global consciousness of Civil Rights and Black Power activists illustrating the ways in which their understanding of international events and politics helped them to connect local struggles with global events and currents.[31]

In illuminating the intersections of race, politics, and U.S. foreign policy such studies have deepened our understanding of the impact of the Cold War on Black Freedom Struggles within the United States. For instance, as the United States sought to challenge the spread of Communism abroad, the specter of America's race problem proved a major obstacle to foreign policy concerns. The highly publicized school desegregation battle that required federal troops to intervene in Little Rock, Arkansas, led to President Dwight D. Eisenhower's view that "our enemies [are] gloating over" massive resistance to integration.[32] The international spotlight shone so bright on the rampant racial inequities in the United States, that government officials labored to bolster the country's image and this included supporting federal civil rights legislation, as well as a measure of active intervention to quell southern intransigence that threatened to damage the reputation of the United States in the eyes of the world.

African Americans were far from passive in exploiting these concerns. They consciously pointed to racism at home to embarrass the government into action. They also found kindred spirits in foreign leaders fighting anticolonial struggles, particularly those that situated human rights as a global concern. Over the course of the 1950s and 1960s an international host of anticolonial leaders—including Fidel Castro and Che Guevera in Cuba, Patrice Lumumba in the Congo, and Kwame Nkrumah in Ghana—gained popularity among civil rights and Black Power activists in the United States. Adam Clayton Powell, who had addressed protesters in Baltimore in 1942, attended the first Afro-Asian conference, held at Bandung, Indonesia, in 1955. Powell, who actually evoked Black Power during a commencement address at Howard University, was later credited with coining the term—a term which came to represent, problematically, the antithesis of Civil Rights.

Challenging Declension

This speaks to another popular, if problematic, framing of the 1950s and 1960s Black Freedom Struggles—the blaming of Black Power for the degeneration of the heroic phase of the Civil Rights Movement. This declension narrative presents Black Power as the angry twin of the Civil Rights Movement—one spawned by the slow pace of change associated with nonviolent demonstrations. Historian Peniel Joseph vigorously argues otherwise. In fact, Joseph maintains that Civil Rights and Black Power were parallel movements. This idea of parallel movements—with sometimes overlapping and intersecting goals and people—reflects one of the hallmarks of recent Black Power studies scholarship. As with the Civil Rights Movement, these interpretations also tend to re-periodize Black Power, locating its origins in earlier decades, organizations, and people, including Jamaican-born Black Nationalist Marcus Garvey's Universal Negro Improvement Association, the African Blood Brotherhood, and the Moorish Science Temple.

Joseph's description of Black Power as the movement with no name in *Waiting 'Til the Midnight Hour: A Narrative History of Black Power in America* is also important in illustrating the ways in which activists explored alternatives to Black empowerment outside of the confines of the more well known Civil Rights organizations.[33] Within this framework, leaders such as Malcolm X and groups such as the Nation of Islam emerge less as foils to Civil Rights leaders but as vibrant expressions of Black Power well before 1966. Two significant anthologies edited by Joseph, *The Black Power Movement* and *Neighborhood Rebels*, continue this analysis along with a host of significant books and essays seeking to document and explain Black Power's role as an important component of 1950s and 1960s Black Freedom Struggles.

These notable works include Timothy Tyson's *Radio Free Dixie: Robert F. Williams & the Roots of Black Power*, which considers the importance of the controversial head of the Monroe, North Carolina NAACP who advocated many of the tenets associated with Black Power well before the media gave it a label in 1966.[34] Yohuru Williams' *Black Politics/White Power: Civil Rights, Black Power, and Black Panthers in New Haven* (2000) on Black Freedom Struggles in New Haven, Connecticut also points to the existence of a vibrant parallel movement in that city. Studies of key groups, such as Yohuru Williams and Jama Lazerow's *Liberated Territory: Untold Local Perspectives on the Black Panther Party* and Scot Brown's Fighting for US, provides fresh analysis on revolutionary and cultural Black Nationalism.[35] More recently, Rhonda Y. Williams' *Concrete Demands: The Search for Black Power in the 20th Century* (2015) has provided a deeper and more nuanced panoramic look at Black Power. Plumbing a rich array of sources, Williams masterfully illustrates the roots, routes, expressions, and legacy of Black Power in order to understand the ways in which Black men *and* women challenged racial inequality and white power and sought empowerment through activities that privileged Black pride and racial self-determination through cultural, economic, and political independence.

Black Students and Black Arts

One area where Black Power ideologies really resonated was with students—who played a key role in 1950s and 1960s Black Freedom Struggles. Even as images of Black and white college students engaged in nonviolent direct action occupy the public imagination, recent scholarship has shown the impact of Black Power on the nation's college campuses as well. Important works by Martha Biondi, Stephan Bradley, Ibram Rogers, Fabio Rojas, and Joy Ann Williamson have helped to "unsettle," in Biondi's words, what she calls "the usual geography of vanguard student radicalism."[36] In the process, these studies collectively demonstrate the significance of Black colleges and Black college students in this broad era of activism. As with the larger struggle, Biondi notes that "Student activism had been emerging in various locations in isolation" and that the "local political landscape" did as much to shape campus protests as national issues.

While student activists populated the ranks of key Civil Rights and Black Power organizations, they also brought fresh ideas and perspectives to the academy, where they also demanded changes that helped to transform American higher education. Through their collective efforts to secure open admissions, advocate for the hiring of faculty of color, and end the use of standardized tests such as the SAT as the basis for admission, they sought to increase opportunity and make campuses more diverse. On the campuses of the nation's Historically Black Colleges and Universities they confronted faculty and administrators whom they demanded should make curricular changes that acknowledged the importance of Black history and culture. They also sought to organize campuses as bases for protests around local and national issues coalescing around race and poverty.

Reflecting the importance of the post-World War II era, Donna Murch points to the GI Bill and the expansion of public education and the community college system in California as an important precursor to Civil Rights and Black Power activism. The campus served not only as a place of study, but also a place where students from all over the nation could share ideas. The Great Migration that had witnessed the large-scale migration of Blacks out of the South bore fruit on the campuses of institutions like Merrit Junior College in Oakland where two children of migrants, Huey Newton and Bobby Seale, the co-founders of the Black Panther Party for Self-Defense, first met.

The Black Arts Movement also emerged from the fertile ground of 1960s Black Freedom Struggles. As cultural historian James Smethurst notes, "One enormous impact of the Black Arts Movement is the obvious influence it exercised on the conceptions of racial, ethnic, national, gender, and sexual identity in the United States and what might be thought of as movement poetics – whether this influence came through inspiration by Black Arts or reaction against it (or both)."[37] Murch demonstrates this point in connection to the Watts rebellion of 1965, which she describes as both a moment of triumph and despair. Out of the violence and destruction came a new affirmation of Black humanity and Black pride, which she locates in the celebration of Black music and culture that was the Wattstax Festival of 1972, presented on the occasion of the seventh anniversary of the devastating Watts riots. "On the one hand," Murch argues, "Wattstax brilliantly captures how the urban rebellions nurtured a strong sense of community pride that reached its zenith in the Black Power and Black Arts movements of the late 1960s and early 1970s." "Conversely," she continued "the vicious backlash by the state, law enforcement, and National Guard anticipated the rise of mass incarceration and the expansion of the modern 'carceral' state in the decades to come."[38]

Mass Incarceration

It is that backlash that has come to occupy the attention of historians at the present who are considering the rise of the carceral state as a response to Black Freedom Struggles. Murch explains, "Scholars have chosen the term 'carceral'— 'of or belonging to prison'—to invoke a wide range of punitive state action." These include what she describes as "aggressive policing; border patrol, military, and immigrant detention; public and private surveillance; imprisonment of adults, juveniles, and undocumented workers; courts, prosecution, and parole; and even restrictive and means-tested welfare and social service policy, with links to the broader systems of criminal and juvenile justice."[39]

Legal scholar Michelle Alexander's 2010 publication *The New Jim Crow* has garnered the most attention for showing the ways in which mass incarceration rates and punitive drug laws represent a continuation of segregation. Alexander provocatively notes, that in spite of the election of the nation's first Black

President (Barack Obama in 2008) and rhetoric about a new "colorblind" America, "No other country in the world imprisons so many of its racial or ethnic minorities. The United States imprisons a larger percentage of its black population than South Africa did at the height of apartheid."[40] Alexander situates the origins of America's mass incarceration problem in the unresolved folds of the histories of emancipation and Civil Rights deepening the analysis of earlier works that hinted at the connection. Alexander argues that the discriminatory way in which laws are enforced has produced a "Counter-Revolution" representing "the most damaging manifestation of the backlash against the Civil Rights Movement."[41]

Other important works including Ruth Wilson Gilmore's prize-winning *Golden Gulag: Prisons, Surplus, Crisis, and Opposition in Globalizing California* and Heather Thompson's comprehensive 2010 *Journal of American History* article, "Why Mass Incarceration Matters: Rethinking Crisis, Decline, and Transformation in Postwar American History" have been incredibly useful in helping to frame this work. Studies such as Khalil Muhammad, *The Condemnation of Blackness: Ideas about Race and Crime in the Making of Modern Urban America* take a longer view. Muhammad examines reforms pursued during the Progressive era that have had a profound and lasting influence on ideas about crime and punishment and what he aptly describes as the "ideological currency of black criminality" that links present-day inequalities in the criminal justice system with their historical roots in the Jim Crow South.[42]

Other notable studies such as Donna Murch's *Living for the City*, Christian Parenti's *Lockdown America: Police and Prisons in the Age of Crisis*, and Kelly Lytle Hernandez's *MIGRA! A History of the U.S. Border Patrol*, offer other facets of this history as it pertains to migration, education, and the policing of Black and Brown bodies. [43] Finally, historian Robert Chase's groundbreaking work on prison writ writers along with Dan Berger's *Captive Nation: Black Prison Organizing in the Civil Rights Era* explore the intersection between Black Freedom Struggles and the prison rights movement in the United States. Berger, in particular, focuses his scholarly gaze on imprisonment as a central feature of Black life.[44]

Conclusion

As the highly condensed discussion presented here illustrates, over the past two decades popular conceptions of the Civil Rights Movement have shifted with the production of a new robust historiography. The new scholarship has reshaped the dominant narratives of the Civil Rights Movement, Black Power, and Black Freedom Struggles. And, yet, there are more local and synthetic histories to write, as well as other important questions remaining, particularly regarding less visible actors.[45] Examining the Six Degrees of Segregation not only illuminates the familiar terrain of voting rights and access to places of public accommodation, but also encourages us to explore and rethink aspects of Black Freedom

Struggles that illustrate their connection to contemporary issues.[46] This present volume will lay the groundwork for better understanding, and challenging, narratives of the Civil Rights and Black Power Movements by providing a historical survey built around familiar individuals, organizations, and issues that unquestionably shaped one of the most significant periods in American history.

Notes

1 *Keyes v. School District No. 1*, 413 U.S. 189, 217 (1973); see also Christina B. Whitman, "Individual and Community: An Appreciation of Mr. Justice Powell," *Virginia Law Review* (1982): 307.
2 Howell S. Baum, *Brown in Baltimore: School Desegregation and the Limits of Liberalism* (Ithaca: Cornell University Press, 2010), 40–3; *The Afro-American* (Baltimore), April 28, 1942, 2.
3 *The Afro-American* (Baltimore), April 28, 1942, 2.
4 Ibid.
5 Rhonda Y. Williams, *Concrete Demands: The Search for Black Power in the 20th Century* (New York: Routledge, 2015), 8.
6 John Hope Franklin and Abraham Eisenstadt quoted in Melvyn Dubofsky, *Industrialism and the American Worker, 1865–1920* (New York: Harlan Davidson, 1996).
7 For accounts which locate the origins of the Civil Rights Movement in the postwar period see Gunnar Myrdal, *An American Dilemma: The Negro Problem and American Democracy* (New York: Harper, 1944); Cheryl Greenberg, *To Ask for an Equal Chance: African Americans in the Great Depression* (Lanham: Rowman & Littlefield, 2009); Kevin M. Kruse and Stephen Tuck, eds., *The Fog of War: The Second World War and the Civil Rights Movement* (New York: Oxford University Press, 2012); Davidson M. Douglas, *Jim Crow Moves North: The Battle over Northern School Segregation, 1865–1954* (New York: Cambridge University Press, 2005); James Gregory, *The Southern Diaspora: How the Great Migration of Black and White Southerners Transformed America* (Chapel Hill: University of North Carolina Press, 2006); Thomas J. Sugrue, *The Origins of the Urban Crisis: Race and Inequality in Postwar Detroit* (Princeton: Princeton University Press, 2005).
8 Robert Korstad and Nelson Lichtenstein, "Opportunities Found and Lost: Labor, Radicals and the Early Civil Rights Movement," *Journal of American History* 75 (December 1988): 786–811; Robert Korstad, *Civil Rights Unionism* (Chapel Hill: University of North Carolina Press, 2004).
9 Robert Korstad and Nelson Lichtenstein, "Opportunities Found and Lost: Labor, Radicals, and the Early Civil Rights Movement," in Nelson Lichtenstein, *A Contest of Ideas: Capital, Politics, and Labor* (Urbana: University of Illinois Press, 2014), 109; Robert Korstad and Nelson Lichtenstein, "Opportunities Found and Lost: Labor, Radicals and the Early Civil Rights Movement," *Journal of American History* 75 (December 1988): 786–811; for an excellent discussion of this historiography see Adam Fairclough, "Historians and the Civil Rights Movement," *Journal of American Studies* 24, no. 3 (1990): 387–98.
10 Harvard Sitkoff, *A New Deal for Blacks: The Emergence of Civil Rights as a National Issue: The Depression Decade* (New York: Oxford University Press, 1981); Nancy Joan Weiss,

Farewell to the Party of Lincoln: Black Politics in the Age of FDR (New Jersey: Princeton University Press, 1983).

11 Robert J. Norrell, *Reaping the Whirlwind: The Civil Rights Movement in Tuskegee* (New York: Alfred A. Knopf, 1985), x.

12 Sundiata Keita Cha-Jua and Clarence Lang, "The 'Long Movement' as Vampire: Temporal and Spatial Fallacies in Recent Black Freedom Studies," *Journal of African American History* 92 (Spring 2007).

13 Hasan Kwame Jeffries, *Bloody Lowndes: Civil Rights and Black Power in Alabama's Black Belt* (New York: New York University Press, 2009).

14 Ibid., 37.

15 Blair L.M. Kelley, *Right to Ride: Streetcar Boycotts and African American Citizenship in the Era of Plessy v. Ferguson* (Chapel Hill: University of North Carolina Press, 2010).

16 Martin Luther King, Jr., "MIA Mass Meeting at Holt Street Baptist Church," December 5, 1955, in Clayborne Carson, Stewart Burns, Susan Carson, Pete Holloran, and Dana L.H. Powell, eds., *The Papers of Martin Luther King, Jr., Volume 2: Rediscovering Precious Values, July 1951–November 1955* (Berkeley: University of California Press, 1994), 72.

17 Jeff Wiltse, *Contested Waters: A Social History of Swimming Pools in America* (Chapel Hill: University of North Carolina Press, 2007), 121–80; Stephen Grant Meyer, *As Long As They Don't Move Next Door: Segregation and Racial Conflict in American Neighborhoods* (Boston: Rowman & Littlefield, 2000), 204; Andrew W. Kahrl, *The Land Was Ours: African American Beaches from Jim Crow to the Sunbelt South* (Cambridge, MA: Harvard University Press, 2012).

18 David J. Garrow, *Bearing the Cross: Martin Luther King and the Southern Christian Leadership Conference* (New York: William Morrow, 1986); Taylor Branch, *Parting the Waters: America in the King Years 1954–63* (New York: Simon & Schuster, 2007); Taylor Branch, *Pillar of Fire: America in the King Years 1963–65* (New York: Simon & Schuster, 2007); Taylor Branch, *At Canaan's Edge: America in the King Years, 1965–68* (New York: Simon & Schuster, 2006); Harvard Sitkoff, *King: Pilgrimage to the Mountaintop* (New York: Macmillan, 2008); Adam Fairclough, *To Redeem the Soul of America: The Southern Christian Leadership Conference and Martin Luther King, Jr.* (Athens: University of Georgia Press, 1987).

19 Charles M. Payne, *I've Got the Light of Freedom: The Organizing Tradition and the Mississippi Freedom Struggle* (Berkeley: University of California Press, 1995); John Dittmer, *Local People: The Struggle for Civil Rights in Mississippi* (Chicago: University of Illinois Press, 1995).

20 Dittmer, *Local People*, 424.

21 More generalized books and studies on the movement as a whole are quite useful even when employing this paradigm. Notable examples include Richard Kluger's *Simple Justice: The History of Brown v. Board of Education and Black America's Struggle for Equality*, Patricia Sullivan's *Lift Every Voice: The NAACP and the Making of the Civil Rights Movement*, David Garrow's *Bearing the Cross*, and Taylor Branch's impressive trilogy on America in the King years. Harvard Sitkoff's *The Struggle for Black Equality* remains one of the most accessible short studies of the movement. See Richard Kluger, *Simple Justice: The History of Brown v. Board of Education and Black America's Struggle for Equality* (New York: Vintage, 2004); Patricia Sullivan, *Lift Every Voice: The NAACP and the Making of the Civil Rights Movement* (New York: The New Press, 2009); David J. Garrow, *Bearing the Cross: Martin Luther King and the Southern Christian Leadership*

Conference (New York: William Morrow, 1986); Harvard Sitkoff, *The Struggle for Black Equality 1954–1980* (New York: Hill & Wang, 1981).

22　Glenda Gilmore, *Defying Dixie: The Radical Roots of Civil Rights, 1919–1950* (New York: W.W. Norton, 2008).

23　Brenda Gayle Plummer, *In Search of Power: African Americans in the Era of Decolonization, 1956–1974* (Cambridge: Cambridge University Press, 2013); Minkah Makalani, *In the Cause of Freedom: Radical Black Internationalism from Harlem to London, 1917–1939* (Chapel Hill: University of North Carolina Press, 2011); Rod Bush's *We Are Not What We Seem: Black Nationalism and Class Struggle in the American Century* (New York: New York University Press, 1999).

24　Barbara Ransby, *Ella Baker and the Black Radical Tradition* (Chapel Hill: University of North Carolina Press, 2003); Jeanne Theoharis, *The Rebellious Life of Mrs. Rosa Parks* (Boston: Beacon Press, 2013).

25　Danielle McGuire, *At the Dark End of the Street: Black Women, Rape and Resistance— A New History of the Civil Rights Movement from Rosa Parks to the Rise of Black Power* (New York: Knopf, 2010).

26　Sharon Harley, "'Chronicle of a Death Foretold': Gloria Richardson, the Cambridge Movement, and the Radical Black Activist Tradition," in Bettye Collier-Thomas and V.P. Franklin, eds., *Sisters in the Struggle: African American Women in the Civil Rights—Black Power Movement* (New York: New York University Press, 2001), 174–96; Darlene Clark Hine, *Hine Sight: Black Women and the Reconstruction of American History* (Bloomington: Indiana University Press, 1997); Peter Levy, *Civil War on Race Street: The Civil Rights Movement in Cambridge, Maryland* (Gainesville: University Press of Florida, 2003).

27　For Wilkins' comments see John D'Emilio, *Lost Prophet: The Life and Times of Bayard Rustin* (New York: Free Press, 2003), 339. See also Daniel Levine, *Bayard Rustin and the Civil Rights Movement* (New Jersey: Rutgers University Press, 2000); Anne Enke, *Finding the Movement: Sexuality, Contested Space, and Feminist Activism* (Durham, NC: Duke University Press, 2007); Nan Alamilla Boyd and Horacio N. Roque Ramírez, eds., *Bodies of Evidence: The Practice of Queer Oral History* (New York: Oxford University Press, 2012); Rosalind Rosenberg, "The Conjunction of Race and Gender," *Journal of Women's History* 14, no. 2 (2002): 68–73.

28　Jason Sokol, *There Goes My Everything: White Southerners in the Age of Civil Rights, 1945–1975* (New York: Vintage, 2008).

29　Kevin M. Kruse, *White Flight: Atlanta and the Making of Modern Conservatism* (Princeton: Princeton University Press, 2012).

30　Yohuru Williams, *Black Politics/White Power: Civil Rights, Black Power, and the Black Panthers in New Haven* (New York: Brandywine, 2000); Thomas Sugrue, *The Origins of the Urban Crisis: Racial Inequality in Postwar Detroit* (Princeton: Princeton University Press, 1996); Matthew J. Countryman, *Up South: Civil Rights and Black Power in Philadelphia* (Philadelphia: University of Pennsylvania Press, 2005); Patrick Jones, *The Selma of the North: Civil Rights Insurgency in Milwaukee* (Cambridge, MA: Harvard University Press, 2010); Martha Biondi, *To Stand and Fight: The Struggle for Civil Rights in Postwar New York City* (Cambridge, MA: Harvard University Press, 2003); Thomas J. Sugrue, *Sweet Land of Liberty: The Forgotten Struggle for Civil Rights in the North* (New York: Random House, 2009); Jeanne F. Theoharis and Komozi Woodard, eds., *Freedom North: Black Freedom Struggles Outside the South, 1940–1980* (New York: Palgrave Macmillan, 2003); Felicia Kornbluh, *The Battle for Welfare Rights: Politics and Poverty in Modern America* (Philadelphia: University of Pennsylvania Press, 2007);

Rhonda Y. Williams, *The Politics of Public Housing: Black Women's Struggles Against Urban Inequality* (New York: Oxford University Press, 2005).

31 Kevin Gaines, "The Civil Rights Movement in World Perspective," *OAH Magazine of History* 21 (October 2006): 14–18.

32 "Dwight D. Eisenhower's Radio and Television Address to the American People on the Situation in Little Rock," in Steven F. Lawson and Charles Payne, *Debating the Civil Rights Movement, 1945–1968* (Lanham: Rowman & Littlefield, 1998), 60–4; Gerald Horne, *Black and Red: W. E. B. Du Bois and the Afro-American Response to the Cold War, 1944–1963* (Albany: State University of New York Press, 1985).

33 Peniel E. Joseph, *Waiting 'Til the Midnight Hour* (New York: Henry Holt, 2006).

34 Timothy B. Tyson, *Radio Free Dixie: Robert F. Williams & the Roots of Black Power* (Chapel Hill: University of North Carolina Press, 1999).

35 Yohuru Williams and Jama Lazerow, eds., *Liberated Territory: Untold Local Perspectives on the Black Panther Party* (Durham, NC: Duke University Press, 2008); Scot Brown, *Fighting for US: Maulana Karenga, the US Organization, and Black Cultural Nationalism* (New York: New York University Press, 2003).

36 Martha Biondi, *The Black Revolution on Campus* (Berkeley: University of California Press, 2012), 6; Ibram Rogers, *The Black Campus Movement: Black Students and the Racial Reconstitution of Higher Education, 1965–1972* (New York: Palgrave Macmillan, 2012); Fabio Rojas, *From Black Power to Black Studies: How a Radical Social Movement Became an Academic Discipline* (Baltimore: Johns Hopkins University Press, 2007); Stefan M. Bradley, *Harlem vs. Columbia University: Black Student Power in the Late 1960s* (Urbana: University of Illinois Press, 2009); Joy Ann Williamson, *Black Power on Campus: The University of Illinois, 1965–75* (Urbana: University of Illinois Press, 2003); Peniel E. Joseph, "Dashikis and Democracy: Black Studies, Student Activism, and the Black Power Movement," *The Journal of African American History* (2003): 182–203.

37 James Smethurst, "'Pat Your Foot and Turn the Corner': Amiri Baraka, the Black Arts Movement, and the Poetics of Popular Avant-Garde," *African American Review* 37, no. 2/3 (2003): 268.

38 Donna Murch, "The Many Meanings of Watts: Black Power, Wattstax, and the Carceral State," *OAH Magazine of History* 26, no. 1 (2012): 37–40. On the Watts rebellion see Gerald Horne, *Fire This Time: The Watts Uprising and the 1960s* (New York: Da Capo Press: 1997), 45–133; Heather Thompson, "Urban Uprisings: Riots or Rebellions," in David Farber and Beth Bailey, eds., *The Columbia Guide to America in the 1960s* (New York: Columbia University Press, 2001), 109.

39 Murch, "The Many Meanings of Watts."

40 Michelle Alexander, *The New Jim Crow: Mass Incarceration in the Age of Colorblindness* (New York: The New Press, 2012), 6.

41 Ibid., 11.

42 Khalil Gibran Muhammad, *The Condemnation of Blackness* (Cambridge, MA: Harvard University Press, 2010).

43 Heather Thompson, "Why Mass Incarceration Matters: Rethinking Crisis, Decline, and Transformation in Postwar American History," *Journal of American History* (December 2010): 703–734; Donna Murch, *Living for the City; Christian Parenti, Lockdown America: Police and Prisons in the Age of Crisis* (New York: Verso, 1999); Kelly Lytle Hernandez, *MIGRA! A History of the U.S. Border Patrol* (Berkeley: University of California Press, 2010); Muhammad, *The Condemnation of Blackness*; Robert Perkinson, *Texas Tough: The Rise of a Prison Empire* (New York: Metropolitan

Books, 2010); Ruth Wilson Gilmore, *Golden Gulag: Prisons, Surplus, Crisis, and Opposition in Globalizing California* (Berkeley: University of California Press, 2007).

44 Daniel Berger, *Captive Nation: Black Prison Organizing in the Civil Rights Era* (Chapel Hill: University of North Carolina Press, 2014).

45 Regarding less visible actors, see Rhonda Y. Williams, *The Politics of Public Housing: Black Women's Struggles against Urban Inequality* (New York: Oxford University Press, 2004). On synthetic history, see Sugrue, *Sweet Land of Liberty*; and Williams, *Concrete Demands*.

46 For two good recent examples of the nexus of Civil Rights, Black Power, and healthcare, see Alondra Nelson, *Body and Soul: The Black Panther Party and the Fight against Medical Discrimination* (Minneapolis: University of Minnesota Press, 2011); John Dittmer, *The Good Doctors: The Medical Committee for Human Rights and the Struggle for Social Justice in Health Care* (New York: Bloomsbury Publishing USA, 2009).

1

"A CONTINUING EVOLVING PROCESS"

The Predecessors and Origins of the Civil Rights and Black Power Movements

Justice is never given; it is exacted and the struggle must be continuous for freedom is never a final fact, but a continuing evolving process to higher and higher levels of human, social, economic, political, and religious relationship.

A. Philip Randolph[1]

The Civil Rights and Black Power Movements occupy a unique place in recent American history. They have become the backdrop for a continuing conversation about race and democracy that seeks to contextualize the nation's continuing struggle to reconcile elements of racial inequality with its seeming triumph over legal apartheid during the 1960s. The U.S. Supreme Court's overturning of key sections of the Voting Rights Act of 1965, designed to protect Black voting rights, in the summer of 2013 raised serious concerns among many former movement activists about the stability and legacy of the changes they fought to win. Making an appeal to Congress in the aftermath of the Court's 5–4 decision in *Shelby County* v. *Holder* to reestablish those sections that were stricken, Georgia Congressman and longtime Civil Rights activist, John Lewis observed, "People must never forget that the scars and stains of racism are still deeply embedded in every corner, every fiber of American society, even when it comes to our politics." Referencing his great-grandfather whom he noted "had been a slave" and "became a registered voter," during Reconstruction, Lewis tied the Civil Rights victories of his era, to the much longer history of the struggle to end slavery and maintain protections for African American Civil Rights to this day. His observations illustrate one of the new directions in thinking about the Civil Rights Movement as both a unique occurrence and one chapter or phase of a much longer Black Freedom Movement.[2]

Over the past decade, scholars have debated about how to capture the essence of this rethinking of the movement's temporal and spatial boundaries. Traditionally, scholars have treated the movement primarily as a southern phenomenon fixing its dates in the period between 1954 and 1968—roughly from the Supreme Court's decision in *Brown* v. *Board of Education* to the assassination of the Reverend Dr. Martin Luther King in Memphis. There are, of course, significant limitations that Congressman Lewis' comments illustrate, in conceptualizing the movement this way. Scholarship that is more recent has sought to expand this definition of the movement beyond its present boundaries—placing it in the much larger context of what historian Clayborne Carson calls the Modern Black Freedom Struggle that was both national and global. Although the movement arose in response to a unique set of circumstances that coalesced in the period after World War II, it was also part of this much longer freedom struggle. As sociologist Aldon Morris proposed, "Organized protest against white domination has always been one of the cornerstones of the black experience."[3] While respecting yet expanding the chronological boundaries of these events, highlighting the issues, personalities, strategies, and tactics employed by those dedicated to winning full equality for African Americans can be instructive.

Even in specialized studies of the movement, scholars quickly conceded that while the postwar period witnessed a flowering of resistance to American apartheid, the roots of that resistance went much deeper. As historian Robert Korstad observed, in his book *Civil Rights Unionism*, "the key events in this history of working-class insurgency took place between 1942 and 1950 . . . But the institutions and processes that influenced mobilization have a much longer history."[4] This is not to suggest that there has been one continuous movement but rather to highlight the continuities and similarities around those issues and ideas that defined early freedom struggles with the distinct issues and ideas that Civil Rights and Black Power activists later organized and mobilized around. In general, freedom struggles between the end of Reconstruction and the advent of the modern Civil Rights Movement united around certain key issues unique to the African American experience. These include the fight against residential segregation and segregated education coupled with the demand for fair employment, unfettered access to places of public accommodation and equitable treatment within the criminal justice system, which even in the present day remains a persistent obstacles to full equality. Students of the period will find not only a variation in the issues themselves but also among the responses of various individuals and organizations committed to addressing them. Thus, while lynching and the problem of mass incarceration remain distinct issues, they fall under the broad heading of Jim Crow Justice, the roots of which are traceable to the decades after the American Civil War.

Making such connections is certainly not new. Movement leaders often drew such comparisons to emphasize the struggle's longue durée. In 1962, for instance, the Reverend Dr. Martin Luther King joined a distinguished group of guests at the Waldorf Astoria Hotel in New York City to celebrate the induction of Jackie Robinson, the first African American to play major league baseball in the 20th century, into the Baseball Hall of Fame. Robinson, King observed in his brief remarks, referring to an incident in 1944 when the baseball legend refused to give up his seat on a Texas bus, "was a freedom rider before the freedom rides." King's comments were reminiscent of a speech he delivered years earlier on the eve of the Montgomery Bus Boycott. King reminded the audience at the packed Holt Street Baptist Church that the "situation" of segregated transportation that occasioned their gathering was "not at all new." "The problem," he explained, "has existed over endless years." "For many years now," he explained, "Negroes in Montgomery and so many other areas have been inflicted with the paralysis of crippling fear on buses in our community." "On so many occasions," he continued:

> Negroes have been intimidated and humiliated and oppressed because of the sheer fact that they were Negroes I don't have time this evening to go into the history of these numerous cases. Many of them now are lost in the thick fog of oblivion but at least one stands before us now with glaring dimensions.[5]

The "one" case King spoke of, of course, was the arrest of 42-year-old seamstress Rosa Parks. Despite the enduring perception of Parks' courageous act of defiance as an act of impulse, because she was "tired of giving," in fact the longtime Civil Rights activist was connected with several local and national protest organizations operating in the Montgomery area including the NAACP that had been committed to fighting for racial equality. Her act of rebelliousness soon became a successful local then national movement.[6] At the core of the protest was the demand by African Americans in Montgomery for treatment as first-class citizens—a demand that helped to galvanize a national movement.

Joe Azbell, the white city editor of the *Montgomery Advertiser*, who reported on the meeting the following day, captured this sentiment while highlighting the two remarks in King's speech that he observed "drew the most applause." "We will not retreat one inch in our fight to secure and hold our American citizenship," King boldly challenges his fellow protesters. Second was the statement: "And the history book will write of us as a race of people who in Montgomery County, State of Alabama, Country of the United States, stood up for and fought for their rights as American citizens, as citizens of democracy."[7]

During the high point of the movement, the quest for first class citizenship united in protest a disparate and diverse coalition of activists, scholars, unionists, veterans, and persons from across the political spectrum. While they shared similar goals, their methods and manner for achieving them were far from uniform. Dr. King's comments illustrate the complexities of the movement in this regard. In speaking of the long series of injustices, he focused the attention of his audience on the larger denial of justice and equality that bound people of African descent together in pursuit of a common goal. It was not always one unified movement with distinctive leaders and organizations; that would come later. Its origins are important nonetheless because they laid a foundation for the later movement that eventually converged in the more familiar battles of the 1950s and 1960s, including Montgomery, Little Rock, Birmingham, and Selma.

What was evident in these early struggles was an inchoate Civil Rights Movement still in gestation in the riverbed of a Long Black Freedom Struggle. That riverbed not only incubated a struggle for Civil Rights but also an emergent Black Power Movement—a parallel movement seeking to establish a distinct Black cultural identity as well as independent Black institutions and ties with people of African descent across the globe. While often separatist in tone, Black Power advocates also tested the parameters and limits of citizenship and democracy as their demands for self-defense, and self-determination pushed the very boundaries of the constitutional guarantees of free speech and association.

This construction of citizenship, of course, was impossible without the Civil War. Between 1861 and 1865, conflict tore the nation asunder as the Union and Confederate armies battled over competing economic, social, and political systems rooted in slavery. Before the war, the U.S. Supreme Court's decision in *Dred Scott* (1858) declared that people of "African ancestry" were "not intended to be included, under the word 'citizens' in the Constitution," and could "therefore claim none of the rights and privileges which that instrument provides for and secures to citizens of the United States." By the conclusion of the war, there was genuine optimism that the Union would not only abolish slavery but also extend citizenship to the Freedmen. In the decade after the war, three new Constitutional Amendments, abolishing slavery (13th Amendment), granting citizenship (14th Amendment), and outlawing discrimination based on race in voting (15th Amendment) buttressed by additional legislation seeking to establish Civil Rights seemed to argue for a bright future.

In reality, however, the new Amendments proved insufficient against the rising tide of white supremacy. In a series of rulings between 1873 and 1883, a hostile U.S. Supreme Court chose to interpret the scope and meaning of the Amendments narrowly, effectively nullifying the efforts of the Republican Congress to establish African Americans' claim to full citizenship. Lincoln's successor, Andrew Johnson, in the meantime utilized his veto power to attempt to check other legislation aimed at establishing equal rights for people of color. Throughout the former states of the Confederacy, state and local politicians adopted laws and policies designed to return African Americans back to the same position they occupied under slavery. Simultaneously, white terrorist groups such as the Ku Klux Klan used violence and intimidation to undermine Black Civil Rights and disfranchise Black voters. Northern and border states were not immune from the violence or the segregationist impulse. Delaware attempted to bar Blacks' testimony against whites in court while the Pennsylvania State Supreme Court upheld the legality of segregated railroads.

The result, especially in the South, was a quasi-freedom that relegated African Americans to second-class citizenship. Southern author and ex-confederate soldier George Washington Cable best captured the essence of the dilemma that African Americans faced in an extended essay published in *The Century Magazine* in 1885. While advocating for full citizenship for African Americans, Cable grimly acknowledged that to be

> a free man is his still distant goal ... Twice he has been a freedman. In the days of compulsory reconstruction, he was freed in the presence of his master by that master's victorious foe. In these days of voluntary reconstruction he is virtually freed by the consent of his master, but the master retaining the exclusive right to define the bounds of his freedom.[8]

Cable condemned the incipient lines of segregation he saw emerging in many southern states in the wake of the failed efforts at Congressional Reconstruction. Emboldened Democratic southern legislatures, eager to put the war and "the Negro question" behind them, moved swiftly to reestablish white supremacy. They found an ally in the U.S. Supreme Court, which over the period from 1873 to 1896, systematically dismantled many of the protections put in place by the "Radical Republican" Congress to protect African American Civil Rights. Beginning with the Slaughterhouse cases of 1873, the High Court narrowly interpreted the scope of the Amendments while deferring to state police powers in matters of "health, safety, and morals," that became the cornerstone of segregationist laws.

African Americans were far from passive in responding to assaults on their freedom. Tens of thousands left the Jim Crow South, for instance, in search of greener pastures in Kansas, Oklahoma, and other points west, a precursor to the Great Migration that took place in successive waves between 1900 and 1970. Others were more vocal in their resistance. In the years and decades after the war, a number of African American newspaper editors, civic leaders, and ministers spoke out against efforts to restrict Black citizenship. AME Bishop and Civil War veteran Henry McNeal Turner, for instance, sharply criticized the U.S. Supreme Court for its ruling in the Civil Rights cases of 1883, which struck down the Civil Rights Act of 1875. Designed to ensure equal access to places of public accommodation for people of color, the court declared the law unconstitutional and held acts of private discrimination beyond the reach of the federal government. Referring to the "Dred Scott" decision as "only a mole-hill in comparison with this obstructing Rocky Mountain to the freedom of citizenship," Turner could hardly contain his indignation. The "gambler, cut-throat, thief, despoiler of happy homes, and the cowardly assassin," he protested, "need only to have white faces in order to be accommodated with more celerity and respect than are our lawyers, doctors, teachers and humble preachers."[9]

Turner's words foreshadowed state-sanctioned segregation. A little over a decade after its ruling in the Civil Rights cases the High Court issued its decision in *Plessy* v. *Ferguson* holding that Louisiana's 1890 Separate Car Act, requiring African Americans and whites to sit in separate cars, did not violate the citizenship or equal protection clauses of the 14th Amendment. The court ruled further that such segregation placed no "badge of inferiority" on African Americans in violation of the 13th Amendment and, thus, was not illegal. The ruling effectively eliminated barriers to segregation. While segregationists celebrated the decision, it was a clear departure from broader trends toward integration. In the roughly two decades between the end of the war and the court's ruling in *Plessy*, for example, the historian C. Vann Woodward noted significant fluidity in race relations.[10] African Americans, in spite of racial prejudice, were able to start families, carve out successful businesses, and take advantage of educational opportunities. Institutions of higher learning like Howard University and the Tuskegee Institute served as the gateway for a small but influential minority to acquire the experience and training necessary to move into the professions; some African Americans were able to enroll at white institutions.

The Supreme Court's decision in *Plessy*, however, arrested this progress. Empowered by the court's decree, Democratic controlled legislatures in southern states quickly erected legal barriers to equality for African Americans under the doctrine of separate but equal.

Even before the court's decision, African American Civil Rights activists like newspaper editors Ida B. Wells-Barnett and T. Thomas Fortune were quick to protest such denials. Wells devoted her considerable talents as a writer to challenging second-class citizenship, highlighting the numerous social and political injustices African Americans faced. In 1890, Fortune helped to found the Afro-American League that also sought to challenge discriminatory practices that robbed Black people of their Civil Rights. The *Plessy* decision provided a new sense of urgency that spurred the growth of numerous Black organizations focused on establishing equal rights and promoting self-help in the face of government indifference. African American activists organized in earnest.

The Black Women's Club Movement that emerged during the 1890s represented one response. From 1890 to 1920s, African American female activists organized hundreds of African American women's clubs including more than 150 in the city of Chicago alone. While promoting racial uplift, a sometimes conservative and patriarchal ideology that called for educated African Americans to assume responsibility for the welfare of the entire race, the clubs addressed a host of issues pertinent to the Black community. Their efforts included campaigns to stop lynching and to provide educational opportunities for African

Americans. In 1896, Black Women's Clubs combined to form the National Association of Colored Women's Clubs (NACW). Selecting Mary Church Terrell as the first president, the organization adopted the motto "Lifting as We Climb," illustrating its uplift and Civil Rights agenda.

The year before the NACW's founding, in September of 1895, African American educator Booker T. Washington, also within the uplift tradition, offered a different response. By endorsing the doctrine of separate but equal, Washington hoped to carve out an economic niche for African Americans non-threatening to white supremacy. Invited to give an address on the racial progress made in the South since the war at the much-anticipated 1895 Atlanta Exposition, the founder of the Tuskegee Institute, who had been born in slavery, expressed his willingness to sacrifice political and social equality for economic opportunity. Decrying efforts at agitation for social equality as "the extremist folly," he promised his predominately white audience, "In all things that are purely social we can be as separate as the fingers, yet one as the hand in all things essential to mutual progress."

Embraced by white supremacists and northern philanthropists as a viable solution to the race question, Washington's speech received mixed reviews among African Americans. Some acknowledged the need to build economic power. Many, including African American scholar W.E.B. Du Bois, refused to accept Washington's submissive acceptance of white supremacy. "So far as Mr. Washington preaches thrift, patience, and industrial training for the masses," Du Bois explained, "We must hold up his hands and strive with him."

> But so far as Mr. Washington apologizes for injustice, North or South, does not rightly value the privilege and duty of voting, belittles the emasculating effects of caste distinction and opposes the higher training and ambition of our brighter minds—so far as he, the South, or the Nation, does this—we must unceasingly and firmly oppose them.[11]

Despite this opposition, Washington's message was welcomed among white elites, including President Theodore Roosevelt, whose patronage helped to make the savvy educator the recognized spokesperson for African Americans. Washington used his vast power and political influence, especially over the African American press, to silence his detractors. He also occasionally worked privately to combat barriers to Black equality like debt peonage. Washington's public kowtowing to white supremacy angered and alienated some would-be supporters while his underlying philosophy of self-reliance and self-help appealed to others. His emphasis on building Black economic power, for instance, intrigued Jamaican-born Black Nationalist Marcus Garvey who would later incorporate elements of Washington's philosophy into the bedrock of his Universal Negro Improvement Association (UNIA). Other features of Washington's thought, especially with regard to economic self-sufficiency, also took hold much later within groups like the Nation of Islam (NOI). Both the UNIA and the NOI embraced racial separation—believing for different reasons than Washington that integration was neither possible nor desirable.

The *Plessy* decision set the stage for the next half-century of struggle, standing as a great legal obstruction to full equality for people of color and a central target for individuals and organizations to occasionally mobilize around. It was unquestionably the *Plessy* decision that African American educator and Civil Rights activist W.E.B. Du Bois had in mind when he declared in 1903 that "The problem of the Twentieth Century," would be "the problem of the color line." His forecast proved accurate. He and a host of other women and men in diverse organizations spent the next half-century both directly and indirectly chipping away at racial apartheid.

Such opposition took many forms. Between 1900 and 1906 for instance, largely decentralized efforts to boycott Jim Crow public transportation emerged in some 25 southern cities.[12] A number of small but important Civil Rights organizations developed including Du Bois' own Niagara Movement, forerunner to the NAACP. Founded in Niagara Falls and led by African American elites whom Du Bois identified as the talented tenth, the most educated and best-equipped persons ready to lead the race, the group fashioned an agenda. They promoted racial uplift, but also sought to achieve absolute equality before the law through the restoration of Black voting rights and an end to anti-Black violence.

The NACW also remained active. Consistently weighing in on issues of national import such as lynching, Mary Church Terrell, along with other activists at the time, fought a two-front war on segregation at the local and national levels. "For fifteen years I have resided in Washington," she explained, noting the slowly encroaching divide of separate but equal in the nation's capital, "and while it was far from being a paradise for colored people when I first touched these shores, it has been doing its level best ever since to make conditions for us intolerable." The spread of segregation was not only evident in the South and southern cities like the District of Columbia but in the border states as well. African Americans found conditions in states like Missouri, Kentucky, Maryland, and Delaware as contentious and divided as in the states of the former Confederacy. A Kentucky African American news reporter noted of conditions in his state in 1891, the "Races get along nicely—like oil and water—the whites at the top and the Negroes at the bottom."

In many of these communities, segregation was established not by law (de jure segregation) but custom (de facto segregation). However, after *Plessy*, more overt forms of segregation were imposed even in areas where African Americans had enjoyed equal rights. This was on full display in Kentucky in 1908. Berea College, a private institution that admitted African American students, was compelled to observe a state ordinance dictating racial separation in the state's schools and colleges. The college found no relief from the U.S. Supreme Court, which upheld the Kentucky law. "Have we become so inoculated with preju-dice of race," Justice John Marshall Harlan was moved to ask in dissent, "that an American government, professedly based on the principles of freedom, and charged with the protection of all citizens alike, can make distinctions between such citizens in the matter of their voluntary meeting for innocent purposes, simply because of their respective races?"[13]

Cloaked with the precedent established in *Plessy*, Kentucky and other states erected such statutes using state police powers ostensibly to promote public safety by keeping the races separate and preventing violence between the races, an increasing problem at the turn of the century. A flurry of race riots after 1900, including a serious outbreak in August of 1908 in Springfield, Illinois, spurred the formation of the NAACP. The association melded the Niagara Movement, headed by Du Bois with the interest of prominent northern white liberals including suffragist, socialist, and journalist Mary White Ovington, journalist Oswald Garrison Villard, and labor reformer and socialist William English Walling. They were shocked by the violence in Springfield, the birth-place of Abraham Lincoln. The association pledged to fight for equal rights for African Americans demanding not only political, but also social and economic equality.[14]

The NAACP took two key steps in its early years that helped facilitate Civil Rights struggles later on. In 1910, the Association launched its own magazine, *The Crisis*. Edited by Du Bois, the monthly journal published news of interest to African Americans while also cataloguing incidents of lynching and other social, political, and economic abuses. With the creation of a National Legal Redress Committee in 1911, the association likewise set its sights on combating segregation through the courts. In 1915, it sought to topple one of the barriers to voting rights focusing on Oklahoma's Grandfather Clause. In the aftermath of the Civil War, white supremacists experimented with various methods of disfranchising Black voters including the poll tax, Grandfather Clause, and lit-eracy test. By the time the NAACP formed, 10 southern states amended their state constitutions utilizing one or a combination of these measures to dis-franchise Black voters. Despite triumph in the Grandfather Clause case, African Americans still had to contend with other efforts to restrict or render the Black vote nugatory such as the use of the white primary—which restricted Blacks from participating in primary elections thus denying them any voice over a party's candidates or agenda.

The NAACP was not only concerned with political rights. In 1917, it waged an equally successful battle to have state sanctioned residential segregation over-turned. In the case of *Buchanan* v. *Warley*, which involved a city ordinance from Louisville, Kentucky, the Association showed that city and state residential laws were a violation of the 14th Amendment's privileges and immunities clause. As with the Grandfather Clause case, white supremacists simply found other means to prevent African Americans from purchasing homes in white areas through the adoption of racially restrictive covenants—nominally private contracts that barred Blacks from occupying homes in white neighborhoods except as domestic servants.

While the NAACP battled against segregation, intolerable conditions in the South helped spur the first wave of the Great Migration. Compelled by the lack of economic, social, and political freedom in the South many African Americans began to seek refuge in the urban North and West. Between 1910 and 1970, an estimated six million African Americans abandoned southern states in search of greater economic, social, and political opportunity in northern and Midwestern cities like New York, Pittsburg, and Chicago.

In the first phase of this "Great Migration" that lasted from 1910 until 1930, African Americans found ample work in tanneries, steel mills, and on the railroads. America's entry into World War I also brought additional opportunities for jobs in factories related to the war industries. The war itself, however, divided Black leaders. Some, like W.E.B. Du Bois, saw it as an opportunity to stake a claim to freedom and equality; others, like Black labor leader A. Phillip Randolph, remained skeptical.

African Americans experienced prejudice in America's Jim Crow Army. While some 380,000 Blacks served in the war, only about 42,000 saw combat.[15] Southern plantation owners, in particular, feared the potential impact of the war not only on their profits but also on race relations. In order to preserve their control over Black labor, they were able to delay conscription of Black soldiers until after the harvest season. They also publicly expressed worry, about the impact the war might have on "race relations," especially after a group of armed Black soldiers in Houston during August of 1917 retaliated in response to repeated abuses. These fears were best summed up by racist Mississippi Senator James K. Vardaman who claimed to "know of no greater menace to the South" than the arming of Black soldiers.[16]

In the end, African Americans served with distinction but returned to a nation unwilling to honor their sacrifice. Lynching increased steadily in the years after the war. In 1917, 62 Black people were lynched; two years later, 77 were killed in this manner, including 10 still wearing their military uniforms. Worse still was the rash of race riots that rocked American cities during what became known as the Red Summer of 1919. Thousands of people, Black and white, were killed in racially fueled battles that swept through Washington, Chicago, Omaha, and New York, not to mention numerous other cities both North and South. Fed up with Jim Crow, Black people fought back against indignities as a means of self-defense. Whites blamed the violence on a new attitude of defiance on the part of Blacks returning from the Great War.

This new attitude was reflected in the "New Negro Movement" headquartered in Harlem and sweeping other cities. Significant political overtones emanated from this movement of cultural expression as Black art and literature reflected new images of Black identity and questioned the depth of American democracy.

Emblematic of the period was Claude McKay's 1919 poem, "If We Must Die." Written in response to violence of the "Red Summer" McKay recalled the fear and danger that pervaded the Black community. "Our Negro newspapers," he later recalled, "were morbid, full of details of clashes between colored and white, murderous shootings and hangings." He continued: "It was during those days that the sonnet, 'If We Must Die,' exploded out of me. And for it the Negro people unanimously hailed me as a poet."[17]

McKay was not the only artist or poet to find a voice and approval for speaking out against injustice in his work. Scores of artists, singers, poets, writers, and musicians worked to fashion a new Black aesthetic. Alternatively known as the Harlem or Black Renaissance, the New Negro Movement of the 1920s was also an important precursor to the Civil Rights and Black Power Movements in terms of creating an aesthetic divorced from the racist and stereo-typical views of "Negroes." Distinct forms of cultural expression in song and dance also proved vital to the later movement. The music, art, literature, and poetry coming out of the Black Renaissance inspired the Black Arts Movement of the 1960s that drew upon and expanded themes of racial pride and uplift as seen in the works of author Lorraine Hansberry, journalist William Worthy, and poet and playwright Amiri Baraka.[18]

The violent treatment of African Americans in the war's aftermath confirmed for some the need to look beyond the borders of the United States for answers. Du Bois, who had enthusiastically supported the war with the slogan "Our War Our Country," was deeply disappointed in the meager considerations extended to Black veterans. In the shadow of the international peace process, he embraced Pan-Africanism and in February of 1919, he helped to convene the First Pan African Congress that pushed for the decolonization of and return of home rule in Africa and the West Indies—an agenda that brought him at least partially into line with one of his arch revivals, Jamaican-born Black Nationalist Marcus Garvey. With the motto "One Aim, One God, One Destiny," Garvey's UNIA railed against the "slavery, racial exploitation and alien political monopoly" introduced by European colonization that plagued African as well as Latin American and Caribbean nations.[19]

While racial separation was the crux of Garvey's program, other nationalists strove to create parallel institutions that sought to instill race pride while bolstering American citizenship. In 1913, Prophet Noble Drew Ali (Timothy Drew), for instance, launched the Moorish Science Temple in Newark, New Jersey. While embracing elements of Garvey's organization and programming, the Moors nevertheless privileged American citizenship and sought to make Blacks model citizens by adhering to strict guidelines also within the uplift tradition. Promulgating a message that identified Blacks as "Asiatic" Moors and descendants from the Holy Land of Canaan, Ali perpetuated a Black-centered theology that gained significant traction during the 1920s. Over the course of the decade, new temples were established in many of the same cities that proved popular migration destinations for southern Blacks including Detroit, Philadelphia, and New York, not to mention Washington, DC. Drew actually relocated to Chicago in 1925. The Moorish Science Temple's brand of religious Black Nationalism continued to flourish into the 1930s, becoming the hallmark of other faith leaders such as Father Divine who blended elements of religion and Black Nationalism into a cohesive force for racial uplift. The Moorish Science Temple played a critical role in the formation of the NOI as Ali's successor Wallace D. Fard mentored NOI founder Elijah Poole, better known as Elijah Muhammad.[20]

Marcus Garvey was deported in 1929 for tax evasion but his supporters continued to push his agenda and program. After the stock market crash of 1929 plunged the nation into economic despair, their program and ideology gained new appeal. Segregation and racism ensured that the meager relief efforts undertaken by the Hoover administration and public assistance agencies often ignored African Americans. With an emphasis on self-help, Black Nationalist organizations pursued alternative paths to security and independence including calls for a government-sponsored repatriation back to Africa. In 1933 for instance, Louisiana native and Black Nationalist Mittie Maud Lena Gordon's Chicago-based Peace Movement of Ethiopia secured more than 400,000 signatures on a petition sent to President Roosevelt requesting the repatriation of Blacks back to Africa. Later in the decade, Gordon, a former Garveyite, found an unlikely ally in Mississippi Segregationist Senator Theodore Bilbo who signed off on the initiative to support his own white supremacist agenda.[21]

Gordon was clearly not alone. In 1936, *Newsweek* magazine reported on the resurgence of a "vast new Back-to Africa Movement ... growing in strength." Popularized by Marcus Garvey in the 1920s, the Back to Africa Movement had roots in the 1820s, when abolitionists, such as John Russwurm, situated by the historian Winston James as "Pan-Africanist Pioneer," promoted colonization as an alternative to emancipation. In the late 1930s, reverberations of Marcus Garvey's UNIA could still be felt as Garvey himself remained active on the international scene. The nationalist sentiments of Hitler and Mussolini appealed to Garvey who dreamed of an independent homeland for displaced people of African descent on the continent of Africa. In 1939, Ramon Martinez, the head of the Detroit-based Negro Nationalist Society of America, actually drafted a bill for Bilbo to introduce to Congress requesting the repatriation of African Americans to Africa. In spite of their support and the media coverage, those interested in pursuing a return to Africa remained largely on the fringes.[22]

For the vast majority of African Americans, the better alternative was to work to reform the United States and make it live up to the ideals expressed in its founding documents. Although African Americans loyally supported the Republican Party for its role in the Civil War and Reconstruction, by the 1930s the realities of the Great Depression argued for a change. The reelection of Franklin Delano Roosevelt in 1936 marked the beginning of a transformation in which African Americans in large numbers switched their political allegiances from the Party of Lincoln to the Democrats. From a practical standpoint Roosevelt's program of Relief, Reform, and Recovery proved more attractive than President Herbert Hoover's belief in a natural market recovery. While Roosevelt's New Deal set to work reforming the nation's economy, the government agencies charged with administering New Deal programs abided by Jim Crow standards limiting the impact of relief efforts on African Americans burdened by both economic hardship and racism.[23]

Nevertheless, the New Deal did provide some important opportunities. Roosevelt's willingness to cultivate African American opinion endeared him to some. The support and patronage of First Lady Eleanor Roosevelt earned the respect and admiration of others. The appointment of African American leaders like college founder and club leader Mary McLeod Bethune to the National Youth Administration signaled the willingness of the President to acknowledge African American concerns, even if in the end the results were not as substantive as they had hoped for.

America's entry into World War II however soon shifted the political landscape significantly, affecting the Black Freedom Struggle in several important respects. First, the ideological nature of the conflict forced the nation to contend with the meaning of democracy against the backdrop of Axis propaganda that highlighted American hypocrisy on the issue of race. While American war propaganda focused on a defense of liberty, the denial of basic freedoms to African Americans called the very essence of American democracy into question. Second, from the outset, African Americans saw the war as an opportunity to press for full citizenship. Melding a patriotic defense of democracy with calls for its full implementation, they pressed for what the *Pittsburgh Courier* derived from a January 1942 letter by reader James G. Thompson labeled a "Double V" campaign calling for victory over America's enemies abroad and over racial bigotry at home. Supported by organizations such as the NAACP and the Urban League, the "Double V" gained momentum early, especially in the area of fair employment practices.[24]

The increased labor demands occasioned by the war, for instance, allowed Civil Rights leader and labor organizer A. Phillip Randolph to use the threat of a mass march on Washington as a means to win better pay and equal opportunity for African Americans in the bustling defense industries. Randolph's March on Washington Movement (MOWM) also sought to use direct action protest as a means of communicating African American frustrations with second-class citizenship. Eager to prevent such a potentially embarrassing demonstration in June of 1941, President Roosevelt issued Executive Order 8802 outlawing discrimination in the defense industries. The first executive directive on race since Reconstruction, the historic order also established the Fair Employment Practices Commission (FEPC) to ensure fairness and equality in hiring in industries and unions involved in filling government contracts.

As a result, some two million Black workers gained employment in defense-related industries by the close of the war; another 200,000 secured federal civil service jobs. Union membership among African Americans also skyrocketed, nearly doubling to 1,250,000 by 1945.[25]

Although the MOWM achieved its primary goal of opening employment opportunities, Randolph was not satisfied. He and the other organizers conceived of the march as a demonstration for both jobs and freedom. While 8802 opened up the defense industries, African Americans still suffered from the denial of basic freedoms, including the right to vote. To address these concerns in November 1942, Randolph moved to broaden the MOWM agenda to include demands "to end of Jim Crow in education, in housing, in transportation and in every other social, economic, and political privilege." While these demands were not as easily met as the ones in the area of defense employment practices, they pointed to a basic outline of the Civil Rights Movement to emerge and its chief targets of segregation in housing, education, and places of public accommodation.[26]

Efforts at pressing the government to move into other areas in which it could act unilaterally also proved fruitful. Despite their distinguished service in World War I, African Americans still served in a Jim Crow military. At the start of the war, only about 4,000 Black men were in uniform. Although the Selective Service Act of 1940 officially barred discrimination in recruitment and training of soldiers, draft boards routinely rejected Black recruits. The military further assigned African Americans to non-combat units charged with support functions including maintenance, transport, and supply. While this work played a crucial support role in advancing the war effort, African Americans demanded the opportunity to fight. Civil Rights organizations readily took up the cause. In order to prevent discrimination by draft boards the NAACP petitioned President Roosevelt to certify that Black enlistment numbers fairly mirror population percentages. In most instances, the government willingly obliged. Given the ideological nature of the conflict and the desire to convey widespread support for the war, the government adopted new programs designed to cast a veneer of equality on segregated practices. In response to complaints about the treatment of Black military personnel, army authorities issued a ruling outlawing segregation on military bases. These rule changes provided some protection for Black soldiers. In 1944, three years shy of his historic reintegration of major league baseball, military authorities dismissed a court martial case against Jackie Robinson for his failure to give up his seat on a segregated Texas bus after he reminded the tribunal of the new policy. Civil Rights organizations also pushed the government to allow Black pilots to participate in the Army Air Corp. African American fighters eventually saw training at a segregated base in Tuskegee, Alabama and formed the all-Black Fighter Squadron and bombardier unit better known as the "Tuskegee Airmen" who flew missions into southern Europe as well as North Africa.[27]

These changes however were not enough to overcome the prejudice and discrimination Black soldiers faced at the hands of their fellow citizens. In many instances, German POWs received better treatment. Black soldiers offered a blistering critique of the paradox best captured by the writer Stephen Ambrose of how the "world's greatest democracy fought the world's greatest racist with a segregated Army." Despite this paradox by 1945 approximately 1.2 million African Americans had served in the various branches, including thousands of Black women in the Women's Auxiliary Corps units with a record of distinguished service.[28]

Thus, African American soldiers returned from the war more determined than ever to challenge second-class citizenship. They joined a broad range of other activists including labor organizers, pacifists, communists, and Black Nationalists whose own agendas also targeted the racism and inequality that defined life for African Americans. Over the course of the next two decades, their combined efforts to address the issues of housing, education, unfair labor practices, Jim Crow Justice, voting rights and discrimination in transportation and places of public accommodation launched the Modern Civil Rights Movement.

Notes

1   A. Phillip Randolph quoted in James R. Green and Robert C. Hayden, "A. Philip Randolph and Boston's African-American Railroad Worker," *Trotter Review* 6, no. 2 (1992): 20; see also Jervis Anderson, *A. Philip Randolph: A Biographical Portrait* (Berkeley: University of California Press, 1972 [1986]), v.

2   John Lewis quoted in "Rep. John Lewis Pushes For Updated Voting Rights Act," http://hereandnow.wbur.org/2013/07/17/senate-voting-rights, accessed, July 2, 2015

3   Aldon D. Morris, *The Origins of the Civil Rights Movement: Black Communities Organizing for Change* (New York: The Free Press, 1984), x.

4   Robert Korstad, *Civil Rights Unionism: Tobacco Workers and the Struggle for Democracy in the Mid-Twentieth-Century South* (Chapel Hill: University of North Carolina Press, 2003), 5.

5   Martin Luther King, Jr., "MIA Mass Meeting at Holt Street Baptist Church," December 5, 1955, in Clayborne Carson, Stewart Burns, Susan Carson, Pete Holloran, and Dana L.H. Powell, eds., *The Papers of Martin Luther King, Jr., Volume 2: Rediscovering Precious Values, July 1951–November 1955* (Berkeley: University of California Press, 1994), 72.

6   On Rosa Parks see Jeanne Theoharis "'A Life History of Being Rebellious': The Radicalism of Rosa Parks," in Dayo Gore, Jeanne Theoharis and Komozi Woodard, eds., *Want to Start a Revolution? Radical Women in the Black Freedom Struggle* (New York: New York University Press, 2009); Herbert Kohl, *She Would Not Be Moved: How We Tell the Story of Rosa Parks and the Montgomery Bus Boycott* (New York: The New Press, 2005).

7   King quoted in Stewart Burns, *Daybreak of Freedom: The Montgomery Bus Boycott* (Chapel Hill: University of North Carolina Press, 1997), vii. For a short and

accessible account of the Montgomery Bus Boycott see Donnie Williams and Wayne Greenhaw's *The Thunder of Angels: The Montgomery Bus Boycott and the People Who Broke the Back of Jim Crow* (New York: Lawrence Hill, 2005).

8   George Washington Cable, *The Silent South, Together With The Freedman's Case In Equity And The Convict Lease System* (New York: C. Scribner's Sons, 1899), 16.

9   Henry McNeal Turner, *Civil Rights. The Outrage of the Supreme Court of the United States upon the Black Man. Reviewed in a Reply to the New York "Voice," the Great Temperance Paper of the United States* (Philadelphia: Publication Department A.M.E. Church, 1889).

10 C. Vann Woodward, *The Strange Career of Jim Crow: A Commemorative Edition* (New York and Oxford: Oxford University Press, 2002).

11 Dubois quoted in Francis L. Broderick, *W.E.B. Du Bois, Negro Leader in a Time of Crisis,* Volume 2 (Palo Alto: Stanford University Press, 1959), 69; Robert Oscar Lopez, "The Colors of Double Exceptionalism—The Founders and African America," *Literature Compass* 5, no. 1 (2008): 20–41. On Du Bois' life and work see David Levering Lewis, *W.E.B. Du Bois: The Fight for Equality and the American Century, 1919–1963* (New York: Henry Holt, 2000).

12 On these protests see Blair L.M. Kelley, *Right to Ride: Streetcar Boycotts and African American Citizenship in the Era of Plessy v. Ferguson* (Chapel Hill: University of North Carolina Press, 2010); August Meier and Elliott Rudwick "The Boycott Movement Against Jim Crow Streetcars in the South, 1900–1906," *The Journal of American History* 55, no. 4 (1969): 756–75.

13 *Berea College v. Kentucky*, 211 U.S. 45, 60 (1908) (Harlan, J., dissenting).

14 For a comprehensive account of the history of the NAACP see Patricia Sullivan, *Lift Every Voice: The NAACP and the Making of the Civil Rights Movement* (New York: New Press, 2009).

15 For an accessible account on African Americans, Civil Rights and World War II, see Kevin M. Kruse and Stephen Tuck, eds., *The Fog of War: The Second World War and the Civil Rights Movement* (New York: Oxford University Press, 2012).

16 James Vardaman quoted in James Campbell, *The Color of War: How One Battle Broke Japan and Another Changed America* (New York: Crown Books, 2012), 392.

17 Claude McKay quoted in Anne P. Rice, *Witnessing Lynching: American Writers Respond* (New Brunswick: Rutgers University Press, 2003), 189.

18 For discussions of the connection between Black music and art and Black Freedom Struggles generally see Lawrence Levin, *Black Culture and Black Consciousness* (New York: Oxford University Press, 1977); Brian Ward, *Just My Soul Responding: Rhythm and Blues, Black Consciousness and Race Relations* (Berkeley: University of California Press, 1998); Marc Anthony Neal, *What the Music Said: Black Popular Music and Black Public Culture* (New York: Routledge, 1999); Robin D.G. Kelley, *Africa Speaks, America Answers: Modern Jazz in Revolutionary Times* (Cambridge, MA: Harvard University Press, 2012).

19 Wilson Jeremiah Moses, ed., *Classical Black Nationalism: From the American Revolution to Marcus Garvey* (New York: New York University Press, 1996).

20 Susan Nance, "Respectability and Representation: The Moorish Science Temple, Morocco, and Black Public Culture in 1920s Chicago," *American Quarterly* 54, no. 4 (2002): 623–59.

21 Michael W. Fitzgerald, "'We Have Found a Moses': Theodore Bilbo, Black Nationalism, and the Greater Liberia Bill of 1939," *The Journal of Southern History* (1997): 293–320; Ernest Allen, Jr., "When Japan was 'Champion of the Darker

Races': Satokata Takahashi and the Flowering of Black Messianic Nationalism," *The Black Scholar* (1994): 23–46; George Lipsitz, "Frantic to Join ... the Japanese ... the Asia Pacific War," in T. Fujitani, Geoffrey M.L. White, and Lisa Yoneyama, eds., *Perilous Memories: The Asia-Pacific War(s)* (Durham, NC: Duke University Press, 2001), 347–77.

22 Winston James, *The Struggles of John Brown Russwurm: The Life and Writings of a Pan-Africanist Pioneer, 1799–1851* (New York: New York University Press, 2010).

23 Cheryl Greenberg, *To Ask for an Equal Chance: African Americans in the Great Depression* (Lanham, MD: Rowman & Littlefield, 2009); Harvard Sitkoff, *A New Deal for Blacks: The Emergence of Civil Rights as a National Issue* (New York: Oxford University Press, 1978); Patricia Sullivan, *Days of Hope: Race and Democracy in the New Deal Era* (Chapel Hill: University of North Carolina Press, 1996); Beth Bates' "'Double V for Victory' Mobilizes Black Detroit, 1941–1946," in Jeanne Theoharis and Komzi Woodward, eds., *Freedom North: Black Freedom Struggles Outside the South, 1940–1980* (New York: Palgrave Macmillan, 2003).

24 Rawn James, Jr., *The Double V: How Wars, Protest, and Harry Truman Desegregated America's Military* (New York: Bloomsbury Publishing USA, 2013).

25 Cornelius L. Bynum, *A. Philip Randolph and the Struggle for Civil Rights* (Urbana: University of Illinois Press, 2010).

26 A. Phillip Randolph, "Why Should We March?" in William L. Van Deburg, ed., *Modern Black Nationalism: From Marcus Garvey to Louis Farrakhan* (New York: New York University Press, 1997), 76–7.

27 Jules Tygiel, "The Court Martial of Jackie Robinson," in Jules Tygiel, ed., *The Jackie Robinson Reader* (New York: Penguin Dutton, 1997), 40–51; Michael F. Higginbotham, "Soldiers for Justice: The Role of the Tuskegee Airmen in the Desegregation of the American Armed Forces," *William & Mary Bill of Rights Journal* 8, no. 2 (2000): 273; Todd J. Moye, *Freedom Flyers: The Tuskegee Airmen of World War II* (Cambridge: Oxford University Press, 2010).

28 Stephen E. Ambrose, Citizen *Soldiers: The U.S. Army from the Normandy Beaches to the Bulge to the Surrender of Germany* (New York: Simon & Schuster, 1998), 345–6.

2

AMERICA'S SECOND CIVIL WAR

Nonviolent direct action seeks to create such a crisis and foster such a tension that a community which has constantly refused to negotiate is forced to confront the issue. My citing the creation of tension may sound rather shocking. But I must confess that I am not afraid of the word 'tension.' I have earnestly opposed violent tension, but there is a type of constructive, nonviolent tension which is necessary for growth.

Martin Luther King, Jr. "Letter from Birmingham Jail" (1963)[1]

In his groundbreaking study of the Civil Rights Movement in Mississippi, *I've Got the Light of Freedom*, historian Charles Payne argues that the movement emerged from "two distinct traditions"—a community mobilizing tradition that focused on large-scale, relatively short-term public campaigns and a community organizing tradition that emphasized long-term grassroots community leadership and development. The first, and more familiar of the two, is ultimately what contributed to the major battles of the Second Civil War embodied in Montgomery, Birmingham, and Chicago that are covered in brief in this chapter.

In his yearly executive address to the SCLC on August 11, 1965, just days after the passage of the Voting Rights Act, the Reverend Dr. Martin Luther King summarized the decade of protest from 1955–1965 thusly. "Montgomery," he explained, "led to the Civil Rights Act of 1957 and 1960; Birmingham inspired the Civil Rights Act of 1964, and Selma produced the voting rights legislation of 1965." As in the aftermath of the Civil War, people put their hope and faith into the new legislation, which they assumed would and could shatter unfair law and custom and guarantee absolute equality under the law. They had every reason to be optimistic. Approximately 82 years separated the passage of the Civil Rights Act of 1957 and the last piece of Reconstruction Era legislation.

Only 8 years separated the Civil Rights Act of 1957 and the Civil Rights Act of 1965. For Dr. King and many others, the new national legislation affirming African American Civil Rights was a tangible benchmark of the movement's progress.

Over the past four decades, scholars sought to document the movement's scope and influence outside the boundaries of the South and beyond what historian Jacqueline Dowd Hall described as "limited non-economic objectives."[2] Subsequent chapters will briefly explore some of those initiatives. The present chapter, however, takes the more conventional approach of looking at the progress of the movement squarely through the lens of national politics. At this macro level, the promise and rhetoric of American democracy loomed large, helping to define the movement as an effort completing the arc started by the American Revolution and ensuring absolute equality under the law. Inspired by the movement's emphasis on making the promises of the Declaration of Independence real, former Yale University professor, and SNCC activist Staunton Lynd notably referred to the movement as a Second American Revolution. Similarly, drawing on history, scholar activist Howard Zinn referred to SNCC, of which he was a member, as "the New Abolitionists."[3] Such comparisons sought to put the movement's goals and objectives in the much broader context of the expansion of American democracy.

In 1991, Howard University Professor Arnold Taylor likened the heroic phase of the Civil Rights Movement to a Second Civil War. Highlighting the major contests that ultimately led to landmark court cases and legislation like *Brown* v. *Board of Education* and the Civil Rights Act of 1964, Taylor proposed measuring the movement's progress through its most notable campaigns. Although demonstrations took place throughout the United States historians generally focused on key battles tied to the major organizations like SNCC and leaders such as the Reverend Dr. Martin Luther King. These include the 1955–6 Montgomery Bus Boycott, the 1957 integration of Little Rock Central High School in Arkansas, the 1960s sit-ins and subsequent Freedom Rides, the Albany Movement in 1962, Birmingham, Alabama in 1963, Freedom Summer 1964, Selma, Alabama in 1965, the Meredith March 1966, the Chicago Campaign in 1966, and Memphis in 1968.[4]

The Supreme Court's unanimous decision in *Brown* v. *Board of Education* became the launch pad for these key battles. As University of New Hampshire history professor, Harvard Sitkoff, argued, no single event did more to encourage Black hopes. Nevertheless, in the decade following the decision was far from a panacea. Sitkov notes that while "individual blacks of talent desegregated most professions, the recessions of the 1950's caused black unemployment to soar and the gap between black and white family income to widen." Furthermore, despite the rulings of the Supreme Court and the goodwill and lip service paid by many politicians to Civil Rights, Sitkov explains that massive resistance to desegregation throughout the South remained the rule. This was the context for the second stage of the Civil Rights Movement, as the nation's attempts to slow integration collided with both Black expectations and dissatisfaction with the speed of change. This resulted in activists taking to the streets in a wave of nonviolent protest in what Sitkov describes as "direct-action protests against every aspect of racism still humiliating them."[5]

One of the main reasons the *Brown* decision continues to stand as one of the starting points for the movement stems from to the backlash it produced. Fearful of school integration, *Brown* precipitated a political crisis in the South embodied in the pledges of massive resistance seen most visibly in the 11 states of the Old Confederacy. The *Brown* decision transformed the political landscape of the South, as a chorus of racial demagogues replaced more moderate points of view in a climate of political extremism that pledged massive resistance to school desegregation. Many of the overt actions taken by Southern officials to forestall Brown such as outlawing the NAACP also sought to prevent Black organizing and mobilization. The Montgomery Bus Boycott proved what Black people could accomplish through direct action protest. Segregationists were keenly aware of the power represented by their efforts. Nevertheless, officials such as Virginia Governor J. Lindsay Almond were not dissuaded from pursuing more radical solutions to circumvent and neutralize *Brown*, including suspending public education in the state.

Although there were battles and skirmishes in cities, towns, and communities throughout the country, the major national battles, which involved most of the major Civil Rights organizations, played out in the previously mentioned campaigns. Each, directly or indirectly, helped to set the stage for the passage of momentous legislation or the significant tactical or strategic shifts within the movement itself. After the Albany campaign, for instance, Dr. King recognized that his organization would have to be less haphazard in the way that it engaged in protest activities.

Civil Rights activists fought the major campaigns of the Second Civil War —for the most part in the former states of the Confederacy: Alabama (1955 and 1963) Arkansas (1957), Georgia (1962), and Mississippi (1964). The notable exception is Chicago, Illinois (1966).

This did not mean there were not important campaigns taking place elsewhere in the nation. Dating back to the period just after World War II activists undertook significant protest initiatives in a variety of cities in the West and North including Oakland, California, Philadelphia, Pennsylvania, Detroit, Michigan, New York, New York, and New Haven, Connecticut. While these highly localized struggles may have failed to capture the nation's attention in the same way the national movement identified with King did they nevertheless paved the way for substantive changes in the communities where they took place. They also helped to shape the national movement by helping to keep the pressure on politicians to deal with issues of Black inequality.[6]

After 1955, however, many of these local struggles drew inspiration from a successful boycott of public transportation in the capital of Alabama that also served as the first capitol of the Confederacy. The Montgomery Bus Boycott ushered in a new phase of the Black Freedom Struggle with the widespread adoption of nonviolent direct action protest as a means of challenging racial apartheid.

Montgomery Alabama, 1955–6

As the first "major battle" of Taylor's Second Civil War, Montgomery Alabama holds a unique place in history. Montgomery was not unlike many other cities in the South at this time. The system of segregation was no more, and no less, oppressive than in other cities. The frustration expressed by the Black community was also not unique. The protests began in support of local Civil Rights activist and NAACP chapter officer Rosa Parks after she refused to give up her seat in defiance of local segregation ordinances and soon transformed into a significant mass movement. Organizers called for boycotts, which had been used in the past to challenge southern apartheid and racial segregation. The unprecedented attention and support it drew not only in Alabama but throughout the nation made the protest singular. In the process of securing the first victory of the Second Civil War, events in Montgomery provided a blueprint for the nonviolent armies that secured a national victory for Civil Rights and an end to Jim Crow Segregation in America.

The boycott came at a time when the nation was ripe for change. The legal struggle waged by the NAACP culminating in the *Brown* decision in 1954, coupled with basic socioeconomic changes in American society set in motion by the New Deal and World War II, set the stage for the action in Montgomery. The brutal lynching of 14-year-old Emmett Till a few months before in Mississippi in August of 1955 shocked, saddened, and infuriated many activists.[7] As Bayard Rustin recalled:

> There was a building up of militancy, not so much by going into the streets as by a feeling of we are not going to take this anymore. Some of us had been sitting down in the front of busses for years, but nothing happened. What made '54 so unusual was that the Supreme Court in the Brown decision established black people as being citizens with all the rights of all other citizens. Once that happened, then it was very easy for that militancy, which had been building up to express itself in the Montgomery bus boycott of 55'-56.[8]

In 1955, Ralph David Abernathy, the pastor of Montgomery's First Baptist Church and a founding member of the Montgomery Improvement Association, noted the economic impact of segregation in the city where the majority of

African Americans worked as domestics or laborers. "In the whole state of Alabama," Abernathy explained, "we had probably less than five black doctors ... All of the restaurants were segregated, the hotels and motels were segregated ... Even in the public courthouse, blacks could not drink water except from the fountain labeled 'Colored ...'. You could not use a filling station that was not designated with a restroom for colored ..."[9]

Law as well as custom informed Montgomery's segregation practices. The officers who arrested Rosa Parks on the evening of December 1, 1955 were an important part of the legal enforcement of Montgomery's segregation laws. The exchange between Parks and one of the arresting officers is instructive. As Parks reported:

> One of the policemen asked me if the bus driver had asked me to stand and I said yes. He said, "Why don't you stand up?" And I asked him why do you push us around? He said, "I do not know, but the law is the law and you're under arrest."[10]

Regardless of the officers' sincerity, the judicial system in Montgomery recognized these laws as valid and punished violators accordingly. The roots of Rosa Parks' defiance went far beyond her experience on the bus that afternoon or her encounter with the police however. Her actions emerged from the profound frustration, resentment, and weariness of Black southerners with the humiliating southern racial caste system. In the 18 months preceding the Parks incident, at least four other Black citizens of Montgomery—Claudette Colvin, Mrs. Amelia Browden, a Mrs. Smith, and the Reverend Vernon Johns, King's predecessor as the pastor of the Dexter Avenue Baptist Church—all refused to obey an order to give up their seats to white passengers.[11]

The Montgomery Improvement Association (MIA) that spearheaded the boycott began with the efforts of community leaders to protest Parks' arrest. E.D. Nixon, whose résumé included serving as head of the Progressive Democratic Party in Alabama, showcased the deep organizing traditions within the city; he was among those critical to the early stages of the MIA's development. Nixon also served as president of the Montgomery chapter of A. Phillip Randolph's Brotherhood of Sleeping Car Porters and led the local NAACP. Next, Reverend L. Roy Bennett, President of the Interdenominational Ministerial Alliance, lent his organizational skills to the movement. While Bennett alienated some supporters of the proposed boycott initially, in the end he proved to be a valuable asset to the MIA leadership. Reverend Ralph David Abernathy, who was secretary of the Baptist Ministers Alliance, volunteered his services to Nixon, and encouraged his good friend Martin Luther King of Dexter Avenue Church to get involved as well. Jo Ann Robinson, president of the Women's Political Council, and Rufus Lewis, an Alabama business professional with many ties in the state and the community, who headed

Montgomery's Citizens Steering Committee, were also heavily involved. In addition, a host of ministers from Montgomery's Black churches was involved in the initial meetings of what would become the MIA. Many Black churches lent support to the movement. In fact, the MIA's elected leadership would be comprised primarily of ministers. This network of church, civic, and union leaders provided the MIA with a broad base of support, and clear established lines of communication.

Women played a significant role in challenging segregation in Montgomery. As early as 1946, the Black women of Montgomery organized the Women's Political Council (WPC) in response to scores of arrest of Black riders for violating Montgomery's segregated transportation ordinance. By 1955, the WPC's membership expanded to include a broad cross-section of Montgomery's Black population, providing the organization with ability to mobilize the community to action. As its President Jo Ann Robinson explained, "We were prepared to the point that we knew in a matter of hours, we could corral the whole city."[12] Thus, the WPC provided critical assistance to the MIA in its early stages.

In the meantime, the MIA selected as its president the 26-year-old pastor of the Dexter Avenue Baptist Church, the Reverend Dr. Martin Luther King, Jr. The son of a prominent Atlanta minister, King resided in Montgomery only for a year prior to Parks' arrest. Rufus Lewis, who nominated King, recognized the young pastor's educational achievements and gifted oratorical skills as important assets. Lewis imagined these qualities appealing strongly to the wealthier, professional segment of the Black community, whose support the MIA needed to cultivate in sustaining a boycott. In addition, Lewis believed that King's status as a Baptist minister helped to bring reluctant ministers into the fold to support the boycott. In addition, King's appeal as a minister extended to regular churchgoers in the Black community. Finally, King's brief residency in Montgomery offered a degree of immunity from the past failings of other leaders and kept him out of reach of Montgomery's white leadership that might have otherwise attempt to use his community ties in undermining the MIA.

In exchange for calling off the boycott, the MIA made three modest demands. The first requested more courteous treatment of Black passengers speaking to the humiliation and degradation they felt at paying full fare while subjected to second-class treatment. The other two, which included a call for seating on a first-come, first-served basis that continued the current practice of seating from the rear of the bus forward and the hiring of Black bus drivers on non-integrated routes illustrating the concern for jobs. Though modest, the demands potentially resulted in a complete dismantling of Montgomery's segregated transit system. If local officials had been willing to compromise, segregation would have remained largely intact. They refused, however, believing that the smallest concessions would lead to further demands and a further weakening of the city's system of racial apartheid.

Despite the modest goals of the MIA, opposition to the organization ran high throughout Montgomery's white community. After efforts by Montgomery's white business community failed to end the protest, the opposition turned to intimidation. In February of 1956, officials charged 90 members of the MIA with conspiring to conduct an illegal boycott. A Grand Jury comprised mostly of segregationists returned indictments against King and other leaders of the MIA.

The indictments proved a blessing in disguise as the boycott attracted more national awareness, generating additional sources of funding for the MIA. Illustrating the strong grassroots support for the movement, initially, they operated largely through monies collected at weekly mass meetings. As operating expenses increased, the organization proved less equipped to deal with the heavy costs involved in managing the support apparatus needed to sustain the boycott. In the wake of the indictments, many northern church parishes and human rights organization sent contributions. In addition, King traveled extensively throughout the country, raising money for the organization by giving speeches at colleges and civic events.

When legal methods failed to bring the boycott to a halt, the white citizens of Montgomery resorted to harassment and terror tactics in an attempt to intimidate those in MIA leadership positions, including the systematic bombing of the homes and churches of those prominent leaders. In addition, Montgomery police officers regularly harassed drivers participating in the MIA's car pool, frequently stopping them for minor traffic violations and various other concocted infractions. In his book *Free At Last*, Fred Powledge concludes that this combination of violence and official misconduct helped to win support for the movement even beyond Montgomery. Whenever the nonviolent demonstrators needed a boost, it seemed the white South, and later the white North, served it up with an act of violence, misjudged crudeness, or legal antics that undermined the segregationists' defense, provoke outrage and increased the financial contributions for the activists from outside sources.[13]

Despite the campaign of violence, the MIA adopted as its philosophy the concept of nonviolent direct action protests guided by the agape or redemptive love. Relying heavily on his postgraduate studies in philosophy and theology, King told reporters that Blacks were not the only victims of segregation. He explained that the dehumanizing effects of racism and segregation affected the white community too. What the Black protesters in Montgomery were interested in was extending love or goodwill toward the white populace to join with them in ending the disruptive effects of segregation in their community. King entreated those participating in the boycott to remain faithful to the tactic of nonviolent protest. In graduate school, King studied the works of philosophers such as Reinhold Niebuhr and became acquainted with the methods of Mahatma Gandhi. On the ground in Montgomery, he and the movement benefited from the counsel of longtime nonviolent activists such as Ella Baker, the Reverend Glenn Smiley and Bayard Rustin who helped to direct the movement and establish its philosophical base. Each provided critical organizing support in Montgomery and beyond.

One of the participants of the original 1947 Freedom Rides, the southern-born white Methodist Smiley arrived in Montgomery and emerged as one of the key white supporters of the movement. A National Field Secretary for the Fellowship of Reconciliation, Smiley was introduced to King by one of his most influential advisors, Bayard Rustin. A veteran Civil Rights campaigner, Rustin also participated in the original March on Washington and travelled south in 1947 with the Congress on Racial Equality as part of the Freedom Riders. A brilliant writer and organizer with keen insight into the nature of the race problem in America, Rustin assumed a lower profile in the movement after concerns over his sexuality forced him to take a more behind-the-scenes role. King, however, came to value his association over the next several years, as Rustin continued to provide tactical advice and support after Montgomery. Rounding out the circle of advisors was Ella Baker, a longtime Civil Rights organizer whose activism at the time of the boycott spanned nearly four decades.

Baker cut her teeth in the 1930s as an organizer for the Young Negroes Cooperative League in Harlem. By the 1940s, she became a field secretary and later the National Director of branches for the NAACP. One month into the bus boycott on January 5, 1956, Baker along with Bayard Rustin and Stanley Levinson co-founded the New York-based group In Friendship (IF). Representatives from some 25 organizations committed to labor, religious, and humanitarian concerns comprised IF; they provided direct economic support to the southern Civil Rights initiatives. By the time Baker arrived in Montgomery, she was committed to helping the MIA build a sustainable protest movement. At the close of the campaign, she played a key role as one of the key organizers and, later, as the first Executive Director of the SCLC. In 1960, she assumed a pivotal role in the founding of SNCC.

Despite the opposition of a large segment of Montgomery's white community, some expressed support for the effort. Wealthy white couple Clifford and Virginia Durr, for example, provided crucial legal advice and tactical support to the MIA in its early stages. The Durrs accompanied Nixon to the Montgomery jail after Rosa Parks' arrest and became involved in the MIA. Indirectly, many white homemakers supported the MIA, by providing rides for their Black domestics, a large majority of whom patronized the Montgomery bus lines. In addition, other white homemakers complained to City Hall, pressuring them to resolve the boycott, fearful of losing their domestics for any prolonged period. The campaign also won favor among white supporters from outside the South such as Harris and Claire Woolford, students of Ghandi's philosophy of nonviolence; they saw in Montgomery the potential for a wider movement in the United States.

In what became standard operating procedure during the early phase of the movement, the federal government took a passive role in the situation in Montgomery, monitoring but for the most part steering clear of the issues of citizenship and justice posed by the MIA. Despite King's continual appeals to the Justice Department for protection, those in power remained aloof, at least publicly, to events in Montgomery. Critical support eventually came from the U.S. Supreme Court, supplying the MIA with a much-needed victory. In November of 1955, it affirmed the decision of the lower court ending bus segregation in Montgomery. Despite this initial victory, the Court was not forthcoming in a request made by the MIA to make the ruling immediately effective, allowing the city to appeal. Any hope of stalling integration on the buses finally collapsed a little less than one month later on December 17, when the Supreme Court rejected the city's final appeal. After 381 days, Montgomery's Black community returned to the buses without restrictions on seating and service. While segregation remained in other areas of public life in Montgomery, the MIA produced a tangible blueprint for victory, a host of qualified organizers, and the man who emerged as the national symbol for the struggle for nonviolent Civil Rights, Martin Luther King, Jr.

In 1957 in an effort to replicate the success of Montgomery throughout the region, Dr. King helped to found the SCLC that evolved into one of the most significant forces in the national movement. That year national attention fixated on a developing crisis over school desegregation in Little Rock, Arkansas. Events in Little Rock helped segregationists articulate their opposition to Civil Rights. Perhaps Alabama Governor John Patterson best summed up the opposition to integration in a speech he delivered in January of 1959:

> There can be no compromise in this fight. There is no such thing as a "little integration." The determined and ruthless purpose of the race agitators and such organizations as the NAACP . . . is to destroy our culture, our heritage, and our traditions. If we compromise or surrender our rights in this fight, they will be gone forever, never to be regained or restored.

The Reverend Benjamin Mays, President of Morehouse College where Dr. King earned his bachelor's degree, sought to correct this view. Shortly after the *Brown* decision, he explained "Negroes want segregation abolished . . . because they want the legal stigma of inferiority removed and because they do not believe that equality of educational opportunities can be completely achieved in a society where the laws brand a group inferior."[14]

Eradicating that legal stigma took many forms, especially in the first half of the 1960s. Commencing with the student sit-ins and culminating with the passage of the Voting Rights Act of 1965, significant battles at the local and national level coupled with events beyond the borders of the United States accelerated the pace of change. At the opening of the new decade, Black college students took center stage as they launched a spontaneous direct action campaign to desegregate lunch counters and other places of public accommodations throughout the South. Beginning with the courageous actions at North Carolina A&T of four freshmen students, Joseph McNeil, Franklin McCain, David Richmond, and Ezell Blair, Jr., whose attempt to desegregate the lunch counter at a downtown Woolworth's department store in Greensboro soon galvanized students across the South. The sit-ins that quickly spread to other communities precipitated a different type of crisis for the leadership of older movement figures who wondered if the demonstrators, who were often subjected to extreme forms of brutality and violence, could and would remain nonviolent. One response to that crisis, a conference convened at Shaw Raleigh University by Ella Baker, to consider methods of coordinating student protest initiatives and according to nonviolent tactics, resulted in the creation of one of the most important Civil Rights groups of the period, SNCC.

The Freedom Rides, 1960–5

Along with CORE, the NAACP, and SCLC, SNCC was a major actor in many of the dramatic showdowns between Civil Rights demonstrators and segregationists in both local and national campaigns between 1960 and 1965. Although instrumental in laying the groundwork for the battles in this period, the NAACP strategy of attacking segregation in the courts gave way to more dramatic forms of direct action protest and coalition building; such efforts were often guided by SNCC and CORE. One of the critical early battles occurred as CORE revived the idea of a Freedom Ride to test whether southern states abided by two rulings of the Supreme Court effectively outlawing segregation in interstate transportation. In the 1940s, CORE introduced many of the tactics such as the sit-ins that developed into the staple of activism during the early 1960s.

One of the chief architects of the Freedom Ride and a former divinity student, James Farmer headed CORE from 1961 to 1966. Farmer, also instrumental in CORE's founding, soon emerged as one of the leaders of the national movement for both his organizing abilities and the organization's deep involvement in nonviolent Civil Rights campaigns in both the South and North.

The first wave of Freedom Riders boarded buses in Washington, DC on May 4, 1961, slated to arrive in New Orleans on May 17 on the anniversary of *Brown* v. *Board of Education*. They left filled with optimism and a healthy dose of fear. According to the plan, racially mixed groups of riders along the route entered bus stations and asked for service and access to the dining and restroom facilities on a non-segregated basis; their requests were consistent with the rulings of the U.S. Supreme Court. As expected, they encountered significant violence and hostility from the outset. In addition to denials of service, Farmer and his colleagues endured beatings and imprisonment. The most egregious incident occurred after a mob of angry white men assaulted the riders and bombed their bus outside Anniston, Alabama, 10 days into the campaign. Faced with mounting legal costs, pressure from the federal government and the possibility of even greater violence, CORE elected to call off the ride. Unwilling to concede the fight, SNCC determined to finish the campaign and issued a call for new riders.

The young people who came to populate SNCC possessed a fearless determination to end segregation. They continued to be keenly aware of the important groundwork laid by the previous decade, specifically through the *Brown* decision and Montgomery. James Forman, the second Executive Director of SNCC, situated the Montgomery boycott as having "a particularly important effect on young blacks, and helped me to generate the student movement of 1960 . . . It woke me to the real—not merely theoretical—possibility of building a nonviolent mass movement of Southern black people to fight segregation."[15]

Beginning with the reconstituted Freedom Rides and over the course of the next five years SNCC's workers surfaced as the advance guard of many of the movement's most notable campaigns. In small rural communities throughout the South, SNCC activists worked to challenge segregation and help Blacks claim political power. In addition to testing the bounds of legal decisions, SNCC made voter registration one of its main goals and, along with the NAACP, successfully registered Black voters in some of the most dangerous areas of the South.

Along the way, SNCC and CORE helped organize and inspire local people to action. Jackson, Mississippi native Claire Collins Harvey reflected in an interview with journalist Robert Penn Warren:

> I think the presence of the freedom riders did more for Jackson's Negro community than anything that I know has happened in my years living here. Because we were very disunified. We had no sense of unity at all on social issues as Negroes.[16]

Inspired by the protest Collins went on to found Womanpower Unlimited in May of 1961. What began primarily as an effort to provide support for the Freedom Riders soon blossomed into an important local Civil Rights organization that sought to tackle racial and gender inequality in Jackson, Mississippi and beyond. The organization also became heavily involved in voter education campaigns, a cornerstone of many Civil Rights groups' agendas.

Womanpower Unlimited was not a singular phenomenon. Across the country, the bravery of Civil Rights workers stirred people to action. The national movement also helped to shine a light on various localized efforts taking place in communities around a host of related issues including desegregation of schools, voter registration, and unfair labor practices. The emergence of national organizations such as SNCC provided further direction.

At the same time Civil Rights demonstrations, such as the Freedom Rides, brought a reluctant federal government into the fray increasingly on the side of racial equality. This support was by no mean consistent. Although Kennedy had courted the Black vote, his failure to meet his campaign promises, such as wiping away housing segregation in federal housing programs, led to targeted efforts like the Ink for Jack Campaign that involved Civil Rights groups mailing ink pens to the White House in an effort to remind the President of his promise. Kennedy, however, remained aloof. The battles over Civil Rights taking place in the streets proved more of an annoyance and a distraction from his primary concern, the Cold War.

In the aftermath of the Freedom Rides, the Kennedys attempted to harness the energies of the movement by dangling the promise of both financial support and federal intervention if movement leaders turned their attention toward voter registration projects. Some worried that the Kennedys were merely attempting to co-opt the movement by turning it into a giant recruiting tool for the Democratic Party. With finances running low, and no clear plan for where to go next, however, the promise of the program outweighed these concerns. With two large foundations lined up to support the work, the administration succeeded in persuading movement leaders to join the voter registration drive but not without producing a deep rift within SNCC. Many of the students like Diane Nash and Marion Barry felt that the organization should maintain its commitment to direct action protest. Others like Charles Sherrod believed that a voter registration drive—especially one with promised government support—could prove fruitful. The divide was settled when James Forman, a respected member of the group, was elected as chairman. Highlighting the complementary goals of both strategies Forman moved SNCC toward the adoption of a two-pronged strategy, first proposed by Ella Baker, that would allow the student activists to continue their work in both areas. Southern intransigence nevertheless created conditions for showdowns in communities committed to maintaining white supremacy. Voter registration efforts coupled with SNCC's continued penchant for direct action spurred new battlefields as activists explored initiatives in communities where they believed they could continue to dismantle segregation. The small town of Albany in southwest Georgia proved such a place and a key battleground late in 1961.

Albany, Georgia, 1961–2

As part of a campaign to empower African Americans through the ballot box, SNCC workers zeroed in on the town of Albany, Georgia in the fall of 1961. With African Americans making up approximately 40 percent of the town's population, Albany seemed a logical and strategic choice. As Terrell County resident Lucius Holloway conceptualized the problem, even though African Americans comprised 60 percent of the Albany Metropolitan area population "we had fifty-two people registered to vote." Holloway was quick to point out the reasons for the imbalance. "It wasn't simply apathy that kept them away," he explained, "I would say it was fear."[17] When SNCC activists Charles Sherrod and Cordell Reagon arrived in the fall of 1961, they meant to shatter that sense of fear by waging a frontal assault on segregation. Bypassing the established networks represented by local groups including the NAACP, SNCC focused its attentions on mustering local high school and college students in the hopes of building a popular and local mass movement.[18]

SNCC workers recognized both the opportunities and challenges presented by this approach. As in other communities, SNCC reached out to young people to engage them in nonviolent direct action protest. Charles Sherrod explained the utility and appeal of such a strategy, especially to young people accustomed to the violence of segregation but with the courage to press for Civil Rights "with nothing but our bodies and minds, fearlessly standing before the monsters who [k]illed our mothers and castrated our fathers—yet we stand with Love."[19]

It was an inspiring philosophy but one that initially failed to gain traction in SNCC's early voter registration efforts, leaving Sherrod and Reagon anxious to explore other ways of stimulating local protest. An order handed down by the Interstate Commerce Commission in the midst of their strategizing that commanded the desegregation of Interstate terminals in response to the Freedom Rides offered a strong possibility. SNCC hoped to capitalize on the order as a starting point for introducing direct action protest into its efforts. After Albany's terminal employees directly defied the ICC mandate and blocked access to a group of African American students seeking to integrate the facility, SNCC workers knew they had their issue. With the community galvanized around the terminal incident, SNCC workers brokered a partnership with other local Civil Rights groups. Several weeks later, an organization calling itself the Albany Movement moved to the forefront of the protest. An amalgamation of SNCC workers and other local Civil Rights organizations, including the NAACP and CORE, the new umbrella organization banded together under the joint leadership of a local physician named William Anderson and a business owner, named Slater King.

After authorities ordered the arrests of a second wave of Albany State students for attempting to desegregate the bus terminal, the protests kicked into full gear. By November, hundreds mobilized to take part in demonstrations aimed at not only the segregated bus terminal but also other forms of Jim Crow Segregation from libraries to lunch counters.

Hundreds marched on City Hall in the hopes of attracting media coverage and provoking a response from local authorities but Albany Police Chief Laurie Pritchett frustrated their efforts by restraining his police. Pritchett carefully studied Dr. King's book *Stride toward Freedom*, which laid out the basics of direct action protest. Astutely, he recognized how mass arrests and acts of violence—especially by law enforcement—ultimately helped to bring media attention to those campaigns. Pritchett resolved to rob the movement of its two most effective tools, filling the jails and drawing the interest of the press. Projecting the image of a model peace officer publicly, Pritchett treated protestors with marked respect before the cameras. He contacted neighboring jails within a 30-mile radius and, thereby, absorbed the crush of demonstrators without drawing negative attention to Albany. Despite reports of brutality from behind the jail walls, Albany police deflected the claim that they treated the protestors harshly. Without footage of police officers brutalizing demonstrators, movement organizers had a hard time turning public opinion in their favor. The press instead hailed Pritchett as an enlightened public servant and accepted the idea that the demonstrations were the work of outside agitators.

Worse still from the movement's standpoint, internal problems plagued the campaign. From its inception, deep divisions existed among the three organizations that formed the nucleus of the Albany Movement, SNCC, the NAACP and CORE. Differing views on strategies and tactics and a lack of focus led to a trajectory more scattershot than deliberate. With mass arrests and dwindling resources, the Albany campaign seemed destined to fail.

The turning point came in mid-December when Anderson quietly put out a call to Martin Luther King to come to Albany presumably to speak in support of the demonstrations. The invitation rankled SNCC organizers partly because Anderson failed to consult them, but also because of their increasing disdain for what they regarded as a helicopter approach employed by the SCLC. Dr. King declined a SNCC offer to participate in the Freedom Rides, leaving the organization's members with the sense that King placed himself above the movement. While the truth was much more complicated, this negative view of King persisted. When Dr. King arrived in Albany, he merely expected to give a speech and leave. During the program, Dr Anderson surprised King by asking him to lead a march to City Hall the following day. Unprepared but unwilling to disappoint his friend and those in attendance, King accepted. His arrest leading that march now placed him as the default leader of the fledging movement. In an effort to dramatize local conditions and bring much-needed media attention to Albany, King refused bail. Pritchett, in the meantime, exploited King's incarceration to solidify his reputation as an honest broker. With his network of satellite jails, he was able to place King and Ralph Abernathy alone in a large holding cell. As King attempted to convey the inhuman conditions under which other protesters suffered, the spacious cell and collection of food and baked goods from local women, which Pritchett shrewdly allowed to be delivered to the pair, undercut King's narrative.

Clearly unaware of all of the local nuances and with few options, King's lawyer allegedly worked out a deal in his name. If the SCLC chief called off the demonstrations, the city agreed to comply with the ICC's ruling and everyone with no further charges. King consented to an apparently reasonable compromise. Albany's administrators quickly reneged on the deal, once King left town however. The demonstrations resumed in earnest.

By the following July, matters remained at an impasse. With more than 1,200 arrests since mid-December, the movement organizers remained unsuccessful in filling the jails. Hoping to secure a federal injunction against further demonstrations, city officials continued to denounce the movement as the work of outside agitators. Amidst these allegations in July, Dr. King also returned. His second visit proved as problematic as the first. Arrested shortly after his arrival, Pritchett arranged for King's bail to be paid, forcing his hand. When King finally departed, Pritchett triumphantly boasted that the city was "as segregated as ever."[20]

With the Department of Justice closely monitoring the situation, President Kennedy finally weighed in. "I find it wholly inexplicable," he observed during a press conference on August 1, "why the City Council of Albany will not sit down with the citizens of Albany, who may be Negroes, and attempt to secure theme in a peaceful way, their rights . . . The United States Government is involved in sitting down at Geneva with the Soviet Union. I can't understand why the government of Albany, City Council of Albany, cannot do the same for American citizens."[21] Despite the President's clear recognition of African Americans' rights as citizens, state and local officials remained steadfast in opposition to negotiations. In defying the president, Mayor Asa D. Kelley received the full backing of Governor Ernest Vandiver.

The President's words offered little consolation to movement organizers. King and the SCLC, in particular, determined to adapt the hard lessons learned in Albany. After a period of deep reflection, King acknowledged that the organization needed to rethink its model of engagement. Referring to the haphazard way SCLC became involved in the Albany campaign, he pointedly advised his associates at a three-day SCLC retreat that December "I don't want to be a fireman anymore."[22] In the future, the SCLC needed to exercise greater control over demonstrations borne of careful planning and execution. With the pressure of producing a victory on par with Montgomery mounting, they selected Birmingham, Alabama as the SCLC's next target. Despite a failed voter registration effort in that city in 1959, SCLC associate and Birmingham native Fred Shuttlesworth convinced the group that Birmingham was an ideal choice.

Nearly eight long years after the MIA's successful toppling of segregated busing in Montgomery, King and the SCLC were desperate for a victory. Although clearly a failure at least from the national perspective, the Albany campaign taught King and his colleagues some important lessons, which they applied with great effect in Birmingham.

Birmingham, Alabama, 1963

In marked contrast to Albany, the SCLC thoroughly investigated and carefully planned its operation in Birmingham, a city with a well-earned reputation for violence. For more than a decade, local Baptist minister Fred Shuttlesworth commanded Civil Rights efforts there. After Alabama outlawed the NAACP in 1956 for its role in encouraging the Montgomery Bus Boycott, Shuttlesworth established the Alabama Christian Movement for Human Rights that became a prime agent of protest in the city and an important satellite of the SCLC.[23]

Local officials declared open season on Shuttlesworth, who continued to apply pressure in spite of threats of personal harm and the dynamiting of his home on Christmas Eve. When he and his wife elected to enroll their children in the white school nearest to their home, a mob assaulted them while police looked on. In many ways, and for all these reasons, Shuttlesworth remained convinced that Birmingham was just the city for SCLC to highlight southern violence and intransigence. After a detailed study, King and his lieutenants agreed. They began making plans for Project C, targeting Birmingham's retail shops during the busy Easter season.

Despite all of the early preparation, Project C nearly ended before it began after a reform candidate defeated local Commissioner of Public Safety Eugene "Bull" Connor in a tight mayoral race. Given his vicious temperament and violent treatment of the Freedom Riders, SCLC felt certain that its non-violent protests would goad Connor into confrontation. Buoyed by Connor's defeat at the polls and weary of the dangers associated with protest, many local members of the Black community felt that King and the SCLC should back off. They feared possible retaliation from the demonstrations and saw King as an outside agitator concerned with capturing headlines at their expense. Local white moderates also feared the onset of demonstrations that might shatter the fragile deal they worked out and believed that King should allow the political process to play out. The Department of Justice also asked the SCLC to put off its protest. In spite of this opposition, King and the SCLC elected to forge ahead and a few days shy of Easter presented a list of demands to local authorities that included the immediate desegregation of public places of accommodation and the hiring of Blacks in the downtown stores and shops.

Unlike Laurie Pritchett, Bull Connor seemed unable to restrain either his officers or himself. Photographers and television cameras were on hand to capture the brutality as police dogs ferociously assaulted nonviolent demonstrators, vaulting Birmingham into the national spotlight. Just as the protests accelerated, officials secured a state court injunction barring future demonstrations.

Until this point, King refrained from defying a court injunction. With bail money nearly exhausted, morale running low, and the number of demonstrators dwindling, King turned inward. After spending much of Good Friday in contemplation and prayer, he informed his inner circle that he could no longer obey unjust laws. This important turning point for both King and the movement lifted one of the key limitations on the scope of its demonstrations. Heading up protests that afternoon and in defiance of the court injunction, Bull Connor had King arrested and placed in solitary confinement until Easter

Sunday when the Kennedy brothers used their influence to have King moved to a regular holding cell.

As King languished in jail, a group of white clergymen drafted a letter condemning the demonstrations in Birmingham as "unwise and untimely." In response, King drafted a letter of his own outlining his nonviolent philosophy and the reason for the protests in Birmingham and beyond. Parrying claims that he was an outside agitator, King chastised white moderates and the white church for failing to speak out against racial injustice.

Released the following week, King returned to find the campaign in disarray and protesters still hard to come by when the SCLC staffer Reverend James Bevel suggested that they invite Birmingham's young people to participate. It was a risky venture. Bevel persisted, noting the relative lack of restraints on the children compared with their parents; he also highlighted the symbolism of their presence. King listened and finally agreed to the Children's Crusade.

On May 2, hundreds of youth gathered at the Sixteenth Street Baptist Church where they viewed "The Nashville Story" as part of their crash course in nonviolent direct action protest. Next, they marched toward downtown prepared to face the wrath of the Birmingham police. The first wave of protesters was loaded onto school buses and paddy wagons and carted off to jail. As successive waves continued to arrive, Bull Connor grew agitated and ordered firefighters to train their hoses on the young demonstrators. Images of well-dressed youth clubbed and bitten by police dogs and children literally knocked off their feet by powerful blasts wielded by Birmingham's firefighters dominated the evening news broadcasts. The footage provoked an immediate response.

With the eyes of the world fixed on Birmingham and a looming presidential election, Bull Connor's brutality forced the Kennedy administration to intervene. In hopes of alleviating the pressure, Attorney General Robert Kennedy asked the United Auto Workers Union to provide $160,000 in bail money for those arrested while Assistant Attorney General Burke Marshall flew to Birmingham in the hopes of brokering a deal to end the protests. Secretary of the Treasury Douglas Dillon and Defense Secretary Robert McNamara also became involved, pressing large defense contractors like US Steel executive Roger Blough to use his influence with local business leaders. The Kennedys grew also increasingly concerned over the impact the demonstrations might have on foreign affairs.

In the decade after the Montgomery Bus Boycott, the influence of emerging African Nations put pressure on the United States with regard to segregationists' practices, particularly in the nation's capital where increasing numbers of African diplomats suffered the indignities of Jim Crow Segregation. As the historian Michael Krenn observed, "In 1945, there were only four African countries in the UN; five more joined during the 1950s. Between 1960 and the end of 1963, however, twenty- four new African nations became members of the UN; fifteen of those had joined in 1960, just a year before Kennedy came into office."[24] With the Soviet Union vying for influence, the U.S. diplomatic corps urged the President to act expeditiously. The immediate spectacle of violence in Birmingham prompted the President to act. "The civil rights movement should thank God for Bull Connor," President Kennedy remarked after viewing television reports of the demonstrations, "He helped it as much as Abraham Lincoln."[25]

Under intense pressure from the demonstrations, not to mention the financial impact of the boycott, the white business community finally conceded. On May 10, the Chamber of Commerce informed the public that the two sides reached a deal for the integration of downtown stores as well as the hiring of Black clerks. Not everyone was happy with the agreement. Fred Shuttlesworth, for instance, wanted more concessions. King, on the other hand, boasted that the settlement represented "the most magnificent victory for justice we've seen in the Deep South."[26]

With the adoption of an agreement in Birmingham, the national Civil Rights Movement claimed the victory it needed and much more. Over the next few months, the Birmingham effect took hold as officials in approximately 50 cities, mostly in the upper South, undertook voluntary desegregation measures in hopes of staving off similar protests in their own communities.

While white Alabamans pondered the larger meaning of the concessions, officials from Governor George Wallace downwards denounced the men that negotiated the accord as "gutless traitors." Klan Imperial Wizard Robert Shelton warned of the possibility of violence against Dr. King. That night, Klansmen detonated explosives at the home of King's brother and the Gaston hotel where King and the SCLC had stayed. Although King had already left town, violence broke out as Black rioters took to the streets to register their anger at the attempt on King's life. With Birmingham descending into bedlam, the moment of the movement's greatest victory also signaled a serious challenge to nonviolence.

Concerned over the impact of the violence on the movement and the community in Birmingham, King pleaded for nonviolence. At a rally in San Francisco where 15,000 demonstrators assembled in support of the Birmingham protests, Muslim Minister Malcolm X chose to interpret the violence as a sign of progress. "One of the things the Birmingham incident brought to life," he advised those in attendance, "is the lack of fear in the Negro community for whites … Our people in this country," he continued, "have been held in check more by fear than anything else. Today that fear is gone so that when they explode there is nothing that the white man can use to really contain that explosion."[27] The combination of demonstrations, foreign policy concerns, and experiences in Little Rock and Ole Miss, encouraged Kennedy to move decisively. In addition to calling for peace, the president dispatched troops from nearby Ft. McClellan.

The situation in Birmingham served as the backdrop for another showdown between the Kennedy administration and Alabama Governor George Wallace, demonstrating the shifting tide of government action. A federal judge ordered the University of Alabama, proudly claiming to be the last segregated university in the country, to admit two Black students, Vivian Malone and James Hood, for its summer session. Determined to prevent the students from entering the university the Governor first sought to get the pair to withdraw their applications for admission through blackmail, but when officials failed to turn up evidence to use against them, Wallace proclaimed his willingness to provoke a confrontation with the federal government.

The Kennedy administration stood prepared. In advance of Assistant Attorney General Nicholas Katzenbach's visit, Kennedy dispatched federal troops to the University of Alabama to enforce enrollment of two Black students. A defiant Governor Wallace, who had opened his term as governor with a pledge maintaining "Segregation forever," refused to relent.

On June 11, Katzenbach, with the two students in tow, arrived on the campus prepared to execute the judge's orders. Wallace had other plans. With reporters and television crews braced for the confrontation, Wallace raised his hand to stop Katzenbach from entering Foster Auditorium. Katzenbach read a presidential decree ordering Wallace to allow the students to register. Wallace read a proclamation of his own, decrying what he called an "unwelcomed, unwanted, unwarranted, and forced-induced intrusion upon the campus."[28] His political theater concluded, Wallace stepped aside to allow Katzenbach and the students to enter—while Kennedy federalized the Alabama Guard in anticipation of further trouble.

A short time later, the President took to the airways to address the American people. Speaking with a new sense of urgency and conviction, Kennedy decried segregation as a "moral crisis" that necessitated a clear federal response. Boldly declaring it time "for this nation to fulfill its promise," the President shared his intent to ask "Congress to enact legislation giving all Americans the right to be served in facilities which are open to the public" along with other "elementary" rights "including greater protection for the right to vote."[29] He closed by proposing an ambitious new Civil Rights bill to not only guarantee voting rights but mandate equal access to places of public accommodation and jobs. The federal government pledged to withdraw funds from all state and local agencies that refused to comply. Critics quickly noted the limitations of these actions. In his effort to win support from both parties, the Justice Department agreed to intervene only if the aggrieved person brought a lawsuit. The bill's attempts to deal with voting rights only extended to federal, not state and local, elections, focused only on southern school desegregation and failed to address the issues of police brutality and employment discrimination.

Calling the President's speech a breakthrough, King revived labor leader A. Phillip Randolph's call for a massive demonstration in the nation's capital. The SCLC proposed the idea to Randolph, who cited the growing income disparity between Black and white families and high Black unemployment statistics and urged King to make economic justice a key component of the march. Plans for a Jobs and Freedom March, better known as the March on Washington, began in earnest.

If Kennedy's speech inspired hope, it also triggered more violence against Civil Rights workers. Literally hours after the President's address, early on the morning of June 12, 1963, white supremacist Byron De La Beckwith ambushed and murdered Mississippi NAACP organizer Medgar Evers in the driveway of his home as he returned from a day of political organizing. However, the violence only stiffened Civil Rights demonstrators' resolve, leading to dozens of protests across the country.

While the administration proved proactive in the case of Birmingham, many African Americans became impatient, maintaining that the efforts extended by the federal government were insufficient to protect Civil Rights protesters. During the Birmingham campaign, for instance, an assembly of Black artists and entertainers met with Attorney General Robert Kennedy in New York to register their concerns over the widespread violence in the South and the government's failure to protect demonstrators.

Malcolm X, who remained skeptical of both the strategies and goals of the movement, offered a more trenchant analysis. "An integrated cup of coffee isn't sufficient pay for four hundred years of slave labor," he explained in a speech in June of 1963. A "better job in the white man's factory, or a better job in the white man's business, or a better job in the white man's industry or economy is, at best, only a temporary solution," he continued, "the only lasting and permanent solution is complete separation on some land that we can call our own."[30]

While not evident in the national coverage of the King-led movement, Malcolm's ideas had currency among many grassroots organizers and activists who saw greater possibilities in building separate Black institutions than forcing integration into discriminatory white ones. Nevertheless, Civil Rights leaders and their allies used the threat of so-called "Negro extremism" as a tool to encourage federal action. At the opening of House Judiciary Committee hearings on civil rights on June 13, African American Representative Charles C. Diggs, Jr. of Michigan laid down the gauntlet, "If rational counsel is to prevail among the mass of Negroes," he advised, "then Congress will have to give the moderates, such as myself, necessary weapons—and that means the whole civil-rights package . . . If the Negroes don't get their demands," he concluded, "they will turn to other leadership that will produce an even greater crisis than this one."[31]

Events in other parts of the country seemed to bear Diggs out. Concomitant with Birmingham on the eastern shore of Maryland, Gloria Richardson and a collection of local and national Civil Rights groups, including SNCC and CORE, led a local movement to force desegregation in the areas of housing, education, and places of public accommodation. They also worked on improving employment prospects for African Americans.

Highlighting the importance of the emergence of African Nations, protests along the eastern shore of Maryland first began in 1961 after a local restaurant just off Interstate 40 refused service to a diplomat from the Republic of Chad travelling to Washington, DC from the United Nations. In concert with the local Civic Interest Group of Baltimore, CORE sponsored a series of sit-ins and Freedom Rides in the hopes of pressuring the state to desegregate public accommodations. The humiliation of racial segregation as well as significant Black unemployment illustrated the depth and damaging reach of separate but equal. Route 40 Freedom Rides led to confrontations in Cambridge, Maryland. Throughout the spring, Richardson and others engaged in a series of non-violent protests to dramatize conditions in the border community. Two incidents of rioting in June and July of 1963 finally forced the federal government to intervene. On July 23, Robert Kennedy met with Civil Rights leaders and local officials to hammer out an agreement to end the demonstrations. Among other things, the arrangement allowed for the immediate desegregation of schools, the erection of low-cost public housing, and the appointment of a human relations commission to continue to work toward the peaceful settlement of other issues.

By the end of July, national Civil Rights organizers concentrated squarely on the March on Washington that took place on August 28. Some 200,000 marchers from across the nation marched from the Washington Monument to the steps of the Lincoln Memorial where the National leaders addressed the participants. Dr. King delivered his celebrated "I Have a Dream" speech which called upon the Nation to make real the promises of the Declaration of Independence.

Even as those in attendance listened to King's soaring oration, others remained on the front lines. James Farmer could only send a word of greeting while he sat serving a sentence for defying Louisianan segregation laws. Behind the scenes, tensions were also brewing over the language of a proposed speech by SNCC Chairman John Lewis. Calling the Civil Rights Bill "too little," the 23-year-old Lewis demanded to know in an early draft of his speech, "which side is the Federal Government on?" Although Lewis later removed the language at the request of King and Randolph his address still challenged Congress and the administration to do more. "If we do not get meaningful legislation out of this Congress," Lewis bellowed in the shadow of the Lincoln Memorial, "the time will come when we will not confine our marching to Washington. We will march through the South, through the streets of Jackson, through the streets of Danville, through the streets of Cambridge, through the streets of Birmingham. But we will march with the spirit of love and with the spirit of dignity that we have shown here today."[32]

In the meantime, Arkansas NAACP chief Daisy Bates was a hasty substitution for Myrlie Evers, who was delayed by traffic. She took the last minute gesture to include women on the program as an opportunity to make a statement demonstrating the unity of the movement despite the clear sexism represented by the omission. Addressing the male speakers gathered with her on the platform she nevertheless pledged that the "women of this country" would "kneel in," "sit in" and, squarely facing the reality of death, "will lie in if necessary until every Negro in America can vote. This we pledge to the women of America."[33] If movement leaders failed to recognize the importance of women, the reality of nondiscriminatory bounds of hate soon provided a grim reminder.

With Congressional debate over the Civil Rights Bill continuing in spite of strong southern opposition and fears of a possible Dixiecrat filibuster, in the streets, the simmering tensions of the summer had yet to dissipate. Just weeks after the march, in Birmingham white supremacists bombed the 16th Street Baptist Church, killing four young girls as they prepared for Sunday school. The callous murders were a painful reminder of the lengths to which some segregationists were prepared to go to preserve the status quo.

With the Civil Rights Bill still in jeopardy, John F. Kennedy flew to Dallas on November 22, 1963 and into the crosshairs of an assassin's bullet. His successor, Vice President and former Senate Majority Leader Lyndon Johnson made clear his intention to continue to push for the Civil Rights Bill, despite strong southern opposition. A political insider with a long history in Washington that stretched to the New Deal, Johnson threw his full weight behind the bill whose passage was by no means assured.

The New Year brought another victory, passage of the 24th Amendment outlawing the poll tax in January of 1964 and signaled the toppling of yet another barrier to voting rights. That February, the Civil Rights Bill passed in the House of Representatives by a vote of 290 to 130. A filibuster, however, delayed consideration in the Senate. In the meantime, Civil Rights organizations set their sights on Mississippi as the next target for mass organizing.

Mississippi Freedom Summer 1964

"Everything that took place in Mississippi during the 1960s," observed historian Charles Payne, "took place against that state's long tradition of systematic racial terrorism."[34] When SNCC activist, former Harlem teacher and Harvard graduate Robert Moses initiated a voter registration campaign there in 1961, he squarely confronted that tradition. According to historian Clayborne Carson, "many student activists saw Mississippi as the stronghold of segregation and thus the ultimate testing ground for their idealism and commitment."[35]

SNCC's organizational efforts in Mississippi dated back to the Freedom Rides. Mississippi jails had been the baptism by fire for many SNCC members. In spite of the violence and terror they routinely faced, many remained in the hopes of organizing the state's large African American population. SNCC established a strong base in McComb, Mississippi led by Robert Moses. Strongly committed to Ella Baker's model of developing indigenous leadership, Moses helped to develop a paradigm of community organizing that privileged building that kind of leadership. This became especially evident in 1962 after Moses became director of the Council of Federated Organizations (COFO), an alliance of groups headed by SNCC that sought to coordinate statewide Civil Rights activities. Strategically, Moses positioned himself behind the scenes, allowing local leaders to emerge and guide the movement. He hoped that local organizing and agitation would continue in the event of SNCC's departure. Even after taking on a leadership role in the statewide COFO, Moses kept the focus on local organizing.[36]

Mississippi remained one of the most dangerous and inhospitable environments for Civil Rights activism, especially in its rural environs. There Civil Rights workers encountered types of violent resistance far more severe and effective in hampering direct action campaigns than in southern cities like Montgomery and Birmingham. In May of 1955 for instance, white supremacists murdered the Reverend George Lee after he refused to suspend efforts to register Black voters. Six years later in September of 1961, Mississippi state legislator E.H. Hurst shot and killed 52-year-old NAACP organizer Herbert Lee, in front of a number of witnesses in broad daylight in Liberty, Mississippi for similar efforts. When a witness later came forward to say it was a case of homicide, he was murdered.

Despite the violence, SNCC saw enormous potential in Mississippi— especially in terms of voter registration. In much of the state, African Americans were the numerical majority, yet deprived of the right to vote by a combination of law and terror. After a mock election in the fall of 1963 revealed the possibility of a registering thousands of potential voters, Moses hatched the idea of enlisting an army of white students from the nation's elite colleges and universities to come to the state as part of a massive voter registration drive. Moses wanted the campaign to not only register Black voters but also bring national attention to the problem of voting rights. The plan was not without its critics. Some saw it as a blow to the growth of indigenous leadership. Moses persisted however and a major recruitment effort began for the 1964 Freedom Summer project.

After months of planning and organizing, the first of the approximately 1,000 volunteers arrived at the Western College for Women in Oxford, Ohio on June 14. Most were middle to upper class white northern students from some of the nation's top schools. Designed to help the volunteers carry out the work of the summer including registering Black voters, establishing Freedom Schools, and promoting the Mississippi Freedom Democratic Party (MFDP), the training sessions also addressed the potential for violence.

As Freedom Summer training kicked into full gear, a motion for cloture in the Senate helped to dislodge the logjam over the Civil Rights Bill, paving the way for a vote. With minor alterations, the bill passed the Senate on June 19 by a vote of 73 to 27.

COFO volunteers hardly had time to celebrate the victory. Just two days later on June 21, organizers informed the trainees of the abduction of three Civil Rights workers dispatched to investigate the burning of a church designated as a voter registration and Freedom School site. Black Mississippi native James Chaney, and two white companions, veteran CORE activist Michael Schwerner and Freedom Summer recruit Andrew Goodman, disappeared after local law enforcement officials detained them. COFO reasoned that opponents of the project orchestrated the disappearance of the field workers to intimidate Freedom Summer volunteers but instead it stiffened their resolve. It also provided further proof of the need for the Civil Rights Act.

Federal officials combed the state in search of the missing students. Public outcry over the disappearances resulted in even greater support for the Civil Rights Bill. The House of Representatives adopted the Senate version of the bill on July 2 and Martin Luther King and other national leaders were on hand in Washington when President Lyndon Johnson signed it into law.

On the ground in Mississippi, the search for the three missing Civil Rights workers and voter registration continued in earnest. In addition to its voter registration drive, COFO volunteers created 41 Freedom Schools that served a little more than 3,000 students over the course of the summer. In addition to remedial work in reading and mathematics, the schools also provided courses in African American history as well as leadership training and community development.

In late July, Dr. King travelled to Greenwood at the request of Bob Moses to show the SCLC's support for the campaign and in hopes of encouraging Black Mississippians to get involved in spite of the danger. A reminder of which came less than a month after King's visit when authorities discovered the slain bodies of Schwerner, Chaney, and Goodman buried in an earthen dam, a stark reminder of the risks activists undertook.

Despite a massive effort and demonstrating the deep-seated nature of the problem by the end of the project, local clerks added only 1,600 of the roughly 17,000 Black Mississippians who attempted to register to the voter rolls, dramatically illustrating the need for federal intervention on voting rights. The MFDP hoped to make it an issue at the Democratic National Convention that August in New Jersey. In order to assist Johnson in securing a second term on July 29, several prominent Civil Rights leaders called for a suspension of marches and demonstrations until after the presidential election on November 3. Undaunted, the MFDP arrived at the Democratic Convention in Atlantic City prepared to challenge Mississippi's all-white delegation.

At the Convention, the tension between mass mobilizing and organizing efforts erupted when the MFDP demanded the right to be seated as the legitimate Democratic Party representatives from Mississippi. They ultimately rejected attempts to broker a compromise that guaranteed the party two seats. The MFDP's decision not to compromise reveals as much about SNCC's organizing tradition in contrast to the goal of national victories. As Victoria Gray conceptualized the problem, "Those who were unable to understand why we were unable to accept that compromise did not realize that we would have been betraying the very many people back there in Mississippi whom we represented."[37]

The MFDP also introduced another powerful woman, Fannie Lou Hamer, to the nation. The youngest of 20 children, Hamer had become a fixture in Mississippi Civil Rights organizing by Freedom Summer. Dismissed from her job on a cotton plantation in Ruleville two years earlier after she tried to register to vote, Hamer was jailed and brutally beaten for her attempt. Like so many others, Hamer's work with the MFDP was not her first brush with activism. She attended several conferences in the 1950s but credited a speech and an appeal by SNCC organizer James Bevel in August of 1961 with inspiring her to become more involved. Elected as Vice-Chair of the MFDP, she riveted the convention and, for a short time, the nation with her testimony to the credentials committee before President Johnson preempted coverage with a hastily called press conference.

In spite of the turmoil at the convention and with overwhelming Black support, Johnson, handily won reelection in November. The following month the Nobel Peace Prize committee conferred the award on Dr. King, an affirmation of the movement. However, the major battles were far from complete.

In the end, Freedom Summer proved to be one of the last major interracial initiatives of the national movement. In later efforts, alliances fractured over a variety of issues from the level of white participation to the use of the slogan Black Power. White resentment against the Civil Rights Act of 1964 also triggered a "white backlash"; many white Americans, weary of the violence and protests and alarmed by their own loss of privilege, soured on the movement.

The reception of the MFDP at Atlantic City also signaled the importance of voting rights as a key issue. In spite of the passage of the Civil Rights Act of 1964, many African Americans remained dissatisfied. Malcolm X, now operating independent of the Nation of Islam, summed up the frustration many felt at what they regarded as the hollow victories of 1964. In a speech at the Oxford Union that December, Malcolm declared:

> No matter how many bills pass ... our lives are not worth two cents. And the government has shown its inability, or either its unwillingness to do whatever is necessary to protect black property where the black citizen is concerned.

Others, such as Unita Blackwell, however, remained hopeful and saw great opportunity for the future based on the organizing efforts of COFO. Later she observed, for "black people in Mississippi, Freedom Summer was the beginning of a whole new era. People began to feel that they wasn't just helpless anymore."[38]

Selma, Alabama, 1965

King and the SCLC teamed up with SNCC and the Dallas County Voters League to register Black voters and win national support for new voting rights legislation in early 1965. Despite a population of some 29,000, only a little over 2 percent of registered voters were African Americans. SNCC workers labored in the region since the fall of 1963 without making much headway. Local leaders made an appeal to Dr. King and the SCLC to select the county as their next area of focus. Convinced that the nation was still in need of legislation to protect Black voters, the SCLC agreed to help, hoping that Selma, like Birmingham, would yield an important victory.[39]

Selma had much in common with Birmingham in terms of its local official-dom. Like Bull Connor, Sheriff Jim Clark enjoyed a well-earned reputation for brutality. As SCLC Executive Director Andrew Young recollected, "Jim Clark was a madman. It infuriated him for anybody to defy his authority, even when they just wanted to vote."[40] Selma Mayor Joseph Smitherman later complained, "They picked Selma just like a movie producer would pick a set."[41] Organizers believed that marches might provoke the kind of crisis that would drive Johnson and Congress to pass new national voting rights legislation.

Demonstrations in Selma and neighboring Marion, Alabama began in earnest on January 2. Despite mass arrests, police remained nonviolent. By mid-February, however, law enforcement changed tactics again, increasing the violence against protesters. Tensions reached a boiling point on the evening of February 18 when local police, swelled by the ranks of Alabama state troopers, attacked and seriously injured a number of demonstrators as they participated in a night march in support of a jailed SCLC staff member. Among those injured was 82-year-old Cager Jackson. He was beaten by police as he sought shelter in a café behind the church where the march originated. A state trooper shot Jackson's 26-year-old grandson, Jimmie Lee, as he attempted to shield his mother from the officers' batons when she and Jimmie came to Cager's defense. Jackson's death eight days later came to symbolize the depths of injustice the campaign sought to convey.

Movement leaders announced plans to march from Selma to the capital city of Montgomery on March 7 to protest Jackson's death and ask for greater voter protections. With King attending to business in Atlanta, SNCC chair-person John Lewis teamed up with SCLC minister Hosea Williams to lead the march. On March 7, the marchers made it as far as the Edmund Pettus Bridge on the outskirts of Selma where they confronted police barricades manned by police and troopers under the direction of Sheriff Clark and state police commander Major John Cloud. When the marchers did not heed an order from Cloud to turn back, he commanded his men to disperse them forcibly. The police quickly rushed the demonstrators with tear gas and nightsticks. As the marchers fled, mounted units continued the assault, mercilessly beating them in retreat. Media coverage of the event, dubbed "Bloody Sunday," turned national attention on Alabama. Lewis, who sustained serious injuries in the attack, pondered how it was possible for President Johnson to "send troops to Vietnam" and other parts of the globe but not Selma to protect Americans directly imperiled.

In the wake of the violence, the SCLC sent out a call for religious leaders to join Selma demonstrators on Tuesday for a second march. In the meantime, Federal District Court Judge Frank M. Johnson, Jr. announced his intent to issue a restraining order barring the march until March 11, at the earliest. Johnson personally asked King to postpone the action until he could guarantee federal protection.

On March 9, faced again with the dilemma of directly disobeying a pending court order, King led approximately 2,000 marchers back to the Edmund Pettus Bridge. Confronted by the same police barricades, the marchers yielded. After kneeling to pray, they rose, and returned to Selma, escaping both another clash with police and outward defiance of a federal court order.

Despite criticism from some within the movement who argued that the march should have proceeded, the March 9 action nevertheless had the desired effect. President Johnson swiftly dispatched a communique "deploring the brutality" in Alabama and pledging to introduce a voting rights bill to Congress within days.

Shortly after the President's statement, a group of local men violently assaulted James Reeb, a white Unitarian minister from Massachusetts who answered King's call for support. His death two days later solidified the call for new voting legislation. In a gesture similar to one he made for the families of the white missing Mississippi workers, Johnson phoned Reeb's wife and brought all the pressure of the federal government on Governor George Wallace to not only protect the marchers but ensure the right to vote for African Americans in Alabama. Less than a week later on March 15, Johnson in a televised address to Congress, not only asked for new legislation but also squarely committed the nation to overcoming the bitter sting of inequality, noting, "it is all of us, who must overcome the crippling legacy of bigotry and injustice. And we shall overcome."[42]

After carefully reviewing plans for the march, the following day, Judge Frank M. Johnson, Jr. authorized the SCLC to proceed and further enjoined state and local officials from undertaking any action to halt the march. On March 17, President Johnson presented the draft of a bill guaranteeing voting rights for consideration to Congress.

With all legal hurdles cleared and the prospects of another legislative victory on the horizon, the marchers crossed the Edmund Pettus Bridge on their trek to Montgomery on March 21. Now under the watchful gaze of the FBI and the physical protection of the federalized Alabama National Guard the march proceeded without incident. After five days and 54 miles on March 25, the final stage was set. Although Judge Johnson had limited the actual number of daily participants to 300, on the last day some 25,000 joined with the marchers with King at the helm as they arrived at the capitol steps in Montgomery. There King delivered a rousing address thanking those who sacrificed to make the demonstration possible. The danger, however, was not over yet. Hours later, four Klansmen shot into a car killing a white volunteer named Viola Liuzzo, as she transported demonstrators back home to Selma.

In the end the sacrifices of Jackson, Reeb, and Liuzzo were not in vain, as President Johnson attached his signature to the Voting Rights Act of 1965 on August 6 assuring to Black citizens what he described as "the most powerful instrument ever devised by man for breaking down injustice."[43]

The passage of the Voting Rights Act was in many ways the capstone of more than a decade of organizing and mass mobilizing. From the Supreme Court's decision in *Brown* to the campaign in Selma, the NAACP's legal strategy and nonviolent direct action tactics combined to produce a number of legislative victories. In the years ahead, however, the movement entered into arenas where the battle lines were less clear-cut and often beyond the scope of legislative enactments. This would become painfully evident less than a week after the passage of the Voting Rights Act. After an incident of police brutality during a routine traffic stop in the Watts section of Los Angeles, California, six days of rioting and 34 deaths occurred. With the nation pondering why, movement leaders seemed hard-pressed to explain how, in the moment of triumph, there could be such despair. Describing the source of the Watts rebellion as "the rumblings of discontent from the 'have-nots' within the midst of an affluent society," Dr. King nevertheless acknowledged that the uprising marked "the beginning of a stirring of those people in our society who have been by passed by the progress of the past decade."[44]

In the years ahead, the movement sought to address these issues. They were joined by a nascent Black Power Movement, long in the shadows but no less significant in addressing its contributions to the Long Black Freedom Struggle.

Notes

1 Martin Luther, King, Jr., "Letter from Birmingham Jail," *The Norton Anthology of African American Literature*, edited by Henry Louis Gates, Jr. and Nellie Y. McKay (New York: Norton, 1997), 1854–66.
2 Jacquelyn Dowd Hall, "The Long Civil Rights Movement and the Political Uses of the Past," *Journal of American History* 91, no. 4 (March 2005).
3 Howard Zinn, *SNCC: The New Abolitionists* (Boston: Beacon Press, 2002 [1964]).
4 Arnold H. Taylor, "America's Second Civil War: Review of Fred Powledge, *Free At Last? The Civil Rights Movement and the People Who Made It*," *Book World*, (3 , 1991).
5 Harvard Sitkoff, "The Preconditions for Racial Change," in William Chafe and Harvard Sitkoff, eds., *A History of Our Time* (New York: Oxford University Press, 1991), 157–66. See also Arnold H. Taylor, *Travail and Triumph: Black Life and Culture*

in the South Since Civil War (Connecticut: Greenwood Publishing Group, 1977), 236–8.

6   For examples of local struggles see, Robert Norrell, *Reaping the Whirlwind: The Civil Rights Movement in Tuskegee* (New York: Knopf, 1985); Charles M. Payne, *I've Got the Light of Freedom: The Organizing Tradition and the Mississippi Freedom Struggle* (Berkeley: University of California Press, 1995); Glenn T. Eskew, *But for Birmingham: The Local and National Movements in the Civil Rights Struggle* (Chapel Hill: University of North Carolina Press, 1997); Adam Fairclough, *Race and Democracy: The Civil Rights Struggle in Louisiana, 1915–1972* (Athens: University of Georgia Press, 1995); Peter Levy, *Civil War on Race Street: The Civil Rights Movement in Cambridge, Maryland* (Gainesville: University Press of Florida, 2003); Yohuru Williams, *Black Politics/ White Power: Civil Rights, Black Power, and the Black Panthers in New Haven* (New York: Brandywine, 2000); Thomas Sugrue, *The Origins of the Urban Crisis: Racial Inequality in Postwar Detroit* (Princeton: Princeton University Press, 1996); Matthew J. Countryman, *Up South: Civil Rights and Black Power in Philadelphia* (Philadelphia: University of Pennsylvania Press, 2005); Patrick Jones, *The Selma of the North: Civil Rights Insurgency in Milwaukee* (Cambridge, MA: Harvard University Press, 2010); Martha Biondi, *To Stand and Fight: The Struggle for Civil Rights in Postwar New York City* (Cambridge, MA: Harvard University Press, 2003); Thomas J. Sugrue, *Sweet Land of Liberty: The Forgotten Struggle for Civil Rights in the North* (New York: Random House, 2009); Jeanne F. Theoharis and Komozi Woodard, eds., *Freedom North: Black Freedom Struggles Outside the South, 1940–1980* (New York: Palgrave Macmillan, 2003); Felicia Kornbluh, *The Battle for Welfare Rights: Politics and Poverty in Modern America* (Philadelphia: University of Pennsylvania Press, 2007); Rhonda Y. Williams, *The Politics of Public Housing: Black Women's Struggles Against Urban Inequality* (New York: Oxford University Press, 2005).

7   On the murder of Till see Stephen J. Whitfield, *A Death in the Delta: The Story of Emmett Till* (Baltimore: Johns Hopkins University Press, 1988).

8   Henry Hampton and Steve Fayer, *Voices of Freedom: An Oral History of the Civil Rights Movement from the 1950's through the 1980's* (New York: Bantam Books, 1991), xxvii. The Second Civil War theory has been advanced by Dr. Arnold H. Taylor of Howard University in an article entitled "America's Second Civil War," *Book World Review* (March 1991).

9   Hampton and Fayer, *Voices of Freedom*, 19; on the Montgomery Bus Boycott see also Jeanne Theoharis, *The Rebellious Life of Mrs. Rosa Parks* (Boston: Beacon Press, 2013); Herbert Kohl, *She Would Not Be Moved: How We Tell the Story of Rosa Parks and the Montgomery Bus Boycott* (New York: The New Press, 2005); Donnie Williams and Wayne Greenhaw's *The Thunder of Angels: The Montgomery Bus Boycott and the People Who Broke the Back of Jim Crow* (New York: Lawrence Hill, 2005); Taylor Branch, *Parting the Waters: America in the King Years, 1954–63* (New York: Simon & Schuster, 2007), 143–205; David Garrow, *Bearing the Cross: Martin Luther King Jr., and the Southern Christian Leadership Conference* (New York: Vintage Books, 1988), 11–82; Harvard Sitkoff, *King: Pilgrimage to the Mountaintop* (New York : Hill & Wang, 2008), 30–51; Adam Fairclough, *To Redeem the Soul of America: The Southern Christian Leadership Conference and Martin Luther King, Jr.* (Athens, GA: University of Georgia Press, 1987), 11–29.

10   Hampton and Fayer, *Voices of Freedom*, 20.

11   "Respectability, Class, and Gender in the Montgomery Bus Boycott and the Early Civil Rights Movement," in Peter Lin and Sharon Monteith, eds., *Gender and the*

Civil Rights Movement (New Brunswick: Rutgers University Press, 2004); Phillip Hoose and Claudette Colvin, *Twice toward Justice* (New York: Farrar, Straus and Giroux, 2009).

12 Hampton and Fayer, *Voices of Freedom*, 22–3.

13 Fred Powledge, *Free At Last* (New York: Harper Perennial, 1991), 85.

14 Freddie C. Colston, *Dr. Benjamin E. Mays Speaks: Representative Speeches of a Great American Orator* (Lanham: University Press of America, 2002), 63.

15 James Forman, "American Civil Rights Activist and Author Former Executive Secretary of the Student Nonviolent Coordinating Committee (SNCC)," *Biography Today: Profiles of People of Interest to Young Readers* 14 (2005): 119.

16 http://whospeaks.library.vanderbilt.edu/interview/clarie-collins-harvey, accessed July 2, 2015.

17 Lucius Holloway quoted in Powledge, *Free At Last*, 349.

18 On the Albany Movement, see Garrow, *Bearing the Cross*, 173–230; Fairclough, *To Redeem the Soul of America*, 85–110; Sitkoff, *King: Pilgrimage to the Mountaintop*, 78–87; Stephen G.N. Tuck, B*eyond Atlanta: The Struggle for Racial Equality in Georgia, 1940–1980* (Georgia: University of Georgia Press, 2003), 147; Branch, *Parting the Waters*, 524–631.

19 Charles Sherrod quoted in Wesley C. Hogan, *Many Minds One Heart: SNCC's Dream for a New America* (Chapel Hill: University of North Carolina Press, 2007), 79.

20 Chief Pritchett quoted in Tuck, *Beyond Atlanta*, 147.

21 Kennedy quoted in Philip A. Goduti, Jr., *Robert F. Kennedy and the Shaping of Civil Rights, 1960–1964* (North Carolina: McFarland & Company, 2012), 113; Clayborne Carson, *In Struggle: SNCC and the Black Awakening of the 1960s* (Cambridge, MA: Harvard University Press, 1995), 61.

22 King quoted in Branch, *Parting the Waters*, 632.

23 On the Birmingham Freedom Movement see Glenn T. Eskew, *But for Birmingham: The Local and National Movements in the Civil Rights Struggle* (Chapel Hill: University of North Carolina Press, 1997); Diane McWhorter, *Carry Me Home: Birmingham, Alabama, the Climactic Battle of the Civil Rights Revolution* (New York: Simon & Schuster, 2001); Andrew Manis, *A Fire You Can't Put Out: The Civil Rights Life of Birmingham's Reverend Fred Shuttlesworth* (Tuscaloosa: University of Alabama Press, 1999).

24 Michael Krenn, "The Unwelcome Mat: African Diplomats in Washington, D.C., during the Kennedy Years," in Brenda Gayle Plummer, *Window on Freedom: Race, Civil Rights, and Foreign Affairs 1945–1988* (Chapel Hill: University of North Carolina Press, 2003).

25 Kennedy quoted in Tomiko Brown-Nagin, *Courage to Dissent: Atlanta and the Long History of the Civil Rights Movement* (New York: Oxford University Press, 2011), 218.

26 Sitkoff, *King: Pilgrimage to the Mountaintop*, 107.

27 Malcolm X quoted in "Miles College's Lucius Pitts, Malcolm X discuss Birmingham on ABC News; 15,000 march in San Francisco" (May 26, 1963), http://blog.al.com/birmingham-news-stories/2013/05/miles_colleges_lucius_pitts_ma.html, accessed July 2, 2015.

28 Stephan Lesher, *George Wallace: American Populist* (New York: Addison Wesley Publishing, 1994), 229.

29 John F. Kennedy, "Radio and Television Report to the American People on Civil Rights," John F. Kennedy Library and Museum (1963).

30   Malcolm X quoted in James L. Conyers and Andrew P. Smallwood, eds., *Malcolm X: A Historical Reader* (Durham, NC: Carolina Academic Press, 2008), 114.

31   Representative Charles C. Diggs quoted in Erin Staley, *Martin Luther King Jr. and the Speech That Inspired the World* (New York: Rosen Publishing, 2015), 40.

32   Garth E. Pauley, "John Lewis's 'Serious Revolution': Rhetoric, Resistance, and Revision at the March on Washington," *Quarterly Journal of Speech* 84, no. 3 (1998): 320–40.

33   Davis W. Houck and David E. Dixon, eds., *Women and the Civil Rights Movement, 1954–1965* (Jackson: University Press of Mississippi, 2009), x.

34   Payne, *I've Got the Light of Freedom*, 7.

35   Clayborne Carson, David J. Garrow, Gerald Gill, Vincent Harding, and Darlene Clark Hine, *The Eyes on the Prize Civil Rights Reader: Documents, Speeches, and Firsthand Accounts from the Black Freedom Struggle* (New York: Penguin Books, 1991), 166

36   On the Mississippi Freedom Movement, see Emilye Crosby, *A Little Taste of Freedom: The Black Freedom Struggle in Claiborne County, Mississippi* (Chapel Hill: University of North Carolina Press, 2005); Payne, *I've Got the Light of Freedom*; John Dittmer, *Local People: The Struggle for Civil Rights in Mississippi* (Chicago: University of Illinois Press, 1995); Doug McAdam, *Freedom Summer* (New York and Oxford: Oxford University Press, 1988); Susie Erenrich, ed., *Freedom Is a Constant Struggle: An Anthology of the Mississippi Civil Rights Movement* (Montgomery: Black Belt Press, 1999); CCarson, *In Struggle*; Bruce Watson, *Freedom Summer: The Savage Season That Made Mississippi Burn and Made America a Democracy* (New York: Viking, 2010).

37   Hampton and Fayer, *Voices of Freedom*, 203.

38   Ibid., 193.

39   On the Selma campaign see Gary May, *Bending Toward Justice: The Voting Rights Act and the Transformation of American Democracy* (New York: Basic Books, 2013); David Garrow, *Protest at Selma* (New Haven: Yale University Press, 1978); Garrow, *Bearing the Cross*, 357–430; Taylor Branch, *At Canaan's Edge: America in the King Years 1965–1968* (New York: Simon & Schuster, 2007), 59–65; Mary Stanton, *From Selma To Sorrow: The Life and Death of Viola Liuzzo* (Athens, GA: University of Georgia Press, 2000).

40   Andrew Young quoted in Hampton and Fayer, *Voices of Freedom*, 214.

41   Joseph Smitheran quoted in Hampton and Fayer, *Voices of Freedom*, 216.

42   Johnson quoted in Philip A. Klinkner, and Rogers M. Smith, *The Unsteady March: The Rise and Decline of Racial Equality in America* (Chicago: University of Chicago Press, 1999), 1.

43   David J. Garrow, "The Voting Rights Act in Historical Perspective," *The Georgia Historical Quarterly* (1990): 377–98.

44   King quoted in Clayborne Carson, ed., *The Autobiography of Martin Luther King, Jr.* (New York: Time Warner, 1998), 291–2.

3

POWER TO THE PEOPLE

Black Power

Black Power is giving power to people who have not had power to determine
their destiny.

Huey Newton[1]

As a black woman, my politics and political affiliation are bound up with and flow
from participation in my people's struggle for liberation, and with the fight of
oppressed people all over the world against American imperialism.

Angela Davis[2]

For many years scholars attempted to pinpoint the origins of Black Power in a
moment, rather than as a sustained movement. Typically, in accounts of the
period, that moment was 1966 and Stokely Carmichael's call for Black Power
during the Meredith March in Greenwood, Mississippi. Recent scholarship has
corrected this view revealing a vibrant parallel Black Power Movement that
helped to shape 1950s and 1960s Black Freedom Struggles. While both movements sometimes overlapped in terms of leaders and goals (Stokely Carmichael
for instance, started, with some reservations, as a Civil Rights activist but eventually fully embraced Black Power) there were important distinctions. At its
core, the Civil Rights Movement was about inclusion, focusing on winning
opportunities for African Americans to claim their rightful place within the
American political system. Black Power, on the other hand, focused on self-
determination that could include political inclusion or manifest itself in autonomous social, political, and economic structures. Black Power, like Black
Nationalism, also promoted racial unity as the cornerstone of Black liberation.
It was far from monolithic. Historian William Van Deburg, for example, notes
that Black Power's "essential spirit was the product of generations of black

people dealing with powerlessness – and surviving."[3] People of African descent, its proponents argued, should unify on the grounds of their shared African heritage and culture as well as their shared experience of racial oppression. Although often denounced as separatist, Black Power advocates pursued this goal in a variety of ways. In his book *Black Nationalism in American Politics and Thought*, political scientist Dean Robinson, for instance, observed that Black Nationalism was broad enough to "include both those who favored separate statehood, as well as, self-help identified 'nationalists' who supported the more modest goal of Black administration of vital private and public institutions."[4] In this sense, as historian Peniel Joseph concludes, Black Power was a broad "political movement whose reverberations touched major aspects of American and global intellectual culture–which paved the way for thousands of works both political and polemical, analyzing and advocating multiple political agendas and perspectives."[5]

Rhonda Y. Williams' *Concrete Demands* deepens this analysis, exploring the rich origins and genealogy of the Black Power Movement, extending back to the turn of the century when a rush of new thoughts and ideas from the New Negro Movement to Pan-Africanism broadened African American horizons and complicated their worldview. It included thought leaders like radical socialist and New Negro Movement founder Hubert Harrison whose promotion of race and class-consciousness among people of African descent deeply influenced other Black leaders like A. Phillip Randolph and Marcus Garvey.[6] Through his editorship of the Universal Negro Improvement Association's newspaper, *The Negro World*, Harrison would help to influence countless other Black leaders, like Malcolm X, whose parents were ardent supporters of Garvey. Rarely acknowledged, but no less important, were the scores of women who found a sense of identity and purpose in the inchoate mist of Black Power. Even as Black women filled the ranks and leadership positions within Civil Rights organizations across the nation, importantly, they also helped to shape the contours of what would become the Black Power Movement. This included women like communist political organizer Williana Jones Burroughs, whose political leanings led her to Moscow, but not before she received the Communist Party's nomination for the post of Lieutenant Governor of New York in 1934.[7] Like the singer Paul Robeson and numerous other African American activists who were enamored with Communism, Burroughs was not afraid to explore alternative paths to empowerment and liberation. Her advocacy on behalf of the Scottsboro Boys, nine young men falsely accused and initially sentenced to death for the rape of two white women in 1931, put her in touch with other Black Communists like Angelo Herndon. Georgia authorities arrested Herndon in 1932 for the possession and distribution of Communist literature under a Civil War statute that made it a crime to stir up insurrection. Convicted by an all-white jury he served two years in prison before his release on appeal. Although the Supreme Court later overturned his conviction (1937), Herndon's encounters with Jim Crow Justice reinforced the notion that absolute equality before the law in a segregated society could never be possible.[8]

Such injustices, coupled with the crippling effects of the Six Degrees of Segregation, led some to explore the possibility of leaving the United States. In the tradition of Marcus Garvey, some advocated for the establishment of an African homeland or even an internal colony within the United States. Others like the Nation of Islam focused on Black institution building among its own followers. Still others like the Black Panthers saw no harm in inter-racial cooperation. All, however, were consciously internationalist in their thinking, linking the struggles of Black people in the United States to those of other groups abroad. As singer Paul Robeson explained in his 1956 testi-mony before the House Un-American Activities Committee for allegedly making disloyal statements about why African Americans would never fight in a war against the Soviet Union where discrimination was supposedly outlawed:

> what is perfectly clear today is that nine hundred million other colored people have told you that *they* will not. Four hundred million in India, and millions everywhere, have told you, precisely, that the colored people are not going to die for anybody: they are going to die for their independ-ence. We are dealing not with fifteen million colored people; we are dealing with hundreds of millions.[9]

Robeson's comments came on the heels of the end of the First Afro-Asian Conference held in Bandung, Indonesia in April of 1955. There delegates from 29 "non-aligned" nations in Africa, the Middle East, and Asia gathered to discuss an agenda that denounced racism and colonialism and sought to find a neutral path in the escalating Cold War between the United States and the Soviet Union. Although the United States elected not to send a representative, New York Congressman Adam Clayton Powell attended.

While Black Power had deep roots, its main gestation period also took place in the fertile post-World War II era. As Rhonda Y. Williams powerfully notes, "The edifice of racial inequality had stood firm in the midst of a war fought for freedom, and this had a radicalizing effect. It evoked concrete demands for rights, protection, and power."[10] These "concrete demands" addressed the same Six Degrees of Segregation in ways distinct from the Civil Rights Movement, including exploring alternatives to integration and privileging programs and interventions that placed racial unity as well as survival as the highest priority.

While Black Power thus deeply informed 1950s and 1960s Black Freedom Struggles, after the adoption of nonviolence as a tactic by the leaders of the national King-led Civil Rights Movement, Black Power activists were increas-ingly framed as proponents of retaliatory violence. Their rejection of nonviolence

in favor of armed self-defense erroneously became one of the defining charac-
teristics of a much more complex movement.

Black Power and Armed Resistance

Shortly before embarking on a solo march to encourage the end of racial
segregation in April of 1963, white Civil Rights activist William Moore drafted
a letter to Mississippi Governor Ross Barnett. In it, Moore warned of the
potential disaster that would befall the nation if Mississippi and other southern
states did not meet the legitimate demands for full equality made by African
Americans. Invoking the colonial experience of the British and French,
Moore noted, "The end of Mississippi colonialism is fast approaching. The
only question is whether you will help it to end in friendship like the British
or hold on to what is already lost, creating bitterness and hatred like the French.
For our sake, as well as the Negro's," he concluded, "I hope you will decide to
try the British way." A few days later, as Moore embarked on his trek from
Chattanooga, Tennessee to Jackson, Mississippi, a sniper killed him. A year later
singer Nina Simone paid homage to Moore and other martyrs in her song
"Mississippi Goddam." Chronicling the violence and brutality that marked the
bloody campaigns of 1963 from Birmingham to the murder of Medgar Evers
and the dynamiting of the 16th Street Baptist Church, Simone boldly declared
in the final verse, "You don't have to live next to me. All I want is my equality."[11]

Nina Simone's powerful lyrics at once rejected the cautious mentality that
had pervaded discussions of Civil Rights protest and asserted that integration
and equality were not necessarily synonymous. As Ruth Feldstein has written,
"the denunciations of the well manner politics of 'going slow' in 'Mississippi
Goddam' made manifest the range of political perspectives that developed in
many locations in this period."[12] To be sure, in communities across the country,
activists such as Gloria Richardson in Cambridge, Maryland had no interest in
adjusting the pace of change to accommodate white fear. For segregationists
Moore's letter, however, underscored a serious concern—one that some,
such as Representative Charles C. Diggs, had been playing on to push the
government to respond. What if under the duress of sustained campaigns of
white terror African Americans adopted violence in defiance of nonviolent
movement as a means to secure not only their rights but true liberation? If
responsible white leadership did not deliver results, spokespersons like Diggs
forecast the movement for Civil Rights might descend into chaos with African
Americans electing to meet violence with violence.

It was a real, if exaggerated, fear that created a false dichotomy over the use
of violence and traditions of self-defense in the African American community. A dichotomy that would unfortunately come to overshadow other aspects
of the Black Power Movement that encompassed much more than calls for
armed self-defense.

Significantly, one of the persons most identified with this view was also one of the best examples of the deep philosophical roots of Black Power. In the early 1960s, Muslim minister Malcolm X gained national attention for his fiery rhetoric. As a "Black Nationalist Freedom Fighter," he drew a sharp distinction between what he called the "Black Revolution" and the "Negro Revolution," which he equated with the integrationist goals of the nonviolent mainstream Civil Rights Movement. Comparing the struggle for Black equality to the American Revolution, Malcolm provocatively pondered:

> If George Washington didn't win independence for this country nonviolently and if Patrick Henry didn't come up with a nonviolent statement, and you taught me to look upon them as patriots and heroes, then it's time for you to realize that I have studied your books well.[13]

Malcolm X, however, often spoke in two voices, one that encouraged Black self-determination and political and economic independence including claiming and exercising the right to vote, and one that dealt with the reality of segregation. In his 1964 "The Ballot or the Bullet" Speech, for instance, Malcolm articulated the archetypal Black Power response to the Six Degrees of Segregation. Although his comments about self-defense garnered the most attention, he dedicated most of the speech to instructing African Americans on how to harness political power and live free from white political and economic domination. These were lessons he learned early on from his parents, both of whom were followers of Marcus Garvey and adherents to the philosophy of racial unity and self-help Garvey and his equally influential, if less visible, second wife Amy Jacques Garvey extolled. Speaking on housing, for example, he explained, "the political philosophy of Black Nationalism only means that if you and I are going to live in a black community – and that's where we're going to live." He continued because as "soon as you move out of the black community into their community, it's mixed for a period of time, but they're gone and you're right there all by yourself again." He also shared a vision of mutual support and community investment that he postulated would allow African Americans not only to elect politicians, who would be responsive to their votes, but also to open businesses, create jobs, and build communities, which they would control and in which they could be proud.

To be clear, the type of armed self-defense that Malcolm counseled, at least in "The Ballot or the Bullet" had deep roots among African Americans living in the South. Recent scholarship by Emilye Crosby, Akinyele Umoja, and memoirs like movement veteran Charlie Cobb's *This Nonviolent Stuff Will Get You Killed* illustrate how traditions of armed resistance peacefully co-existed and even enabled organizing in the South. In his book *We Will Shoot Back*, Umoja writes for instance that, "without armed resistance, primarily organized by local people … activists would not have been able to organize in Mississippi."[14]

Before the arrival of Bayard Rustin in Montgomery in 1955, for instance, and in the face of threats, armed supporters guarded King's family and home. It was the type of "informal and loosely organized" resistance Umoja argues typified self-defense in African American communities before 1964. Problematically, of course, many perceived calls for self-defense as calls for retaliatory violence. Once national Civil Rights organizations, like the NAACP and SCLC, embraced nonviolence, it became difficult for them to reconcile these traditions with individuals, such as Monroe, North Carolina NAACP head Robert F. Williams, who regarded them as essential to survival.[15]

Williams helps us illustrate the intricacies of the relationship between Black Freedom Struggles and self-defense. Born in Monroe in 1925, encounters with the Six Degrees of Segregation punctuated much of his early life experiences. In 1936, at the age of 11, for instance, he witnessed a jarring incident of police brutality when a white police officer violently arrested a Black woman, in Williams' words, with "her dress up over her head, the same way that a cave man would club and drag his sexual prey." Williams was additionally struck at how none of the Black men who witnessed the scene came to the woman's defense, instead lowering "their heads in shame and hurried silently from the cruelly bizarre sight."[16] After moving to Detroit in the early 1940s in search of work in the city's auto industry, Williams felt northern white brutality after he and his brother battled with angry white mobs during the Detroit race riot of 1943, one of the deadliest racial conflicts in U.S. history. Drafted into the army in 1944, Williams returned to North Carolina in 1946, profoundly altered by his experience and his service. As the historian John Dittmer observed, "typical of the generation of southern blacks who launched the civil rights movement in the 1950s" he promptly joined the NAACP in search of answers to the concrete demands outlined by Rhonda Y. Williams. However, Williams struggled with some of the policies set by the national office and, in 1957, ruffled feathers after he publicly proposed that Black people in Monroe arm themselves in defense against white terrorists.[17]

His candor in articulating this and other positions alienated him within the organization and, in 1959, the NAACP suspended him after he suggested that Blacks retaliate against members of an all-white jury that failed to convict a white man charged with sexually assaulting a Black woman. Fearful that Williams' position might be mistaken as being more widespread, Martin Luther King also chose to respond. In a carefully crafted article, King argued that non-violent direct action protest would yield greater victory than what he termed "a few acts of organized violence." Williams remained unconvinced and in 1960 found himself in trouble again, this time on false charges of kidnapping after he granted a white couple sanctuary in his home during a local Black protest. Under indictment and disaffected with the direction of the movement, Williams fled to Cuba where he became a voice in exile. He hosted a radio show, *Radio Free Dixie*, that promoted his alternative vision to Black empowerment. Eschewing integration, he, appealed to a broader Black Internationalism that placed the Black Freedom Struggles taking place in the United States in the larger context of international and anticolonial struggles.

Williams' position was not new. In cities throughout the North and South, organizations and activists had been professing similar views and experimenting with various forms of resistance for more than a century. In this way, as historian Peniel Joseph has observed, "Black power activism existed alongside civil rights struggles of the 1950s and early 1960s, and certain activists simultaneously participated in both movements."[18]

In this way, Black Power was about much more than armed resistance. It was about creating a program of survival that sought political power, cultural autonomy, and economic self-sufficiency. Dating back to the turn of the century, Black Nationalists such as Marcus Garvey had promoted the idea of a broad and unified movement of Black people throughout the African Diaspora. Consciously international, such activists saw the struggle for Black equality in the United States as intimately tied to the struggle of people of African descent throughout the world. Garvey, in particular, privileged the West Indies and the continent of Africa where he argued that European economic exploitation, slavery, and alien political monopoly denied Blacks the right to determine their own laws and destiny. Although no fan of Garvey, W.E.B. Du Bois also embraced the concept of Pan-Africanism that professed similar goals. Dedicated to establishing independence for African nations and cultivating unity among Black people throughout the world, Pan-Africanism expanded to include a range of social, economic, and political initiatives and activities that sought to establish ties between African-descended people. A rise of anticolonial actions in the 1950s also encouraged a vision of Black liberation.

In addition to their conscious internationalism, Black Power advocates focused less on interventions aimed at reshaping America and more on those that might result in Black self-determination—on par with what was happening with many "Third World" liberation struggles. By 1963, the rise of more than two dozen Independent African and Asian Nations convinced Malcolm X that African Americans should take their case before the United Nations in hopes of bringing international pressure to bear on the U.S. government to end segregation and achieving Black liberation. Malcolm encouraged African Americans to see themselves as part of this larger struggle. In his speeches and writings, however, he provided a more traditional view of political revolution. "Revolutions," he proclaimed in "The Black Revolution," "overturn systems. And there is no system on this earth, which has proven itself more corrupt, more criminal, than this system that in 1964 still colonizes 22 million African-Americans, still enslaves 22 million Afro- Americans."[19]

Though oversimplified, Malcolm drew a sharp line between what he called the Black Revolution and the "Negro Revolution." As he conceptualized the problem, commenting on both nonviolence and interracial cooperation:

Who ever heard of angry revolutionists all harmonizing "We shall overcome ... Suum Day ..." while tripping and swaying along arm in arm with the very people they were supposed to be angrily revolting against? Who ever heard of angry revolutionaries swinging their bare feet together with their oppressors in lily pad park pools, with gospels and guitars and "I have a Dream" speeches?[20]

While the range of the debate over tactics extended well beyond Martin Luther King and Malcolm X, their contrasting views remain instructive. "Our history," King seemed to answer Malcolm in his second book *Why We Can't Wait?*, "teaches us that wielding the sword against racial superiority is not effective." He concluded that the

Negro's method of nonviolent direct action is not only suitable as a remedy for injustice; its very nature is such that it challenges the myth of inferiority. Even the most reluctant are forced to recognize that no inferior people could choose and successfully pursue a course involving such extensive sacrifice, bravery, and skill.[21]

In the face of continued violence against Civil Rights demonstrators and the victories of Third World revolutionary struggles, King's defense of nonviolence did not recognize the critical power of alternative strategies and tactics. Such triumphs of indigenous people over colonial powers also provided Black Power advocates, like Robert F. Williams, Queen Mother Audley Moore, and Malcolm X with the opportunity to contrast the illusion of American democratic practice against the realities of Jim Crow. After a Florida Congressman raised the possibility of military intercession in Cuba to assure free elections in 1960, Robert F. Williams, for instance, pondered how "as an oppressed American negro now enjoying the greatest freedom of my life in revolutionary Cuba" could be concerned with Cuba when "many Negroes have been without free elections for almost 200 years." The admiration was not one-sided as Third World revolutionary leaders looked to American Civil Rights and Black Power activists for support. The cross-fertilization of ideas greatly influenced Black Power advocates who freely experimented with political ideas from Marxism/Leninism to Nkrumaism—a political ideology tied to Kwame Nkrumah who helped guide the African nation of Ghana to independence.[22]

Black Power on Campus

One of the places where Black Power found a welcome audience was on college campuses. Just as these intellectual spaces of knowledge and study had proved incubators for activism associated with the Civil Rights Movement, they also provided the space for Black Power activists to explore, contemplate, and debate alternative pathways to Black empowerment. The nation's Historically Black Colleges and Universities were especially receptive to Black Power. At both Historically Black Colleges and Universities and on the campuses of predominately white universities, African American students pushed for the hiring of diverse faculty, the creation of Black Studies programs and programs to aid in the recruitment and retention of a diverse student body. The vehicles for these demands were often Black Student Unions that brought students together to discuss important issues relative not only to the collegiate experience but also to the wider world.

The democratization of education, occasioned by the GI Bill, also made education more affordable, opening up campuses across the nation to new pools of students whose interests extended beyond acquiring skills for employment. In collectives, student unions, and in study groups, Black students and their allies read and discussed the speeches and written works of Black Power leaders like Malcolm X and pondered their place in a much larger war against global oppression exemplified by Asian, African, and Latin American and Caribbean revolutionary struggles such as the Cuban Revolution.

These debates and discussions often moved students to act, and several important Black Power organizations grew out of campus dialogues. There was significant diversity in these conversations, often spawning multiple approaches rooted in a desire for Black liberation. In 1962, for instance, activist Donald Warden established the Bay Area Afro-American Association. In addition to political independence, Warden championed a community-based philosophy of social engagement that emphasized the importance of maintaining a distinct cultural identity. Ron Maulana Karenga embraced this aspect of Warden's philosophy and worked to establish an offshoot of the Association in Los Angeles that became the starting point for an important cultural nationalist group called US. In the meantime, Warden's critique of nonviolence captivated Oakland Merritt College students Huey Newton and Bobby Seale who eventually incorporated into another significant organization, the Black Panther Party for Self-Defense, whom historian Donna Murch rightly observes began with a study group.[23] In 1962, students at Central State College in Wilberforce, Ohio, formed the basis of what would eventually become the Revolutionary Action Movement or RAM. Heavily influenced by Robert F. Williams' call for armed self-defense, the group sought to combine the direct action methods of SNCC with the Nation of Islam's Black Nationalist ideology. Demonstrating foreign influences, such as Fidel Castro, Kwame Nkrumah, and Mao Tse Tung, RAM's philosophy also incorporated elements of Marxism and Third World internationalism.[24]

Black Power and Urban Unrest

In the midst of these political stirrings came the Watts rebellion of August 1965. The violent uprising forced Americans to confront the reality of the pervasive scope of poverty and racism, which author Michael Harrington in his 1962 publication *The Other America: Poverty in the United States* defined as largely poor, Black, and urban.[25] While the national media focused almost exclusively on the states of the Old Confederacy as the key battlegrounds within the movement, significant fighting was taking place in cities across the country—but especially in the North and West, often overlooked in the discussions of racial inequality. Typically portrayed as oases of equality when compared with the South, or Promised Lands, most cities presented their own version of Jim Crow Segregation, including racially restrictive covenants that barred access to decent housing, unfair labor practices that froze African Americans out of labor unions and relegated them to the lowest paying jobs, and de facto segregation in schools.

There was also significant police brutality. The unrest in Watts that lasted six days and resulted in 34 deaths and an estimated 40 million dollars in property damage proved to be only the first in a series of hundreds of incidents of civil unrest over a three-year period. The events that led to the disturbance in Watts were typical of what would become somewhat of a pattern. Just after dusk on the evening of August 11, 1965, white California Highway Patrol officer Lee W. Minikus stopped 21-year-old Marquette Frye on suspicion of driving under the influence. In view of a large crowd of spectators, a scuffle between officers, Frye, and his family generated grossly exaggerated, but nonetheless believable, rumors of police misconduct. Over the next six days, rioters registered their discontent by overturning cars, looting and burning businesses, and skirmishing with police. Order returned only after Governor Pat Brown called in the National Guard and imposed a 45-mile-wide curfew.[26]

In a desire to downplay the local issues that produced the unrest, politicians and police attempted to fix the blame for the rebellion on outside influences—namely political agitators. An official investigation launched by the Governor, however, dismissed these claims, and instead blamed the uprising on mounting dissatisfaction with poor schools, lack of jobs, substandard housing, and well-documented complaints against the police. Importantly, when Martin Luther King, Jr. cut short his vacation to fly to Los Angeles, where he pled for calm, residents rebuffed him. Later, King prophetically cast events in Watts as "the beginning of a stirring of those people in our society who have been by passed by the progress of the past decade."[27]

Two years later, in 1967, events in Watts replayed in cities across the country with more than 100 documented disturbances, the most destructive taking place in Detroit, Michigan. As in Watts, the violence in Detroit also highlighted the problems accompanying demographic shifts that had begun decades before in many big cities. Black migrants from the South flooded cities like Chicago and Detroit in the postwar eras in search of work. Detroit's booming auto industry provided a strong pull. Unlike other immigrant groups, the response to Black people was less than welcoming. They were forced to live in substandard housing and often found employment precarious. Even before the riots, many white middle-class Detroiters began relocating to new suburban communities. The construction of new highways facilitated this exodus, which had the added impact of decreasing the city's tax base and rapidly shifting the city's racial demography. Whites who remained in Detroit fought to preserve racially homogenous communities. Adopting the language of war, they referred to Black entrees as invasions and described schools and communities in the midst of integration as battlegrounds. They also blamed problems associated with the process of deindustrialization and a rise in crime on the growing Black population. Typical of police forces across the country at that time, the Detroit police force, which was 95 percent white, in a city whose population was one-third Black, became notorious for its mistreatment of Black residents. The rampant poverty and disparities in policing mattered little to public officials interested in "preventing" uprisings in their own communities. On the heels of the Watts riot the then chief of police warned of the potential for a Watts style rebellion in the Motor City.[28]

Tensions between police and the Black community finally ruptured in the wee hours of the morning of July 23, 1967, after police executed a raid on an unlicensed after-hours club in one of the city's predominately Black neighborhoods. Within hours, rioters had taken to the streets to register their frustrations. During a week of fierce combat in which police deployed military tanks, 43 people died and clashes and fires left nearly 700 buildings badly damaged or destroyed. While police claimed to be under assault from snipers, a presidential commission later determined that police officers and National Guardsmen perpetrated the majority of the killings.

That commission, appointed by President Lyndon Johnson and chaired by Illinois Governor Otto Kerner, went even further in its final report on the causes of the riots. "Segregation and poverty," the commissioners observed, "have created in the racial ghetto a destructive environment totally unknown to most white Americans." "This is our basic conclusion," the report boldly contended, "our nation is moving toward two societies, one black, one white-separate, and unequal." "What white Americans have never fully understood," the commission concluded, "is that white society is deeply implicated in the ghetto. White institutions created it, white institutions maintain it, and white society condones it."[29]

If urban rebellions awakened the nation to the festering problem of poverty and racism, they also accelerated the exodus of people from out of the city to the suburbs. Many businesses also left, taking valuable jobs with them and decreasing the tax base for essential city services. As a result, Detroit's population plummeted from 1.6 million to 992,000. The glut of abandoned homes and buildings left behind illustrated the depth of the problem, a problem for which Civil Rights activist Bayard Rustin saw only one solution. "The negro slums today," he explained in 1966, "are ghettoes of despair. In Watts, as elsewhere, there are the unemployable poor: the children, the aging, the permanently handicapped. No measure of employment or of economic growth will put an end to their misery, and only government programs can provide them with a decent way of life."[30]

Swept into office on his own right in 1964, President Lyndon Johnson bristled at the implications of the Kerner Commission Report, which seemed to be an indictment on his administration. Johnson had hoped to make the amelioration of racism and poverty the cornerstones of his Great Society programs and had committed the government to an expansion of social welfare programs unseen since the New Deal. The nation's escalating involvement in the Vietnam War, however, claimed much of the President's and the nation's attention after 1965.

Chicago and the Meredith March

Martin Luther King and the SCLC hoped to put the focus back on poverty and racial inequality by setting their sights on Chicago, Illinois as the location of their next campaign. Responding to a request from the Chicago-based Coordinating Council of Community Organizations in 1966, King and the SCLC sought to dramatize conditions using the same tactics they had utilized successfully in the South. Under the aegis of the Chicago Freedom Movement, and with the slogan "End Slums" as its official rally cry, in January of 1966 the SCLC set up operations in the Windy City. To dramatize the substandard conditions that many Black Chicagoans lived under, Dr. King and his family moved into one of the city's most poverty-stricken South Side tenements. King then promptly persuaded his fellow tenants to participate in a rent strike.

While the move had great symbolic import, King faced an uphill battle from the outset. Like many northern elected officials, Mayor Richard J. Daley had publicly supported the Civil Rights Movement, contributing money to Civil Rights organizations and articulating support for desegregation in the South. One of the most popular and seasoned politicians in the Democratic Party, Daley politely responded to all of the movement's complaints and moved quickly to undermine the SCLC's claims of an unresponsive government. As the chief executive of the country's second largest city, Daley further instructed the Chicago police to act with restraint to deflect attention away from the protestors.[31]

Unable to provoke the desired confrontation with the city officials, the SCLC was wholly unprepared for what it would experience—lack of support by the city's Black leadership and a violent backlash by the city's white citizens. Largely dependent on the patronage of the Daley administration, Black leaders refused to support the SCLC's campaign. This helped to make the city, what King termed, the very definition of "a system of internal colonialism." While Black leaders remained inactive, local white ethnic residents formed mobs and shouted racial slurs. Waving Nazi and Confederate banners, they viciously attacked demonstrators during a march through a neighborhood. Taken aback, King confessed that "even in Mississippi" he had never encountered "mobs as hostile and as hate filled."[32]

By the close of the nearly year-long campaign, King and the SCLC had little to show for their efforts—beyond some hollow promises by the Daley machine to better address issues of housing and poverty. After the Chicago Movement disbanded, one of SCLC's young lieutenants, Jesse Jackson, remained and continued to work through a local Civil Rights organization, Operation Breadbasket, to pursue solutions to the problems of Chicago's poor and Black. From the standpoint of the Civil Rights Movement's tried and true practices of precipitating a crisis and drawing national attention, however, Chicago was a failure.

While Rustin and King held out hope for government intervention, leading King to plan for a Poor People's Campaign in Washington, Black Power activists within SNCC were experiencing internal changes that would ulti- mately help give the nation a label for the parallel movement "with no name." In June of 1966, James Meredith, who had successfully integrated Ole Miss, started out on what he billed as a March against Fear from Memphis, Tennessee to Jackson, Mississippi. Meredith selected Mississippi in order to demonstrate to southern Blacks that they needed to continue to stand up against white terro- rism.[33] However, Meredith had a difficult time generating interest. The media seemed fatigued by Civil Rights reporting and more heavily invested in cover- ing the Vietnam War, and the other major Civil Rights leaders, unconvinced of the utility of the march, declined his invitation to participate. So Meredith elected, as William Moore had three years prior, to continue alone. With a handful of newspersons and a few well-wishers in tow, Meredith began his solo trek on June 5, 1966.

By the next day, however, Meredith gained national attention when a white sniper ambushed him on a lonely stretch of highway and sprayed him with birdshot. Transported to a local hospital for treatment, Meredith survived the attack. In the meantime, once skeptical representatives of all of the major Civil Rights organizations now rushed to Meredith's bedside and pledged to continue his march. Among them were King, representing the SCLC, Floyd McKissick from CORE, Whitney Young from the Urban League, and Roy Wilkins from the NAACP, and arriving late the newly elected chairperson of SNCC, Stokely Carmichael.[34]

Born and raised in Trinidad, Carmichael immigrated to New York at the age of 11 where he excelled in school and earned a scholarship to Howard University. While at Howard, Carmichael was initially skeptical of the move- ment. Impressed with accounts of the sit-ins, however, he nevertheless traveled to Fayette County, Tennessee in December 1960 several months ahead of the formation of SNCC to join the waves of student protesters. Carmichael quickly earned the reputation as a committed activist. Yet, similar to Robert F. Williams he claimed to have never fully subscribed to the philosophy of nonviolence. As he explained in an interview with journalist Robert Penn Warren in 1964: "I think that the issue of nonviolence is very important in the question of solving certain things, but it's not true that it necessarily brings us closer together and makes us love each other."[35] Nevertheless, in the same interview, Carmichael said of Malcolm X: "I told him, you keep your talk, and you say what you want, I don't think you put me in a better bargaining position, you know, because you don't say anything." Just two years later, however, Carmichael began speaking of "picking up where Malcolm left off."[36] His reasons for doing so illustrate some of the appeal of Black Power, especially in SNCC.[37]

Carmichael's embrace of Black Power was also evident among the membership of SNCC. After Malcolm's death in 1965, there was heightened interest in many of Malcolm's ideas among many in SNCC, CORE, and other organizations. These young activists, however, had become disenchanted with certain aspects of the movement, especially in the face of rampant racism and murders in the South. Along with Frantz Fanon, author of *Wretched of the Earth*, Malcolm X would emerge as the biggest inspiration for these activists. They also were keeping a watchful eye on events beyond the United States, including Ghana, Cuba, and China. At the time, journalist Peter Goldman documented the supposed shift. "The older leaders never quit believing that (King's dream)," he wrote, "but the radical young did cool off; they went into the 1960's as King's children and came out Malcolm's."[38] Scholarship that is more recent challenges Goldman's notion of a dichotomized Civil Rights and Black Power Movement. Even so, in many organizations, such as SNCC, activists did engage in a process of rediscovery. They began rethinking, and incorporating, some of the foundational ideas floated by Black Power advocates dating back, in some cases, to the turn of the century. An acceptance of nonviolence did not mean that they could not find inspiration also in expressions that were more militant.[39]

One of these ideas was that SNCC should be an all-Black organization. Shortly before James Meredith announced his plans for a March against Fear, those in favor of a change orchestrated what John Lewis later described as an organizational coup that saw the election of Carmichael as chairperson. This new leadership team promptly went about making changes, including expelling white members from the group. White people could remain allies, they maintained, but their organizing efforts should be concentrated on building indigenous Black leadership in the South as well as equal respect for the lives of Black Civil Rights workers. SNCC would later lay out its views on the expulsion in a position paper. "In an attempt to find a solution to our dilemma," the paper began, "we propose that our organization should be black-staffed, black controlled, and black financed." Reflecting the long-standing push in Black Power for self-sufficiency, the authors continued, "If we are to proceed toward true liberation we must cut ourselves off from white people. We must form our own institutions, credit unions, co-ops, political parties, write our own histories."[40]

Against the backdrop of these changes, Carmichael arrived at James Meredith's bedside to help plan the continuation of his march. He promptly demanded that the march de-emphasize white participation, highlight the need for independent Black political units, and include militant Civil Rights groups such as the armed Deacons for Defense and Justice to provide security for the marchers.[41] His demands prickled Wilkins and Young, who hoped to send out a nationwide call for whites to join the marchers. They also insisted that the controversial Deacons for Defense not be included and pressed that the group issue a joint statement reaffirming their commitment to nonviolence.[42] Despite considerable pressure from Wilkins and Young, Dr. King who held the swing vote refused to repudiate Carmichael's demands. Frustrated, Wilkins and Young left, announcing that their organizations would not participate in the march. In the weeks that followed, and with King travelling back and forth between Mississippi and Chicago, SNCC and Carmichael attempted to turn the march into a showcase for Black Power. While at a Civil Rights symposium in Boston five years earlier, King had believed unity possible, despite the existence of philosophical differences among the various organizations; the Meredith March presented a different reality. SNCC and Carmichael definitely saw it as a moment of opportunity and frankly had a distinct advantage. Mississippi was SNCC country. The organization had been deeply involved in organizing Blacks there. Shortly after his release from jail after authorities arrested him for trespassing on the evening of June 16, Carmichael ascended a platform in Greenwood, Mississippi to deliver a speech. Advised by his lieutenants who had been making what he called mini-Black Power speeches throughout the march to gauge the people's reaction, Carmichael elected to make public SNCC's shift. "This is the 27th time that I've been arrested," he defiantly informed his audience, "and I ain't going to jail no more . . . We want black power!" Carmichael engaged the crowd of roughly 600 in a call and response where each time they roared in unison, "Black Power."[43]

In the larger scheme of an entire movement, the Carmichael speech was just a moment, but a defining one. The following day the press reported on what for them was a new slogan and a strident call for revolution. Carmichael had provided ample material for them in his speech. "We have begged the president. We've begged the federal government" he told those gathered, "Every courthouse in Mississippi ought to be burned down tomorrow!" Carmichael's rhetoric obscured the deep grassroots organizing and voter registration that SNCC had been doing in the region.[44]

Months later, on the television program, *Meet the Press*, King, via satellite from Chicago, joined Carmichael, McKissick, and Meredith to discuss the meaning of Black Power. Illustrating CORE's new direction, McKissick dismissed nonviolence as "something of the past," declaring, "Most people will not agree to be nonviolent, not agree to be hit and passively stand there and not return the blow." Meredith agreed, adding, "Nonviolence is incompatible with American ideas." He continued, "This is a military minded nation and it always has been." Carmichael concurred, but framed his answer within a broader discourse about self-defense. Black people, he observed:

> are the only people who have to protect ourselves from our protection. We have to protect ourselves against state troopers, against the police in Mississippi. And if we don't protect ourselves ... then who will protect us! And I agree 150% that Black people have to move to the position where they organize themselves and they are in fact their protection for each other.[45]

Carmichael's explanation was largely lost on white reporters who continued to try to define Black Power in terms of violence. As scholar William Van Deburg conceptualized the problem:

> The unprecedented scourge of civil disturbances which took place during the mid-sixties convinced many that every ghetto contained hundreds— even thousands—of irreconcilable extremists whose singular goal was to foment rebellion. Terrified whites conjured up visions of campus radicals, Muslim separatists, and black teenage gang members banded together in an unholy pact to kill whitey or force him to his knees.[46]

It was not only white people but also many Civil Rights leaders who were concerned with the concept of Black Power. Some feared that Carmichael's message would lead to a white backlash against the movement and might alienate sympathetic white supporters whose contributions had sustained the movement. "Though it be clarified and clarified again," NAACP Executive Director Roy Wilkins bemoaned in July of 1966, "'black power' in the quick, uncritical, and highly emotional adoption it has received from some segments of a beleaguered people can mean in the end only black death." Wilkins likened the Black Power Movement to "a reverse Mississippi, a reverse Hitler, a reverse Ku Klux Klan."[47] "Far from prodding the white power structure into action the new militant leadership," Bayard Rustin likewise observed, "has obscured the moral issue facing this nation, and permitted the President and the Vice President to lecture to us about racism in the reverse instead of proposing more meaningful programs for dealing with the problems of unemployment, housing and education."[48]

In an article in the *New York Review of Books*, in September, Carmichael sought to silence the opposition while also explaining the urgency of the change. While Wilkins and Rustin remained concerned about how whites would perceive the shift, Carmichael made clear that SNCC was primarily interested in addressing the needs of the Black masses. As Carmichael explained, "One of the tragedies of the struggle against racism is that up to now there has been no national organization which could speak to the growing militancy of young black people in the urban ghetto." Carmichael continued:

> I blame ourselves – together with the mass media – for what has happened in Watts, Harlem, Chicago, Cleveland, Omaha. Each time the people in those cities saw Martin Luther King get slapped, they became angry; when they saw four little girls bombed to death, they were angrier; when nothing happened, they were steaming. We had nothing to offer that they could see, except to go out and be beaten again. We helped to build their frustration.[49]

Dr. King continued to try to carve out a middle ground. One month after the Meredith March, the SCLC ran a full-page ad in the *New York Times*, condemning Black Power as a slogan derived from weakness and desperation. When seven national Black leaders met on October 14, 1966 to collectively denounce the concept of Black Power, publicizing their stand in a three-quarter-page advertisement in the *New York Times* and in an NAACP memo, King privately endorsed the principles of their statement but refused to sign it. On October 16, King clarified his position, noting that while he supported the statement's four major tenets, including nonviolence and interracial collaboration, he also did not wish to be a part of any repudiation efforts that could be construed by the press and the public as an attempt to excommunicate SNCC and CORE from the Civil Rights Movement.

The media and the majority of the nation's introduction to Black Power was thus cast in this frame, obscuring those facets of Black pride and community building that made it so attractive to those on the margins. In his final book, *Where Do We Go from Here: Chaos or Community?* published in 1967, King offered a more probing reflection on Black Power. "It is inaccurate to refer to Black Power as racism in reverse," he observed. "Racism," he explained "is a doctrine of the congenital inferiority and worthlessness of a people." The "major proponents of Black Power," he concluded, "have never contended that the white man is innately worthless." King however took a pessimistic view of its ultimate utility. "The Black Power movement of today," he concluded, "like the Garvey 'Back to Africa' Movement of the 1920s, represents a dashing of hope, a conviction of the inability of the Negro to win and a belief in the infinitude of the ghetto."[50]

The Black Panther Party and Beyond

What King saw as a cry of despair and a dashing of hope, Oakland Black Panther Party for Self-Defense co-founders Huey Newton and Bobby Seale saw as misdirected energy that might form the basis of a Black revolution. The Black Panther Party sought to become the political compass that might guide such a revolution. While critical of the lack of political focus associated with urban rebellions, Newton nevertheless perceived that "the insurrections that have been going on throughout the country, in Watts, in Newark, in Detroit ... were all responses of the people demanding that they have freedom to determine their destiny, rejecting exploitation." Newton and Seale pledged to form a new type of organization that would draw its membership from "the Brothers off the block," urban street toughs, hardened by the realities of racism in America and not afraid to fight back. Inspired by the Lowndes County Freedom Organization they chose the Black Panther as their symbol.

Founded in Oakland, California in 1966, the Black Panther Party for Self-Defense (BPP) quickly gained national attention for its confrontational style and embrace of armed self-defense. Although its original focus was local, the founders drafted a 10-point program that laid out basic objectives and a structure easily transferrable beyond its base. Consistent with point number five, which called for an end to police brutality, the Panthers commenced armed patrols of the Oakland police in which they observed police conduct and advised suspects of their rights.

After several high profile confrontations with police, including a shootout in October of 1967 that resulted in the death of an Oakland police officer and the wounding of Newton, the Party launched a series of community programs aimed at both serving the community and rehabilitating its image. While maintaining its revolutionary agenda the BPP also sought to meet the needs of those suffering under what Martin Luther King famously described as the crippling airtight cage of poverty. The Panther community programs took many forms, including providing breakfast for schoolchildren, free health clinics, and community food kitchens. Panther women, in particular, became the stewards of many of these programs, addressing the critical day-to-day needs of the communities they served while exercising significant leadership. In Boston, for example, Audrea Jones rose to the highest leadership within the local chapter directing what would become a model Panther operation.[51]

Still, the Panthers could not seem to shake their violent image or their confrontations with police. On April 6, 1968, just two days after a sniper had gunned down the Reverend Dr. Martin Luther King in Memphis, Oakland police shot and killed 17-year-old Panther Bobby Hutton during what police described as a shootout with Panthers while trying to quiet unrest following King's assassination. Police claimed that the Panthers had initiated the shootout while the Panthers claimed that Hutton was unarmed. The following January, members of the US organization killed two Panthers, Jon Huggins and Alprentice "Bunchy" Carter, on the campus of UCLA as both groups sought to organize students in support of a Black Studies program. That May, Connecticut authorities indicted eight Panthers for the murder of a police informant in New Haven, Connecticut. This included Ericka Huggins, the widow of John Huggins. The parade of violence culminated that December in a pre-dawn assault on the Chicago headquarters of the party by police that resulted in the deaths of Panther leaders Fred Hampton and Mark Clark. An FBI informant, serving in capacity as the party's minister of defense, had supplied the floor plan for the deadly raid.[52]

Evidence later revealed that state and local law enforcement officials as well as the FBI had engaged in a systematic campaign against the BPP and other Civil Rights and Black Power organizations that crossed the line from law enforcement to provocation. On March 4, 1968—a month before Dr. King's assassination, for instance, FBI Director J. Edgar Hoover issued a directive calling on agents to foment counterintelligence initiative to "Prevent the RISE OF A 'MESSIAH' who could unify, and electrify, the militant black nationalist movement. Malcolm X might have been such a 'messiah;' he is the martyr of the movement today." "King," the memo continued, "could be a very real contender for this position should he abandon his supposed 'obedience' to 'white, liberal doctrines' (nonviolence) and embrace Black Nationalism. Carmichael has the necessary charisma to be a real threat in this way." The Black Panther Party was the subject of much of the FBI's intelligence, including the use of paid informants more than willing to cross the line to keep their handlers happy.[53] Even with the level of government repression, the Panthers made significant strides, however the group also exhibited organizational shortcomings such as its loose membership structure that facilitated the government's campaign.

Blind Spots

As Rhonda Y. Williams' 2014 study *Concrete Demands* makes clear, Black Power also had significant blind spots, especially with regard to gender. With Black Power's heavy emphasis on Black masculinity, women remain mostly invisible in the history of the movement. Despite this hyper-masculinism, however, women played an integral role in Black Power organizations. On college campuses, in Black Arts collectives, and in community study groups, Black women not only helped to shape the discourse on Black Power, but also often led those discussions. Their participation and insights were critical—even when iconic male leaders obscured their roles. One of the people on hand to hear Stokely Carmichael's call for Black Power in Greenwood, Mississippi, for instance, was SNCC's newly minted Executive Secretary Ruby Doris Smith. Born in Atlanta, Georgia in 1942, Smith was a skilled organizer in the best tradition of Ella Baker whose leadership helped to sustain SNCC through its transition to Black Power. Carmichael hailed the seasoned activist, who was jailed during the Freedom Rides and helped to coordinate the Mississippi Freedom Summer, as "a tower of strength." Unlike Carmichael, the dictates of marriage and family complicated Smith's life and activism. In October of 1967, at the age of 25, she succumbed to cancer, prompting fellow activist and friend Kathleen Cleaver, to blame her blistering work schedule as much as the disease for her premature death. "What killed Ruby Doris" she later observed, "was the constant outpouring of work, work, work, work, with being married, having a child, the constant conflicts, the constant struggle that she was subjected to because she was a woman. She was destroyed by the movement."[54]

Smith was in many ways symbolic of other female activists within both movements. Commenting on the absence of women in accounts of the Civil Rights Movement, Kathleen Neal Cleaver notes, "The visual record always documents the presence of women, but in the printed texts of academic accounts women's participation tends to fade." Historian Rhonda Y. Williams rightfully contends that the same is true of Black Power.[55] While the stories of women who rose to important positions of leadership, such as Ruby Smith and Elaine Brown, who eventually became the leader of the Black Panther Party, within national organizations remain obscure, accounts of women working at the grassroots have also been lost. Moving beyond the national spotlight into the battles waged by Black women for everything from welfare rights to fair housing, Williams argues that women often emerged as "central actors" in local struggles that bridged both movements.[56]

Women and Black Power

Women were also instrumental in the founding of many key Black Power organizations. Malcolm X's half-sister Ella, for example, financed his second trip to Mecca and was heavily involved with the Organization of Afro American Unity. Robert F. Williams worked closely with Mae Mallory, also a staunch proponent of self-defense. Apprehended in 1962 after fleeing to Cleveland, she returned to Monroe and served time in prison for the alleged kidnapping for which Williams fled to Cuba before the North Carolina Supreme Court threw out the case due to the fact no Blacks had served on her jury. Instrumental in the founding of the Revolutionary Action Movement, Wanda Marshall also often escapes notice in spite of her influence.

One of the best examples of the influence on women on the Black Power Movement is Audley Eloise Moore, better known as Queen Mother Moore. Born in the town of New Iberia, Louisiana, Moore became enamored with Black Nationalism after hearing Marcus Garvey speak in New Orleans. No stranger to the violence and uncertainty of southern life and inspired by the Jamaican Nationalist's message of Black pride and self-help, she moved to Harlem with her sister in the 1920s. There, surrounded by any number of organizations promoting solutions to the "race problem," she embraced radical politics. Over the next 40 years, she became involved with a number of organizations including the Communist Party in search of a blueprint for change.[57]

By the dawn of the 1960s she was a staple in Harlem and became, along with other prominent Harlem Nationalists, one of the key supporters of Robert F. Williams Crusaders. According to Harold Cruse, Queen Mother Moore and other Nationalists thought they recognized in events in Monroe, North Carolina "an immediate revolutionary situation."[58] While Cruse was not convinced, Williams' reception in Harlem among avowed Nationalists like Moore and Malcolm X helped to elevate his status. Consistent with the local, national, and international interests of Black Power advocates Queen Mother Moore was also deeply involved in local struggles participating in a number of important demonstrations in favor of open housing, organized labor, and community control of schools in the city of New York. A strong proponent of reparations for slavery, she was also deeply interested in establishing a Black homeland. Queen Mother Moore brought her deep knowledge and experience to every endeavor. Yet she, like other women, remained relatively invisible in the larger male-dominated narrative of Black Power.

Black women, for instance, were a major force within one of the organizations most associated with the Black Power Movement, the Black Panther Party. Within the Black Panther Party, women faced similar challenges. While the BPP adopted rules that should have encouraged gender equity, in reality Panther women also had to navigate the terrain of the group's masculinism. Elaine Brown, who would eventually take over the highest post of leadership in the party in the 1970s, recorded an album, *Seize the Time*, of Panther-inspired songs in 1968, including "The End of Silence," with the memorable refrain, "We'll just have to get guns and be men." While the song clearly emphasized the role of males, men were not the only ones to "pick up the gun." As the historian Tracye Mathews has observed:

> Ideas about gender and gender roles were far from static within the BPP. As the Party spread numerically and geographically, class and gender diversity within its ranks increased. New members brought new (and old) ideas with them. Despite the initial self-conscious creation by the leadership of a masculine public identity for the Panthers, some women and men in the Party challenged the characterization of the struggle as one mainly for the redemption of black manhood, and worked within its constraints to serve the interests of the entire black community.[59]

This would be less true in other organizations like the Nation of Islam or Ron Karenga's US organization where gender hierarchy was rigidly set. In their desire to approximate traditional society and culture, they adopted gender politics that emphasized the need for women to be submissive. It is important to note that not all women embraced women's liberation and actually put the advancement of the race before gender. Part of this was predicated on some of the concerns articulated by the Women's Liberation Movement that did not match the interests or concerns of Black women.

As Matthews documented, at least with regard to Panther women, criticisms included the fact that the Women's Liberation Movement did not "address class struggle or national liberation, that they faced dramatically different challenges given the different demographics (black, working-class and predominantly white, middle-class) and some had a tendency towards anti-male and female separatism which they disagreed with." Examining the myriad ways that Black women functioned as "agents of revolutionary change," historian Stephen Ward concludes that far from "simply challenging expressions of male chauvinism," "black feminists were also advancing arguments for deeper revolutionary purpose, theory, and commitment" that resulted in their "applying and extending Black Power thought." Even as Black Power did not eliminate, or even always acknowledge, issues of gender, Black women still challenged its proponents to see the interconnectedness of race and gender struggles.[60]

Black Power Behind Prison Walls

The influence of the Black Power Movement was, perhaps most deeply appreciated by those on the margins. The worst manifestations of Jim Crow Justice existed in prisons. Locked away from the gaze of the media and polite society, prisoners endured serious abuses far beyond the scope of humane punishment. African Americans, of course, were well aware of this brutal reality. While going to jail for violating unjust segregation laws became a badge of honor for many Civil Rights activists, the Black Power Movement's reach behind prison walls gave voice to those often forgotten by mainstream society, whether movement activists or American prisoners. Laws that disproportionately penalized poor minority offenders led to a burgeoning prison population—predominately urban and Black. Early on Malcolm X emerged as a hero among prisoners. The Black Muslims had long been recruiting in American prisons and Malcolm's story helped to widen the appeal of the organization behind prison walls. With its emphasis on discipline and education, the Black Muslims' program of self-help provided a degree of stability as well as a means of resistance for inmates.

It was perhaps only natural that prisoners would also find affinity with the Black Panther Party. In its original Ten-Point Program, the party squarely addressed the issue of Jim Crow Justice. In point eight, the BPP demanded "freedom for all black men held in federal, state, county and city prisons, and jails." In point nine, the Panthers called for African Americans to be "tried in court by a jury of their peer group or people from their black communities." In addition, many of the Black Panther leaders were former inmates. Minister of Information Eldridge Cleaver, for instance, had served time for rape at Folsom State Prison and published a widely read collection of essays, *Soul on*

Ice, about his own experience. Although the Panthers would later distance themselves from Cleaver, his perspective on prison life and culture made him a popular figure among inmates.[61]

Sentenced to a term of 2–15 years on a charge of voluntary manslaughter in September of 1968 in connection with the killing of an Oakland police officer, BPP Minister of Defense Huey P. Newton (he later successfully appealed his conviction) also enjoyed iconic status among prisoners. Many recognized in his story a shared struggle against biased laws, brutal police, and a tainted justice system. The Panthers' engagement with prisoners expanded as incarcerated party members sought to recruit new members as well as politicize and organize the prisons and penitentiaries themselves. On trial for the murder of an alleged police informant in New Haven, Connecticut, Black Panthers Ericka Huggins and Bobby Seale, for example, both engaged in successful efforts to organize prisoners.[62]

The most celebrated of the Panther prison organizers was California inmate George Jackson who also emerged as one of the primary leaders of the Prisoners' Rights Movement. Jackson was literally the poster child for the arbitrary and capricious nature of American punishment. Born in Chicago, Illinois in 1941, his family subsequently relocated to Los Angeles, where Jackson was first confined in the California Youth Authority at 16 for allegedly stealing a motorcycle. Shortly after his parole in 1958, police charged Jackson with driving the getaway car for an acquaintance that stole 71 dollars from a service station. Showing little mercy, the judge in the case sentenced the teenager to a term of one year to life.

During his early years in prison, officials frequently placed Jackson in solitary confinement where he began to read and study the works of Karl Marx, Mao Tse Tung, and prison activist and fellow inmate W.L. Nolen among others. In 1966, Jackson and Nolen helped to found a revolutionary group called the Black Guerrilla Family, which embraced Marxism, and in the spirit of Black Power avowed the right to self-defense for Black inmates. Shortly before authorities had Jackson transferred to Soledad prison in January of 1969, the Black Panther Party drafted Jackson as a Field Marshall. A year later, in January of 1970, Jackson became one-third, along with Fleeta Drumgo and John Clutchette, of the Soledad Brothers. Authorities charged the trio with the killing of Soledad prison guard John Mills allegedly in retaliation for the killing of Nolen by guards a few days earlier. The more vocal and political of the three, Jackson authored two books, *Soledad Brother* and *Blood in My Eye*, that raised public consciousness about prisons and gave voice to the plight of inmates. Typical of the depictions of prison in the letters in *Soledad Brother* was Jackson's bleak commentary from June 7, 1970. "I haven't seen the night sky for a decade," he explained to a friend. "During the early sixties in San Quentin," he continued, "'lockup' meant just that, twenty-four hours a day, all day, a shower once a week, and this could last for months (it's not changed much)."[63]

Placing the plight of prisoners within the broader context of the fight for Black liberation, Jackson argued that any effort at social or political revolution would be incomplete without addressing the issue of incarceration. "I'm of the opinion," he later wrote, "that, right along with the student movement, right along with the old familiar workers' movement, the prison movement is central to the process of revolution as a whole . . . We've got to organize our resistance once we're inside . . . turn the prison into just another front of the struggle, tear it down from the inside."[64]

Jackson's words resonated with an emergent prisoners' movement that witnessed not only efforts to organize prisons but challenge through lawsuits the very foundations of American justice. Although Jackson and the Black Guerrilla Family addressed themselves primarily to the concerns of Black prisoners, they had a much wider influence. Beginning in the late 1960s, prisoners sought to organize around shared concerns regardless of race. So-called "Unity" strikes took place around the nation, but most notably in California. An inmate work stoppage and hunger strike at Folsom in November of 1970, for instance, included a proposal for a prisoner's Bill of Rights that spoke to the collective needs of prisoners.

If George Jackson helped male prisoners find a voice, women in prison, and especially Black women, as in other aspects of American life, remained largely invisible. Toward the close of the decade, Jackson's comrade and girlfriend Angela Davis would give a face, at least, to the experience of women political prisoners.

Born in Birmingham, Alabama, in January of 1944, like many women in the Black Freedom Struggle, Davis played a significant if unheralded early role. While never a formal member of the Black Panther Party, her attraction to the party grew out of both her appreciation for its politics and her background. Like many southern migrants, Angela Davis was no stranger to armed self-defense. Growing up in Birmingham, Alabama during the tenure of Bull Connor, Davis became accustomed to the routine violence and terror that permeated the city. As she later recalled, "I remember the sounds of bombs exploding across the street. Our house shaking. I remember my father having to have guns at his disposal at all times, because of the fact that, at any moment, we might expect to be attacked."[65]

The violence hit especially close to home for Davis in the fall of 1963 when she learned of the bombing of the 16th Street Baptist Church. Her personal acquaintance with the families of several of the murdered girls sparked a sense of pain that she described as "deeply personal." Struggling to come to grips with the cruelty of the murders, she later observed, "The people who planted the bomb in the girls' restroom in the basement of the 16th Street Baptist Church were not pathological, but rather the normal products of their surroundings." Because of the bombings, Davis explained, "all the men organized themselves into an armed patrol. They had to take their guns and patrol our community every night because they did not want that to happen again."[66]

It was partly this tradition of self-defense that drew the young philosophy professor and member of the Communist Party to the Black Panther Party. If Davis appreciated the party's Black self-determination politics, including its belief in self-defense, she was less enamored with its gender politics—or those of the freedom struggle as a whole.

The outright sexism that she encountered as an activist left her frustrated. While working with SNCC, for instance, Davis noted that:

> whenever we women were involved in something important, they [male members of SNCC] began to talk about "women taking over the organization"—calling it a matriarchal coup d'état. All the myths about Black women surfaced. Bobbie, Rene, and I were too domineering; we were trying to control everything, including the men—which meant by extension that were trying to rob them of their manhood. By playing such a leading role in organization, some of them insisted, we were aiding and abetting the enemy, who wanted to see Black men weak and unable to hold their own.[67]

The hyper-masculine Black Power Movement magnified these sentiments. While supportive of many of the larger aims and objectives Davis was critical of the ideologies of many of the Black Power and Black Nationalist organizations in her orbit. She was also critical of the subservient roles many organizations attempted to impose on women. In her autobiography, for instance, Davis recounted an incident in 1967 at the University of California at San Diego, where she helped to found the Black Student Union, in which she "was criticized very heavily, especially by male members of Karenga's US organization, for doing a 'man's job.' Women should not play leadership roles, they insisted. A woman was supposed to 'inspire' her man and educate his children."[68]

Davis experienced these contradictions in both the Civil Rights and Black Power Movements—but saw them as larger problems associated with the male-dominated society. As she later explained:

> After all it had been the voice of the Johnson administration, Daniel Moynihan, who in 1966 had rekindled the theory of the slavery-induced Black matriarchate, maintaining that the dominant role of Black women within the family and, by extension, within the community was one of the central causes of the depressed state of the Black community.[69]

Like many other female activists, Davis endured the sexism—out of a deeper commitment to the struggle for Black Liberation. When the University of

California at Los Angeles terminated her position as a professor of philosophy due to her ties to the Communist Party in 1969 the 26-year-old Davis split her time between fighting to regain her job and involvement in radical politics.

In the midst of a protracted legal battle to reclaim her position, Davis befriended Jonathan Jackson, the 17-year-old brother of George Jackson with whom she had been corresponding in prison. Davis found in George Jackson a kindred spirit and became one of the driving forces behind the effort to win support for him and the other Soledad Brothers. Denouncing their indictments as the most recent in a "long series of repressive and genocidal measures taken by the prisons in the state" in June of 1970, Angela Davis helped to found the Soledad Brothers Defense Committee.

Impatient with the work of the defense committee and unbeknownst to Davis, in August of 1970, Jonathan hatched his own plan to liberate the Soledad Brothers. After securing several firearms, which he covertly registered in Davis' name, the 17-year-old stormed a Marin County courthouse, where he intended to take hostages, whose lives he planned to bargain in exchange for the freedom of the Soledad Brothers. His plan quickly fell apart and in an ensuing shootout, four people, including Jonathan, lay dead.

Authorities quickly zeroed in on Davis who, under duress, admitted to owning the guns—but denied any role in the planning or execution of the courthouse attack. Convinced, given her political affiliations and the nature of the crime, that she would never receive a fair trial, Davis fled. Placed on the FBI's 10 Most Wanted list, she spent two months on the lam before authorities apprehended her in New York in October of 1970.

Her arrest, much to the surprise and dismay of the authorities, sparked an international "Free Angela" campaign, making her one of the most recognizable faces and voices of Black Power in the United States. Davis used her celebrity to educate the world about race, poverty, and injustice toward Black people in the United States including in prisons.

Although eventually acquitted by an all-white jury in any involvement in the courthouse attack, Davis spent 18 months awaiting trial at the Women's Detention Center in New York. While she was in prison, on August 21, 1971, San Quentin guards shot and killed George Jackson during a purported escape attempt. Conflicting accounts of the killing fueled anger and suspicion—especially among prison activists and within the African American community. "No Black person," James Baldwin boldly declared, "will ever believe that George Jackson died the way they tell us he did."[70]

Attica prison, located outside Buffalo in upstate New York, was one of the facilities where prisoners felt Jackson's death most acutely. In mourning hundreds of prisoners donned black armbands and participated in a daylong silent protest. Even before Jackson's slaying, the inmates, inspired by the Prisoners' Rights and Black Power Movements, had already begun to unite in protests against conditions. In addition to the brutal treatment by guards, prisoners sought to organize in order to secure better medical care as well as job and education programs that would prepare them for life outside of prison. The month before Jackson's death a group known as the Attica Liberation Faction submitted a petition to prison officials.

After the State Department of Corrections Commissioner Russell Oswald met with but refused to discuss the prisoners' demands on September 2, the mood within the prison soured. A week later, on the morning of September 9, a scuffle between prisoners and guards resulted in a breach in which approximately 1,300 prisoners took over the prison yard.[71]

With 40 hostages, the prisoners issued a set of demands addressing many of the same issues they had broached in July. Twenty-one-year-old prisoner L.D. Barkley, in the meantime, emerged as one of the inmate leaders, and read a statement that positioned the uprising as "part of the long struggle of people demanding that their basic needs be met." Asserting the humanity of the inmates, he declared, "The entire prison populace has set forth to change forever the ruthless brutalization and disregard for the lives of the prisoners here and throughout the United States." "What has happened here," he continued, "is but the sound before the fury of those who are oppressed."[72]

The prisoners' demands themselves showed the nexus between prisoners' rights and the Black Power Movement. In addition to calls for basic civil liberties, including freedom of speech and religion, they asked that leaders from the Black Panther and Young Lords Party observe and participate in negotiations.

In the midst of their initial euphoria emerged concerns over the potential for a violent response from the state. Those fears crystallized when negotiations reached an impasse four days into the rebellion and New York Governor Nelson Rockefeller authorized state police to reclaim the prison by force. State troopers prepared for a military style assault. In a haze of tear gas, they entered the prison with orders to shoot to kill. When the state troopers' task was completed 29 inmates and 10 hostages lay dead and close to a hundred more injured. Despite efforts by authorities to lay the blame for the carnage on inmates slashing the throats of hostages, the medical examiner later revealed that all those killed on the final day of the takeover, including hostages, died from shots fired by police. Inmates, in the meantime, were responsible for the deaths of a guard and three inmates, in the initial days, bringing the final death toll to 43.

Along with the tragedy of the hostages and prisoners who lost their lives in the violent assault was the failure of the nation to heed their warning. While the population of state and federal prisons steadily declined during the 1960s with 196,429 persons in custody in 1970, over the next two decades inmate populations skyrocketed. New statutes such as the Rockefeller Drug Laws in New York State and mandatory minimums throughout the nation imposed stiff penalties on those offenders unable to afford good counsel. The disproportionate victims were African American and Latino.

The Black Arts Movement

Black Power also spawned new artistic expressions in every form with both political and cultural overtones. Poet Amiri Baraka and Maulana Karenga were critical influences in what became known as the Black Arts Movement. Heavily influenced by Cultural Black Nationalism, a belief that African-Americans were part of a "Nation within a nation" living in the United States but set apart from whites by a distinct set of attitudes, values, and beliefs, cultural nationalists focused on reclaiming Black history and culture as a means of reversing the psychological impact of slavery that distorted a proud African history and replaced it with the legacy of enslavement and oppression.[73]

Noting the myriad ways that slavery and white supremacy privileged Eurocentric standards, cultural nationalists declared that the first step toward Black Liberation must begin with the restoration of African cultural values. They saw politically and culturally infused music and the arts, as well as styles of dress and speech, as key vehicles for achieving this. In Los Angeles, Karenga promoted a set of African centered beliefs and practices called the Kawaida that he hoped would assist African Americans in the process of rejecting Eurocentric paradigms in favor of an African centered worldview with global Black Liberation as the ultimate goal.[74]

Along the eastern seaboard, Baraka, and a host of other talented artists and thinkers including Roland Snellings (Askia Muhammad Toure) and Larry Neal contributed to the Black Arts Movement. Growing out of Baraka's Black Arts Repertory Theater-School in Harlem the Black Arts Movement helped to spread Black Power's message. The performances at the theater were cultural, promoting a positive image of Black life. Importantly Baraka also used the Theater-School as incubator to expose youth to African and African American history, African art and culture, as well as languages and customs.[75]

By the time Stokely Carmichael spoke at the Black Arts Festival in Newark, New Jersey at Baraka's invitation in 1966, the Black Arts Movement had already moved forcefully into the world of politics. During this period, those Black women and men inspired by the Black Arts Movement helped to found more than 800 African-American cultural centers and theaters in communities across the nation from San Francisco, California to Bridgeport, Connecticut.[76]

Black Power Conferences

In 1967, Baraka and Karenga united with other Black Power activists to sponsor the first of several Black Power Conferences that took place between 1967 and 1971. The first, which took place in Newark, New Jersey only weeks after urban unrest engulfed the city, set the tone for what was a more decidedly Nationalist agenda. More than 4,000 participants converged to explore issues ranging from Black unity building to political and economic self-determination along with specific objectives and strategies to achieve the same. Dr. Nathan Wright, a prominent Black sociologist and activist, agreed to chair the conference but critics remained reticent about its purpose. "What was accomplished at the Black Power Conference?" *The Amsterdam News*, for instance, baldly posed on July 29. "Despite the encomiums of success from many at the conference," the author continued, "a definitive meaning for the phrase Black Power eluded circumscription and remained . . . dangerously ambiguous."[77]

One of the organizations to emerge with a highly defined blueprint for Black Power was the Republic of New Africa. Born out of the urban rebellion in Detroit it sought to establish an actual Black state. Shortly after the riot, siblings Imari Abubakari Obadele and Gaidi Obadele (Richard and Milton Henry) convened a meeting, attended by some 500 participants, to discuss the possibility of establishing a Black homeland within the territorial bounds of the United States. Inspired by Malcolm X, as well as the Black Arts Movement, the brothers envisioned an autonomous Black state run by and for people of African descent. On March 31, 1968, they and approximately 100 other attendees adopted a Declaration of Independence that also included the blueprint for a provisional government, the Republic of New Africa (RNA).[78]

Consistent with the larger goals associated with the Black Power Movement the RNA pledged, among other things, to liberate Blacks living in the United States from the stifling grip of political repression. Approximating other guarantees of liberty found in the American original Declaration of Independence the group also promised to support community building through co-operative economics designed to minimize poverty and promote economic development.

As part of a reparations package for slavery, the RNA demanded that the United States cede five southern states, Alabama, Georgia, South Carolina, Mississippi, and Louisiana, as the site of the new government. In addition, it demanded that the government pay every Black person 10,000 dollars to settle the unfulfilled promise of "forty acres, and a mule," pledged to the freedmen during Reconstruction. The RNA's demands were strategic. These states had the highest concentration of Black residents.

Wedding elements of both Revolutionary and Cultural Black Nationalism, the leaders of the RNA embraced the Ujamaa, meaning "oneness" and "unity," a culturally infused system of economics and politics deeply informed by African collectivism. At the very minimum, RNA members postulated that government had a duty to afford its inhabitants the basic requirements for life, including food, shelter, and clothing, along with access to education, personal and national security, and free medical care. A system of equilibriums in politics balanced the power of the nation's President with that of the People's Center Council, who he was to legislate with overseeing all aspects of life and governance.[79]

While less visible than groups like US and the Black Panthers, the RNA nevertheless established a stronghold especially at Tugaloo College, a small

Historically Black College located in Jackson, Mississippi. As with the US and the Black Panthers, law enforcement agencies were quick to establish surveillance and in many instances engage in acts of disruption and provocation against the RNA. Its members were involved in several altercations with police including one in August of 1971, in which a local police officer was shot and killed while participating in an FBI orchestrated assault on RNA headquarters. Of the 11 members of the group arrested for the killing, eight, including President Imari Obadele, were ultimately convicted and given life sentences. Several members were later exonerated based on new evidence suggesting government collusion.

While its critics continued to demand a clear explanation of what Black Power meant, Stokely Carmichael refused to be locked into a single definition. As he explained in the *New York Review of Books* in September of 1966:

> We have no infallible master plan and we make no claim to exclusive knowledge of how to end racism; different groups will work in their own different ways. SNCC cannot spell out the full logistics of self-determination but can only address itself to the problem of helping black communities define their needs, realize their strength and go into action along a variety of lines which they must choose for themselves.[80]

The legacy of Black Power found its expression in the call of college students for Black Studies programs, in revolutionary movements like the Black Panther Party for Self Defense, and a renewed interest in Black Nationalism not to mention a new Black aesthetic that elevated Black heritage through a celebration of history and culture. In the 1970s efforts at harnessing Black political power would reach their fruition in the Gary Convention and efforts by the Black Panther Party to succeed in local politics by calling all of its chapters back to Oakland in an effort to capture the mayor's office.

Hosted by Gary Mayor Richard Hatcher, the second African American to be elected chief executive of a major city, the Gary Convention spanned three days in March of 1972 with the central goal of establishing Black unity. With some 8,000 persons from all over the country in attendance the conveners hoped to craft a cohesive political agenda that would address issues of concern to the Black community including poverty and joblessness. The convention brought together both the previous generation of leaders with new voices including Amiri Baraka, Queen Mother Audley Moore, Coretta Scott King and the Rev. Jesse Jackson Sr. who delivered one of the most important speeches of the convention in which he reminded delegates "We are grown. We ain't taking it no more." "We are 25 million strong," he continued, "Cut us in or cut it out. It is a new ball game."[81]

Despite tensions and disagreements over ideology, strategy, gender, and political agendas, the 3,000 official delegates were finally able to settle on a statement, the Gary Declaration, that clearly stated their terms. "The American system does not work for the masses of our people," they affirmed, "and it cannot be made to work without radical, fundamental changes." "The challenge," they continued, "is thrown to us here in Gary. It is the challenge to consolidate and organize our own Black role as the vanguard in the struggle for a new society. To accept the challenge is to move to independent Black politics. There can be no equivocation on that issue. History leaves us no other choice. White politics has not and cannot bring the changes we need."[82]

While the convention was never replicated on the same scale, it nevertheless stimulated Blacks to pursue politics, and over the next decade the number of Black elected officials more than doubled from 2,200 to over 5,000. At the center of Black political organizing, Black Arts, dashikis, Afro hairstyles and African inspired music and dance was a movement that above all else celebrated Blackness and the quest for self-determination both personally and collectively.

Notes

1 "Huey Newton Talks to the Movement about the Black Panther Party, Cultural Nationalism, SNCC, Liberals, and White Revolutionaries," quoted in Philip S. Foner, ed., *The Black Panthers Speak* (New York: Da Capo Press, 2002), 61.
2 Angela Davis quoted in "UCLA Red Lays Ouster Proceedings to Racism," *Los Angeles Times*, September 24, 1969, 3, 30.
3 William L. Van Deburg, *New Day in Babylon: The Black Power Movement and American Culture, 1965–1975* (Chicago: University of Chicago Press, 1992), 34.
4 Dean Robinson, *Black Nationalism in American Politics and Thought* (Cambridge: Cambridge University Press, 2001), 2.
5 Peniel E. Joseph, "Black Liberation Without Apology: Reconceptualizing the Black Power Movement," *The Black Scholar* 31, nos 3/4 (2001): 2.
6 Jeffrey B. Perry, *Hubert Harrison: The Voice of Harlem Radicalism, 1883–1918* (New York: Columbia University Press, 2009); Mark Solomon, *The Cry was Unity: Communists and African Americans, 1917–36* (Jackson: University of Mississippi Press, 1998).
7 Clarence Taylor, *Reds at the Blackboard: Communism, Civil Rights, and the New York City Teachers Union* (New York: Columbia University Press, 2011).
8 On Angelo Herndon see Glenda Elizabeth Gilmore, *Defying Dixie: The Radical Roots of Civil Rights, 1919–1950* (New York: W.W. Norton, 2008); Frederick T. Griffiths, "Ralph Ellison, Richard Wright, and the Case of Angelo Herndon," *African American Review* 35 (winter 2001): 615–36. On African Americans and the Communist Party see Mark Solomon, *The Cry Was Unity: Communists and African Americans 1917–1936* (Jackson: University Press of Mississippi, 1998); *Hammer and Hoe: Alabama Communists During the Great Depression* (Chapel Hill: University of North Carolina Press, 1990).
9 Paul Robeson's testimony reprinted in Tony Perucci, *Paul Robeson and the Cold War Performance Complex: Race, Madness, Activism* (Ann Arbor: University of Michigan Press, 2012), 171.
10 Rhonda Y. Williams, *Concrete Demands: The Search for Black Power in the 20th Century* (New York: Taylor & Francis, 2015), 38.

11 Nina Simone, "Mississippi Goddam," *Nina Simone in Concert* (1964).

12 Ruth Feldstein, *How It Feels to Be Free: Black Women Entertainers and the Civil Rights Movement* (New York: Oxford University Press, 2013), 87.

13 Jeffrey O.G. Ogbar, *Black Power: Radical Politics and African American Identity* (Baltimore: Johns Hopkins University Press, 2004).

14 Akinyele Omowale Umoja, *We Will Shoot Back: Armed Resistance in the Mississippi Freedom Movement* (New York: New York University Press, 2013), 2.

15 Emilye J. Crosby, "'You Got a Right to Defend Yourself': Self-Defense and the Claiborne County, Mississippi Movement," *International Journal of Africana Studies* 9, no. 1 (Spring 2004): 133–63; Emilye J. Crosby, "'This nonviolent stuff ain't no good. It'll get ya killed.' Teaching about Self-Defense in the African-American Freedom Struggle," in Julie Buckner, Houston Roberson, Rhonda Y. Williams, and Susan Holt, eds., *Teaching the Civil Rights Movement* (New York: Routledge, 2002), 159–73. On armed self-defense also see Akinyele Omowale Umoja, *We Will Shoot Back: Armed Resistance in the Mississippi Freedom Movement* (New York: New York University Press, 2013); Lance Hill, *The Deacons for Defense: Armed Resistance and the Civil Rights Movement* (Chapel Hill: University of North Carolina Press, 2004); Christopher Strain, *Pure Fire: Self-Defense as Activism in the Civil Rights Era* (Athens, GA: University of Georgia Press, 2005); and Simon Wendt, *The Spirit and the Shotgun: Armed Resistance and the Struggle for Civil Rights* (Gainesville: University of Florida Press, 2007).

16 Williams quoted in Timothy B. Tyson, "Robert F. Williams, 'Black Power,' and the Roots of the African American Freedom Struggle," *Journal of American History* (1998): 540; see also Timothy B. Tyson, *Radio Free Dixie: Robert F. Williams and the Roots of Black Power* (Chapel Hill: University of North Carolina Press, 1999).

17 Armed self-defense became synonymous with Black Power. Part of the problem was the intent of the weapons. While both Civil Rights and Black Power activists saw weapons as a key means of staving of white violence as a means of survival, many Black Power groups also hoped to build the base for a Black Revolution. Emilye J. Crosby, "'You Got A Right To Defend Yourself': Self-Defense and the Claiborne County, Mississippi Civil Rights Movement," *The International Journal of Africana Studies: The Journal of the National Council for Black Studies, Inc* (2003): 133; Charles E. Cobb, Jr., *This Nonviolent Stuff'll Get You Killed: How Guns Made the Civil Rights Movement Possible* (New York: Basic Books, 2014); Simon Wendt, "Protection or Path Toward Revolution? Black Power and Self-Defense," *Souls* 9, no. 4 (2007): 320–32; Lance Edward Hill, *The Deacons for Defense: Armed Resistance and the Civil Rights Movement* (Chapel Hill: University of North Carolina Press, 2004); Simon Wendt, "'They Finally Found Out that We Really Are Men': Violence, Non-Violence and Black Manhood in the Civil Rights Era," *Gender & History* 19, no. 3 (2007): 543–64.

18 Peniel E. Joseph, "The Black Power Movement: A State of the Field," *The Journal of American History* 96, no. 3 (2009): 775.

19 George Breitman, ed., *Malcolm X Speaks: Selected Speeches and Statements* (New York: Merit Publishers, 1965), 50.

20 Malcolm X quoted in Malcolm X, *The Autobiography of Malcolm X* (New York: Grove Press, 1966), 280–1.

21 Martin Luther King, Jr., *Why We Can't Wait* (New York: Penguin, 2000).

22 Robert Williams quoted in Tyson, *Radio Free Dixie*, 225.

23 Donna Jean Murch, *Living for the City: Migration, Education, and the Rise of the Black Panther Party in Oakland, California* (Chapel Hill: University of North Carolina Press, 2010); Donna Jean Murch, "The Campus and the Street: Race, Migration, and the Origins of the Black Panther Party in Oakland, CA," *Souls* 9, no. 4 (2007): 333–45. Also see Joy Ann Williamson, *Black Power on Campus, The University of Illinois, 1965–75* (Urbana: University of Illinois Press, 2003); Martha Biondi, *The Black Revolution on Campus* (Berkeley: University of California Press, 2012); Ibram H. Rogers, *The Black Campus Movement: Black Students and the Racial Reconstitution of Higher Education, 1965–1972* (New York: Palgrave Macmillan, 2012).

24 On Black student activism see Peniel E. Joseph, "Dashikis and Democracy: Black Studies, Student Activism, and the Black Power Movement," *The Journal of African American History* (2003): 182–203; Biondi, *The Black Revolution on Campus*, 6; Rogers, *The Black Campus Movement*; Fabio Rojas, *From Black Power to Black Studies: How a Radical Social Movement Became an Academic Discipline* (Baltimore: Johns Hopkins University Press, 2007); Stefan M. Bradley, *Harlem vs. Columbia University: Black Student Power in the Late 1960s* (Urbana: University of Illinois Press, 2009); Williamson, *Black Power on Campus*.

25 Michael Harrington, *The Other America* (New York: Simon & Schuster, 1997).

26 On the Watts rebellion see Gerald Horne, *Fire This Time: The Watts Uprising and the 1960s* (Charlottesville: University of Virginia Press, 1995); see also "144 Hours in August 1965," The McCone Report, http://www.usc.edu/libraries/archives/cityinstress/mccone/part4.html, accessed July 2, 2015; John A. McCone and W.M. Christopher, "Violence in the City—An End or a Beginning? A Report by the Governor's Commission on the Los Angeles Riots," *Los Angeles: State of California, Governor's Commission on the Los Angeles Riots* (1965); Heather Thompson, "Urban Uprisings: Riots or Rebellions," in David Farber and Beth Bailey, eds., *The Columbia Guide to America in the 1960s* (New York: Columbia University Press, 2001), 109; Donna Murch, "The Many Meanings of Watts: Black Power, Wattstax, and the Carceral State," *OAH Magazine of History* 26, no. 1 (2012): 37–40.

27 King quoted in Clayborne Carson, ed., *The Autobiography of Martin Luther King, Jr.* (New York: Warner Books, 2001).

28 Heather Ann Thompson, *Whose Detroit? Politics, Labor, and Race in a Modern American City* (Ithaca: Cornell University Press, 2001); Thomas Sugrue, *The Origins of the Urban Crisis: Racial Inequality in Postwar Detroit* (Princeton: Princeton University Press, 1996); Sidney Fine, *Violence in the Model City: The Cavanagh Administration, Race Relations, and the Detroit Riot of 1967* (Ann Arbor: University of Michigan Press, 1989); Tom Craig and Robert Shogan, *The Detroit Race Riot: A Study in Violence* (New York: Da Capo Press, 1976).

29 National Advisory Commission on Civil Disorders, and Otto Kerner. Report of the National Advisory Commission on Civil Disorders, March 1, 1968. US Government Printing Office, 1968.

30 Bayard Rustin, "The Watts 'Manifesto' & the McCone Report," *Commentary* 41, no. 3 (1966): 29–35.

31 On King and the Chicago Campaign see James Ralph, *Northern Protest: Martin Luther King, Jr., Chicago, and the Civil Rights Movement* (Cambridge, MA: Harvard University Press, 1993); David J. Garrow, *Bearing the Cross: Martin Luther King Jr., and the Southern Christian Leadership Conference* (New York: Vintage Books, 1988);

Taylor Branch, *At Canaan's Edge: America in the King Years, 1965–68* (New York: Simon & Schuster, 2007).

32 King quoted in Chris Hedges, *Death of the Liberal Class* (New York: Nation Books, 2010), 186; in addition to the literature on King see Adam Cohen and Elizabeth Taylor, *American Pharaoh: Mayor Richard J. Daley – His Battle for Chicago and the Nation* (Boston: Little, Brown, 2000).

33 K. Fleming, "March Meredith Began," *Newsweek*, June 20, 1966, 30; "Heat on the Highway," *Time*, June 17, 1966, 7; "Walk in South to Conquer Old Fears," *Life*, June 17, 1966, 30–5.

34 "Strange March through Mississippi," *U.S. News and World Report*, June 27, 1966, 48; Lionel Lokos, *House Divided* (New Rochelle: Arlington House, 1968), 330–3.

35 Robert Penn Warren, *Who Speaks for the Negro* (New York: Random House, 1965), 397.

36 This quote comes from a speech delivered by Stokely Carmichael at a CORE meeting in Cleveland, Ohio. This particular quote is reprinted in an article written by Gene Roberts in August Meir and Elliot Rudwick, eds., *Black Protests In The Sixties* (New York: Marches Wimer, 1991), 153.

37 Peniel E. Joseph, *Stokely: A Life* (New York: Basic Civitas, 2014); Kwame Ture with Ekueme Michael Thelwell, *Ready For Revolution: The Life and Struggles of Stokely Carmichael (Kwame Ture)* (New York: Scribner, 2003); Peniel E. Joseph, *Waiting 'Til the Midnight Hour: A Narrative History of Black Power in America* (New York: Macmillan, 2007).

38 "Malcolm X: Witness for the Prosecution," Peter Goldman in August Meier and John Hope Franklin, eds., *Black Leaders of the Twentieth Century* (Illinois: University of Illinois Press, 1982), 325.

39 Williams, *Concrete Demands*, 112–15.

40 SNCC Position Paper, August 5, 1966, at 150–1.

41 Cleveland Sellers, *The River Of No Return* reprinted in Voices of Freedom Clayborne Carson, 228.

42 Clayborne Carson, David J. Garrow, Gerald Gill, Vincent Harding and Darlene Clark Hine, eds., *The Eyes on the Prize Civil Rights Reader* (New York: Viking, 1991), 280–1.

43 Peniel E. Joseph, "Revolution in Babylon: Stokely Carmichael and America in the 1960s 1," *Souls* 9, no. 4 (2007): 281–301; Peniel E. Joseph, *Stokely: A Life* (New York: Basic Civitas, 2014); Kwame Ture with Ekueme Michael Thelwell, *Ready For Revolution: The Life and Struggles of Stokely Carmichael (Kwame Ture)* (New York: Scribner, 2003); Peniel E. Joseph, *Waiting 'Til the Midnight Hour: A Narrative History of Black Power in America* (New York: Macmillan, 2007).

44 Taylor Branch, *The King Years: Historic Moments in The Civil Rights Movement* (New York: Simon & Schuster, 2013), 144.

45 "Riots, Battles, Power Marches; its Still a Hot Summer," *U.S. News and World Report*, August 15, 1966, 7; Martin Luther King, Jr., "Nonviolence: The Only Road to Freedom," *Ebony*, October 1966, 30. C.T. Rowan, "Crisis in the Civil Rights Leadership," *Ebony*, November 1, 1966, 30; Raymond Hall, *Black Separatism in the United States* (Hanover, NH: University Press of New England, 1978), 172–3; "Meet The Press" (Washington, DC: Merkle Press) Sunday August 21, 1966, 8–10; "Negro Leaders Dividing," *U.S. News and World Report*, July 18,

1966, 4; Bradford Chambers, *Chronicles of Black Protest* (New York: The New American Library, 1969), 217.

46 William L.Van Deburg, *New Day In Babylon:The Black Power Movement And American Culture, 1965–1975* (Chicago: University of Chicago Press, 1992), 167.

47 Roy Wilkins quoted in Yohuru Williams, "'A Red, Black and Green Liberation Jumpsuit': Roy Wilkins, the Black Panthers, and the Conundrum of Black Power," in Peniel Joseph, ed., *The Black Power Movement: Rethinking the Civil Rights-Black Power Era* (New York: Routledge, 2006), 174; see also David C. Carter, *The Music Has Gone Out of the Movement: Civil Rights and the Johnson Administration, 1965–1968* (Chapel Hill: University of North Carolina Press, 2009).

48 Bayard Rustin, *Down The Line* (Chicago: Quadrangle Books, 1971), 157.

49 Stokely Carmichael, *Black Power: The Politics of Liberation in America* (New York: Random House, 1967); Stokely Carmichael and Kwame Ture, "Power and Racism: What We Want," *The Black Scholar* (1997): 52–7.

50 Martin Luther King, Jr., *Where Do We Go From Here: Chaos or Community?* (Boston: Beacon Press, 2010).

51 On the role of women in the Black Power Movement see Williams, *Concrete Demands*; Tracye Matthews, "'No One Ever Asks, What a Man's Role in the Revolution Is': Gender and the Politics of the Black Panther Party, 1966–1971," 267–304, and Angela D. LeBlanc-Ernest, "'The Most Qualified Person to Handle the Job': Black Panther Party Women, 1966–1982," 305–34, both in Charles Earl Jones, *The Black Panther Party Reconsidered* (Baltimore: Black Classic Press, 1998), 267–304, 305–34.

52 On the Black Panther Trails in New Haven see Yohuru Williams, *Black Politics White Power, Civil Rights, Black Power, and the Black Panthers in New Haven* (Blackwell Press, 2008); Yohuru Williams and Jama Lazerow, eds., *In Search of the Black Panther Party: New Perspectives on a Revolutionary Movement* (Durham, NC: Duke University Press, 2006); Yohuru Williams and Jama Lazerow, eds., *Liberated Territory: Untold Local Perspectives on the Black Panther Party* (Durham, NC: Duke University Press, 2008).

53 On the FBI's campaign against the Civil Rights and Black Power Movements, Ward Churchill and Jim Vander Wall, *The COINTELPRO Papers: Documents from the FBI's Secret Wars Against Domestic Dissent* (Boston: South End Press, 1990; Classics Edition, 2002); Ward Churchill and Jim Vander Wall, *Agents of Repression:The FBI's Secret Wars Against the Black Panther Party and the American Indian Movement* (Boston: South End Press, 1988; Classics Edition, 2002); Kenneth O'Reilly, *"Racial Matters": The FBI's Secret File on Black America, 1960–1972* (New York: Free Press, 1989); David J. Garrow, *The FBI and Martin Luther King, Jr.: From "Solo" to Memphis* (New York: W.W. Norton & Company, 1981); Frank J. Donner, *The Age of Surveillance: The Aims and Methods of America's Political Intelligence System* (New York: Alfred Knopf, 1980).

54 Kathleen Cleaver quoted in Bettye Collier-Thomas and V.P. Franklin, eds., *Sisters in the Struggle: African American Women in the Civil Rights–Black Power Movement* (New York: New York University Press, 2001), 210. For a comprehensive discussion on gender and Black Power see Williams, *Concrete Demands*.

55 Kathleen Neal Cleaver, "Racism, Civil Rights, and Feminism," in Adrien Katherine Wing, ed., *Critical Race Feminism: A Reader* (New York: New York University Press, 1997), 36.

56   Rhonda Y. Wiliams, "Black Women and Black Power," *OAH Magazine of History* 22, no. 3 (2008): 22–6.

57   Erik S. McDuffie, "'I wanted a Communist movement, but I wanted to have the chance to organize our people': The Diasporic Radicalism of Queen Mother Audley Moore and the Origins of Black Power," *African and Black Diaspora: An International Journal* 3, no. 2 (2010): 181–95; Erik S. McDuffie, *Sojourning for Freedom: Black Women, American Communism, and the Making of Black Left Feminism* (Durham, NC: Duke University Press, 2011); Erik S. McDuffie, "'For full freedom of … colored women in Africa, Asia, and these United States': Black Women Radicals and the Practice of a Black Women's International," *Palimpsest: A Journal on Women, Gender, and the Black International* 1, no. 1 (2012): 1–30.

58   Tyson, *Radio Free Dixie*, 204.

59   Matthews, "'No One Ever Asks, What a Man's Place in the Revolution Is'," 270.

60   Stephen Ward, "The Third World Women's Alliance: Black Feminist Radicalism and Black Power Politics," in Peniel Joseph, ed., *The Black Power Movement: Rethinking the Civil Rights-Black Power Era* (New York: Routledge, 2006), 144.

61   Eldridge Cleaver, "Soul on Ice. 1968. Reprint" (1991); Kathleen Rout, *Eldridge Cleaver,* Volume 583 (Boston: Twayne Pub, 1991); Eldridge Cleaver, *Eldridge Cleaver: Post-Prison Writings and Speeches* (New York: Random House, 1969).

62   Yohuru R. Williams, "In the Name of the Law: The 1967 Shooting of Huey Newton and Law Enforcement's Permissive Environment," *Negro History Bulletin* 61, no. 2 (1998): 6–18; Donald F. Tibbs, *From Black Power to Prison Power: The Making of Jones V. North Carolina Prisoners' Labor Union* (New York: Palgrave Macmillan, 2012); Nico Slate, ed., *Black Power Beyond Borders: The Global Dimensions of the Black Power Movement* (New York: Palgrave Macmillan, 2012).

63   George Jackson, *Soledad Brother: The Prison Letters of George Jackson* (Chicago: Chicago Review Press, 1970).

64   "Remembering the Realt Dragon: An Interview with George Jackson by Karen Wald," http://historyisaweapon.com/defcon1/jacksoninterview.html, accessed July 2, 2015.

65   Angela Davis, *Angela Davis: An Autobiography* (New York: International Publishers, 1988 [1974]), 161.

66   Ibid.

67   Ibid., 182.

68   Ibid., 161.

69   Ibid., 182.

70   James Baldwin quoted in Brian Conni, "8. The Prison Writer as Ideologue: George Jackson and the Attica Rebellion," *Prose and Cons: Essays on Prison Literature in the United States* (2005): 147.

71   On Attica see Heather Ann Thompson, "Why Mass Incarceration Matters: Rethinking Crisis, Decline, and Transformation in Postwar American History," *The Journal of American History* 97, no. 3 (2010): 703–34; Ethan Sachs, "A State and Its Prison: The Attica Riot of 1971 and Untold Stories Since," PhD diss., University of Michigan, 2012; Heather Ann Thompson, "Rethinking Working-Class Struggle through the Lens of the Carceral State: Toward a Labor History of Inmates and Guards," *Labor* 8, no. 3 (2011): 15–45; Andrew B. Mamo, "'The Dignity and Justice that Is Due to Us by Right of Our Birth': Violence and Rights in the 1971 Attica Riot," *Harvard Civil Rights-Civil Liberties Law Review* (CR-CL) 29, no. 2 (2014); Sue Mahan, "An 'Orgy of Brutality' at Attica and the 'Killing Ground' at Santa Fe:

A Comparison of Prison Riots," *Prison Violence in America* 2 (1994): 92–127; Tom Wicker, *A Time To Die: The Attica Prison Revolt* (Lincoln: University of Nebraska Press, 1994).

72 L.D. Barkley quoted in Justin Brooks, "How Can We Sleep While the Beds Are Burning—The Tumultuous Prison Culture of Attica Flourishes in American Prisons Twenty-Five Years Later," *Syracuse L. Rev.* 47 (1996): 159; see also Cynthia Young's *Soul Power: Culture, Radicalism, and the Making of a U.S. Third World Left* (Durham, NC: Duke University Press, 2006), 165.

73 Komozi Woodard, *A Nation Within A Nation: Amiri Baraka and Black Power Politics* (Chapel Hill: University of North Carolina Press, 1999), xi–xv; William Sales, *From Civil Rights to Black Liberation* (Boston: South End Press, 1994), 170–83; Clayborn Carson, *The Eyes on the Prize: Civil Rights Reader* (New York: Penguin Books, 1991), 273–8; E.U. Essien-Udom, *Black Nationalism: A Search for Identity in America* (Chicago: University of Chicago Press, 1962); Dean E. Robinson, *Black Nationalism in American Politics and Thought* (Cambridge: Cambridge University Press, 2001), 4; Ward Churchill and Jim Vander Wall, *Agents of Repression: The FBI's Secret Wars Against the Black Panther Party and the American Indian Movement* (Boston: South End Press, 1990).

74 Scot Brown, *Fighting for US: Maulana Karenga, the US Organization, and Black Cultural Nationalism* (New York: New York University Press, 2003).

75 Komozi A. Woodard, *Nation Within A Nation: Amiri Baraka (Leroi Jones) and Black Power Politics* (Chapel Hill: University of North Carolina Press, 1999); James Edward Smethurst, *The Black Arts Movement: Literary Nationalism in the 1960s and 1970s* (Chapel Hill: University of North Carolina Press, 2005).

76 Smethurst, *The Black Arts Movement*; Peniel E. Joseph, "The Black Power Movement: A State of the Field," *The Journal of American History* 96, no. 3 (2009): 751–76.

77 The *Amsterdam News* quoted in Harold Cruse, *Rebellion or Revolution?* (New York: William & Morrow, 1968), 199. On the Newark Black Power Conference see Woodard's *A Nation Within a Nation*; Jeffrey O.G. Ogbar's *Black Power: Radical Politics and African American Identity* (Baltimore: Johns Hopkins Press, 2004); Joseph, *Waiting 'Til the Midnight Hour*; Jeanne F. Theoharis and Komozi Woodard, *Groundwork: Local Black Freedom Movements in America* (New York: New York University Press, 2005); Kevin Mumford, *Newark: A History of Race, Rights and Riots in America* (New York: New York University Press, 2007).

78 Christian Davenport, "Understanding Covert Repressive Action: The Case of the US Government against the Republic of New Africa," *Journal of Conflict Resolution* 49, no. 1 (2005): 120–40; Donald Cunnigen, "Bringing the Revolution Down Home: The Republic of New Africa in Mississippi," *Sociological Spectrum* 19, no. 1 (1999): 63–92; Peniel E. Joseph, "Dashikis and Democracy: Black Studies, Student Activism, and the Black Power Movement," *The Journal of African American History* (2003): 182–203.

79 Chokwe Lumumba, "Short History of the U.S. War on the Republic of New Africa," *Black Scholar* 12 (January–February 1981); Cunnigen, "Bringing the Revolution Down Home"; Christian Davenport, "Understanding Covert Repressive Action."

80 Stokely Carmichael, "What We Want," *The New York Review of Books* 7 (September 22, 1966): 5–6, 8; also Peniel E. Joseph, *Stokely: A Life* (New York: Basic, 2014); Stokely Carmichael, *Stokely Speaks: From Black Power Back to Pan-Africanism* (New York: Vintage, 1971).

81 Jesse Jackson quoted in Eyes on the prize II [video recording]: America at the racial crossroads 1965–1985, *Ain't Gonna Shuffle No More (1964–72)*, Boston, MA: Blackside, Inc. Distributed by PBS Video, 1989.

82 William Strickland, "The Gary Convention and the Crisis of American Politics," *Black World* 21, no. 12 (1972): 18–26; Komozi Woodard, "Amiri Baraka, the Congress of African People, and Black Power Politics from the 1961 United Nations Protest to the 1972 Gary Convention," in Joseph, *The Black Power Movement*, 55–77.

4

THE ART OF WAR

The Cultural Productions of the 1950s and 1960s Era Black Freedom Struggles

Inspiration is a very strange thing, sometimes it just happens like a light.

Nina Simone (1969)[1]

Thus all Art is propaganda and ever must be, despite the wailing of the purists. I stand in utter shamelessness and say that whatever art I have for writing has been used always for propaganda for gaining the right of black folk to love and enjoy. I do not care a damn for any art that is not used for propaganda.

W.E.B. Du Bois (1926)[2]

Once social change begins, it cannot be reversed. You cannot uneducate the person who has learned to read. You cannot humiliate the person who feels pride. You cannot oppress the people who are not afraid anymore. We have seen the future and the future is ours.

Cesar Chavez (1984)[3]

The fingerprints of 1950s and 1960s Black Freedom Struggles are evident in both the political changes they wrought and the cultural makings they produced. In addition to changing the political landscape of the country, they affected its language, music, fashion, and art as well. Over the past two decades, numerous scholars from a variety of disciplines, as well as movement participants, have sought to capture not only the essence of the movement but the culture that fed it. Notable works by Robin D.G. Kelly, James Smethurst, Peniel Joseph, Rhonda Williams, Brian Ward, Ruth Feldstein, Suzanne Smith, and others have tackled the subject of the cultural productions of 1950s and 1960s Black Freedom Struggles.[4] Collectively, they documented among activists of the period an important subculture that helped to nourish their activism. Over the course of two decades, a new cultural aesthetic emerged that celebrated the strength and beauty of Black people and Black culture. To be sure, there was still twoness—what Civil Rights leader and pioneering scholar W.E.B. Du Bois described as a "double consciousness"—to these productions that spoke both to a desire for mainstream acceptance and cultural independence. Nowhere, perhaps, was this more evident in the period than in the realm of music.

I Hear a Symphony

On November 1965, Motown Music singing sensation Diana Ross and the Supremes appeared on the Mike Douglass show to perform their sixth chart-topping hit, "I Hear a Symphony." Beamed into the homes of million Americans, the impeccably dressed trio, singing in perfect harmony and moving in lock step, were the models of respectability as they belted out the lyrics to the popular ballad. Both the group's presentation and the song's lyrics in celebration of a love "so exciting and so inviting" were a stark contrast to Nina Simone's "Mississippi Goddam." The straightened coiffures of the Supremes conformed to white mainstream standards of beauty. Years earlier, however, Nina Simone began to wear her hair natural, allowing it to grow into an "Afro"—a popular hairstyle that became synonymous with Black Power and the rejection of white beauty norms. She frequently appeared at her concerts elegantly decked out in African gowns with her hair tightly braided in styles evocative of African women. While the Supremes continued to play bigger and bigger venues, Simone never lost her touch with the grassroots. She frequently performed at Black colleges and universities and in big open-air rallies in Harlem. Her music, like her sense of style, was an affirmation of Black beauty and cultural autonomy. She was the very embodiment of Black Power on stage, but her evolution was a slow one. Her journey from nightclub performer to Black Power icon illustrates the tensions that Black artists faced as they navigated the powerful currents of 1950s and 1960s Black Freedom struggles. This twoness, these cultural productions and their historical footprints, are the focus of this chapter.

The Eye of the Beholder: Preconditions for Change

In his 1926 essay "Criteria of Negro Art," pioneering Black scholar and Civil Rights activist W.E.B. Du Bois championed support for "Negro" Art as an important part of the struggle for equal rights. At the outset, he posed a provocative question. "Suppose the only Negro who survived some centuries hence was the Negro painted by white Americans in the novels and essays they have written. What would people in a hundred years say of black Americans?" Such art, he observed, would not reflect fair and accurate representations of Black life and culture, but those that catered to the fantasies and desires of white audiences who, "want Uncle Toms, Topsies, good 'darkies' and clowns." In response, he posed three primary concerns. The first focused on the idea of beauty and the power to define it. The second focused on the purpose of art, which, he observed, served a dual function to reveal beauty but also to advance the cause of Black equality. "I do not care a damn for any art that is not used for propaganda," he argued. Lastly, he pondered the criteria society used to judge African American art. Whatever the lens, he concluded, such recognition would validate not only African American art but the humanity of the individuals who created it. African American artists, he thus concluded, had a duty to produce works that advanced the cause of freedom. Du Bois used his editorship of *The Crisis* magazine to display such beauty and culture, printing articles, paintings, and poems that sought to uplift the race.[5]

During the 1920s, the Harlem or Black Renaissance that emerged alongside the New Negro Movement resulted in a flowering of artistic expression that affirmed the humanity and inventiveness of people of African descent. It reflected the political philosophy of the gifted socialist organizer and race leader, Hubert Harrison, who defined the "The New Negro," in his celebrated essay of the same name in 1919 as, "Negro first, Negro Last and Negro always." The "New Negro" he continued, "needs not the white man's sympathy; all he is asking for is equal justice under the law and equal opportunity in the battle of life."[6]

Along with this affirmation of equal rights, more often than not, the art produced in the Harlem Renaissance reflected the reality of life under segregation. Consistent with Du Bois and Harrison, African American artists, writ large, produced works that captured the travails and triumphs of the Black experience while challenging notions of Black inferiority. Duke Ellington's controversial 1929 motion picture *Black and Tan Fantasy*, for instance, offered strong portrayals of Black characters even in roles that were stereotypical. Significantly, many artists were not afraid to tackle political subjects. Poets like Langston Hughes and Claude McKay captured the angst of the period while announcing a new attitude of resistance in their artistic expression. Writers like Alain Locke, Alice Dunbar Nelson, Zora Neale Hurston, and Angelina Grimké joined them in producing bold works of fiction and nonfiction. Visual artists like sculptor May Howard Jackson and painter Aaron Douglass produced majestic works representing Black life while film and stage performers such as Josephine Baker and Paul Robeson contributed to shaping a new Black cultural aesthetic.

The New Negro Movement also inspired scholarship affirming the contributions of people of African descent to American history and enterprise. In the 1910s, for instance, Carter G. Woodson pushed for the adoption of Negro History Week as a celebration of Black history and a reminder of the myriad ways in which African Americans substantively contributed to the social, economic and cultural development of America and the world. In the 1920s, Black Nationalist organizations such as Marcus Garvey's UNIA and the Moorish Science Temple, the precursor to the Nation of Islam, likewise emphasized the importance of African and African American history as anchors for nation building.[7] The documents and essays these groups and individuals produced spoke powerfully to the next generation of activists who resurrected them in their own process of personal and political discovery.

White interest in Black music and culture during this period opened up new avenues of influence. Overseas, foreign audiences eagerly embraced Black American artists and entertainers. At home, the stinging rebuke of segregated dance and concert halls where Blacks could enter as performers and servants but never patrons offered a clear challenge to the idea that culture alone could break down barriers.

The influence of Black artists on two uniquely American forms of musical expression, Jazz and the Blues, nevertheless showcased Black creativity and also provided artists with a platform, however limited, to contest inequality. Early on, Black Arts Movement Founder Amiri Baraka posited that Jazz was not merely a form of artistic expression but a musical record of the African American experience. The popularity of Jazz in the 1930s and 1940s helped to make Black singers and musicians such as singer Ella Fitzgerald and trumpeter Louis Armstrong household names. At the dawn of the Cold War, the United States Department of State commissioned Jazz tours to the Soviet Union and other countries in the hopes of reducing tensions and highlighting American arts and culture. In the 1950s and 1960s, worldwide news coverage of Black Freedom Struggles made it especially difficult for Black cultural diplomats to contain their disappointment in the failure of democracy at home. The crisis in Little Rock, Arkansas proved especially distasteful. After seeing coverage of the Little Rock school situation, Jazz musician Louis Armstrong denounced Orval Faubus as an "uneducated plowboy," called President Eisenhower "two faced" and told a reporter, "My people—the Negroes—are not looking for anything—we just want a square shake. But when I see on television and read about a crowd in Arkansas spitting and cursing at a little colored girl—I think I have a right to get sore—and say something about it." Cancelling a scheduled cultural tour of the Soviet Union sponsored by the State Department, Armstrong further explained: "The people over there ask me what's wrong with my country. What am I supposed to say. The way they are treating my people in the South, the government can go to hell." If these comments were surprising coming from the otherwise apolitical Armstrong, they barely compared to the response of Jazz musician Charles Mingus who memorialized his disgust in a song named for Arkansas' recalcitrant Governor entitled "Fables for Faubus."[8]

Both Civil Rights and Black Power organizations recognized the importance of music and art as tools for Black liberation. As historian Jen Woodley has documented in the 40 years between 1910 and 1960, the NAACP instituted a number of cultural initiatives that sought to uplift the race through the promotion of Black art and culture. Importantly, Woodley argues that from the beginning the NAACP's integration of cultural activities into its publications "was directly linked to its legal and legislative efforts."[9] This included, but was not limited to, the incorporation of literature and art in its magazine *The Crisis*, edited early on, of course, by Du Bois. Although political, *The Crisis* offered a regular platform for poets, writers, cartoonists, and painters to display their work; it served as a powerful rebuke to race prejudice and popular depictions of African Americans in mainstream media. "The NAACP," Woodley explained, "was convinced that it had to change this perception of African Americans in order to open the door for such advancements as the franchise, desegregated education, and ultimately full civil rights."[10] In order to do so, the association pledged itself to a three-pronged attack that included recognizing and promoting Black achievement in music and the arts and the encouragement of more positive portrayals of African American life and culture. Similar to the NAACP's approach, A. Phillip Randolph and Chandler Owen also promoted art and culture in their magazine *The Messenger*, and Black newspapers such as the *Chicago Defender* also proved a popular forum and venue for Black arts and culture celebrating Black achievement that challenged notions of Black inferiority.

1950s and 1960s Black Freedom Struggles

A new generation of artists and writers who came of age during the postwar period took up the debate started by Du Bois over the purpose of art during the turbulent, if hopeful, decades of the 1950s and 1960s. Dating back to the 1940s, a host of artists and writers such as Richard Wright (*Native Son*, 1940), Lorraine Hansberry (*A Raisin in the Sun*, 1959), and Ralph Ellison (*Invisible Man*, 1952) produced works and plays that supported the argument made by Du Bois and Harrison that Black artists had a responsibility to produce works that were socially conscious and directed toward the progress of the race. Hansberry, in particular, was a part of an important group of intellectuals including writers James Baldwin, John Killens, and Julian Mayfield, actors Ossie Davis and Ruby Dee, journalist William Worthy, and poet Leroi Jones (later known as Amiri Baraka) who converged in Harlem, New York in the 1950s. There they became the core of what historian Peniel Joseph describes as a "Black Intellegentsia" that not only promoted music and art but also activism. Davis and Dee, for instance, were instrumental in introducing Malcolm X to the vibrant collection of artists and musicians in Harlem who shared many of his ideas on the race problem in the U.S. In organizations like the Harlem Writers Guild, they debated ideas, critiqued each other's work, mentored young artists, and engaged in acts of protest such as the 1961 demonstration at the United Nations to protest the assasination of Congo Prime Minister Patrice Lumumba in what historian Peniel Joseph has called "Black Power's formal arrival on the national political scene." The impetus behind the UN protest was a group called the Cultural Association for Women of African Heritage (CAWAH) which had been formed by Abbey Lincoln and others.[11]

The activism in groups like the CAWAH was a counterbalance to other artists coming of age during the heroic phase of the movement that saw their art as an important corollary force for liberation even if they themselves steered clear of protests. The success of Black recording artists such as Diana Ross and the Supremes and others signaled a degree of mainstream acceptance that seemed to match the pace of the Civil Rights Movement. Yet there were those, especially in the Black Arts Movement, who believed that "success," especially if it meant being judged solely by white standards of talent and beauty, was not enough.

By 1965, the Black Arts Movement directly took up the challenge, providing the space for Black artists and entertainers to ponder the meaning of art, in all forms, and its relationship to Black Freedom Struggles. As one of the luminaries of the Black Arts Movement, poet Larry Neal explained, citing his fellow poet, Etheridge Knight:

> Unless the Black artist establishes a "Black aesthetic" he will have no future at all. To accept the white aesthetic is to accept and validate a society that will not allow him to live. The Black artist must create new forms and new values, sing new songs (or purify old ones); and along with other Black authorities, he must create a new history, new symbols, myths and legends (and purify the old ones by fire). And the Black artist, in creating his own aesthetic, must be accountable for it only to the Black people.[12]

The Black Arts Movement thus produced its own cadre of gifted and visionary writers and poets, including Amiri Baraka, Gwendolyn Brooks, Gil Scott-Heron, and the Last Poets, who used their art to provide a panoramic view of Black life.

Scholar C. Eric Lincoln outlined Black Power and the Black Arts Movement's underlying agenda. "Black Power," he wrote, "seeks to change the structure of the black community—its thought forms, values, culture. It tells black people to love themselves and by so doing, confront white racism with a mode of behavior inimical to everything white."[13]

Poet Amiri Baraka echoed these sentiments in discussing the importance of Black Theater. "Our theatre will show victims so that their brothers in the audience will be better able to understand that they are brothers of victims, and that they themselves are victims if they are blood brothers." Baraka's groundbreaking 1964 plays *The Dutchman* and *The Slave*, for instance, inspired playwrights across the country to use the dramatic arts to reimagine pathways to Black resistance. Baraka's decision to start the Black Arts Repertory Theater and School (BARTS) in Harlem created a conduit for other Black artists to hone their craft. The larger movement produced an unmistakable and significant wave of radical and revolutionary music, art, theater, poetry, and fiction that accompanied the political organizing and rhetoric of revolution of the Black Power Movement. While the hyper-masculinity of the Black Power Movement often obscured the role of women, Black female voices gave force and design to the movement as female artists and activists articulated their own profound vision of Black oppression and liberation. The first African American to win a Pulitzer Prize, Gwendolyn Brooks, for example, used her poetry to speak truth to power and give voice to the voiceless. In one of her lesser-known poems, "Riot" (1969), set against the backdrop of the urban protests that followed the assassination of the Reverend Dr. Martin Luther King, Brooks' description of the protesters asserted the right of Blacks to define for themselves acceptable forms of grief and frustration. She wrote: "They were black and loud . . . And not detainable. And not discreet."

Dressing the Revolution

This new assertiveness was not restricted to speech. The cultural reverberations of the movement surfaced in new forms of style and dress. The politics of respectability that encouraged African Americans to present themselves as dignified and non-threatening at all times gave way to more aggressive forms of speech and dress that exalted cultural differences and challenged notions of white middle-class respectability as the yardstick by which people of color would be judged. The adoption of African-inspired fashions such as the dashiki and the Afro hairstyle in the late 1960s, for instance, spoke to the need for Black unity and Black pride, the adoption of a new cultural aesthetic rooted in a shared African heritage. As writer Phyl Garland observed in a 1973 article in *Ebony* magazine, "Back in 1965, the year of the battle at Watts and the murder of Malcolm X, black Americans undertook a quiet revolution. This struggle was not waged in the streets, but in the more complex passages of the mind where brothers and sisters grappled with concepts of themselves. Some, sooner than others arrived at the conclusion that pride in one's racial heritage should be seen as well as heard and felt." "Thus," he concluded, "The era of the Afro hairstyle, was ushered in."[14]

Like most aspects of the Black Freedom Struggles, however, Garland's attempt to fix a clear date for the turn in fashion is problematic. In founding the CAWAH in 1960, Abbey Lincoln remembered that "one of the stipulations was that the women would wear African hairstyles and we would explore our culture, our African ancestors."[15]

To be sure, the turn to African inspired hairstyles and new patterns of dress and speech was becoming more widespread. The pomp, dress, and uniforms adopted by earlier organizations such as the UNIA were restricted to membership. Writing about this period, scholars Shane White and Graham White assert that the politics of Black style was essentially the politics of metaphor, necessarily ambiguous and indirect, asserting Black humanity in ways that did not invite ridicule or violent attacks.[16] In the 1950s and 1960s, indirect forms became much more overt. More demure forms of dress and expression remained prominent in the mainstream movement led by organizations like the NAACP, but over time the way African Americans dressed, wore their hair, spoke, danced, and engaged in forms of nonverbal communication helped to create a new, unapologetically Black cultural aesthetic.

Many organizations saw cultural nationalism as an important corollary to Black liberation. Constructing its own creation legend that positioned people of African descent as a chosen people, the Nation of Islam nevertheless promoted a code of conduct and dress that emphasized Black respectability anchored in social responsibility and nation building. On the other hand, U.S. founder Maulana Karenga, who also believed that cultural nationalism was critical to Black liberation, embraced a more Afrocentric perspective promoting the adoption of African inspired forms of dress and even language to build Black unity. The Black Panther Party uniform, powder blue shirts and leather jackets, was a throwback to earlier groups and illustrated the paramilitary turn documented by Akinyele Umoja. Along with their earlier emphasis on armed self-defense, the style of the Panthers communicated the party's larger political aims. The adoption of some elements of African dress and culture signaled an emerging consciousness especially among college students about the importance of African heritage and culture. At first indicative of identification with the movement by the early 1970s, the Afro hairstyle and clenched fist salute that once inspired fear became more of a general greeting and acknowledgment of other people of African descent, an important footprint of Black Power's call for racial solidarity.[17]

Religion

Organizers within the Civil Rights and Black Power Movements often blurred the line between politics and faith. African American clergy, of course, were prominent in both movements and proved adept at incorporating faith texts to the cause of Black liberation. The Reverend Dr. King skillfully utilized biblical texts to challenge white clergy to support integration in the name of human goodwill; other religious leaders pursued different ends. Shrine of the Black Madonna founder Albert Cleage, Jr. fashioned a new theology of liberation, building on many of the tenets of economic and political empowerment central to the Black Power Movement. Born in 1911 in Indianapolis, Indiana, Cleage's 1968 publication *The Black Messiah* not only depicted Jesus as a person of African descent but also a revolutionary leader spearheading a movement by other non-white people to liberate themselves from Roman domination. Adopting the primary tenets of Islam, the Nation of Islam promoted its own creation story that situated white people as a race of "Blue-eyed devils" intent on dominating people of color. The more sensational elements of the story also projected people of African descent as "God's Chosen People" and undergirded a fundamental call for Black unity through a shared history. While the Nation of Islam sought to connect both a real and imagined history as the basis for its religious program, scholarship on the African and African American experience was an important precursor to and byproduct of the movement.

Black Studies

The importance of consciousness raising efforts profoundly impacted the nation's college campuses. Demands for Black history and literature courses became the rallying cry of Black student activists in search of greater representation in the curriculum on campuses across the nation.[18] Tellingly, before the Civil War abolitionists like Frederick Douglass emphasized the importance of education for Black people in the South. After the war, benevolent societies sprang up to provide for an education for the freedmen; some, like Victoria Earle Matthews, called attention to the significance of "Race Literature" in challenging distorted ideas of the Black past. Just as Carter Woodson made the teaching of history a cornerstone of the Association for the Study of African American Life and History agenda (ASALH) in the 1910s, Civil Rights and Black Power activists saw it as essential in their campaigns to educate and organize. SNCC, for example, made the teaching of Black history and culture a prominent part of its Freedom Schools in the South. Later, Black Power organizations such as the Los Angeles-based US organization and the Black Panthers incorporated Black history and literature into political education classes. Both organizations proved instrumental in the founding of Black Studies programs that promoted the hiring of Black professors and the expansion of the curriculum to include subjects that increased students' knowledge of the African Diaspora and all its components.

Growing interest in the African Diaspora and its music and culture fueled new scholarship. The work of Black scholars such as historian John Henrik Clarke, a friend of Malcolm X, gained new audiences as African Americans sought to connect more directly with their African roots. Across the country from Seattle, Washington to Bridgeport, Connecticut, African-inspired performance troupes introduced African drums, dance, drama, and poetry along with culturally based rites of passage programs and cultural celebrations such as Kwanza into communities of color.

As a pioneering academic in history and sociology, W.E.B. Du Bois published the study *The Philadelphia Negro* in 1899, setting the stage for more than a half-century of scholarship that informed both movements. John Gibbs St. Clair Drake and Horace Clayton's *Black Metropolis* focused on Chicago and utilized scholarship in a similar vein. A Pan-Africanist, Drake believed such work was an essential tool in combating Jim Crow. Betraying what political scientist Manning Marable later described as the corollary social mission of contemporary

Black Studies scholarship, Drake referred to himself as an "activist anthropologist"; he documented and offered solutions to the race problem.[19] As a college student, Drake admired Carter G. Woodson, sharing his passion for community-engaged scholarship. In the 1910s, Woodson and his organization ASALH pushed for the adoption of Negro History Week as a dual celebration of Black History and Culture and a reminder of the myriad ways African Americans substantively contributed to American and world history. In the 1920s, Black Nationalist organizations such as Marcus Garvey's UNIA and the Moorish Science Temple, the precursor to the Nation of Islam, also emphasized the importance of African and African American history and culture as anchors for nation building. By the 1940s and 1950s, scholars such as Irene Diggs and Allison Davis had already produced interdisciplinary works that helped the next generation of scholars concentrate on the problems of race and class. Davis, who began his career as an English professor and taught Sinclair Drake in college, was "drawn away from a promising academic career in English literature to social anthropology because the latter seemed to promise analytic tools that could be applied to the fight against racism."[20] Diggs studied under Du Bois and helped him found the journal *Phylon: A Review of Race and Culture*. Eventually, she turned her attention to Latin American history, illustrating the diasporic influence of such scholars and their attempt to see the problem from local, national, and even international perspectives. Diggs' comparative work on racism in the United States and Latin America, along with her meticulous documentation of cultural retentions and Black cultural productions foreshadowed the type of research and scholarly inquiry later demanded by students influenced by the Civil Rights and Black Power Movements.

During the 1950s and 1960s, Black Freedom Struggles study groups were a common feature of many organizations that utilized scholarship like Drake's *Black Metropolis* along with classic works by Black authors and poets like Langston Hughes, Claude McKay, Jessie Redmon Fauset, and Alice Dunbar Nelson. At the same time, an interest in the works of Black artists and entertainers introduced a new generation to powerful performers such as Josephine Baker and Billie Holiday as well as artists and painters such as Archibald Motley and Palmer Hayden.

Music

Music was not simply the backdrop to the Civil Rights and Black Power Movements it was an essential part of Black Freedom Struggles. Given the heavy influence of the African American Church, gospel music, for example, permeated early Civil Rights struggles in which repurposed hymns served as the basis for a new catalogue of Freedom Songs. Those songs eventually became synonymous with the movement. The artists who rendered them also gained popularity. Famed Gospel singer Mahilia Jackson, for instance, opened the 1963

March on Washington with a pair of spirituals "How I Got Over" and "I've Been 'Buked and I've Been Scorned." Opera singer Marian Anderson sang another spiritual, "He's Got the Whole World in His Hands."

Folk singers Joan Baez, Bob Dylan, and Peter, Paul, and Mary also sang at the March, accompanied by the lesser known, but no less significant Freedom Singers. Cordell Reagon, Bernice Johnson Reagon, Matthew Jones, Charles Neblett, and Rutha Mae Harris were not only performers but also activists. While they joined Baez in singing "We Shall Overcome" on the Mall in 1963, their participation in anti-Jim Crow demonstrations and time in southern jails had chiseled their voices and their resolve. As a key player in the Albany campaign, Bernice Reagon, for example, recognized the power of music to unify and uplift as a means to inspire morale as well as pass the time—especially when demonstrators were imprisoned.

As previously noted, some musicians were deeply affected by Black Freedom Struggles and used their music to profess support as well as encouragement. In 1960, for instance, Jazz singer Abbey Lincoln participated in a groundbreaking recording session organized by Jazz musician Max Roach in New York City. With the sit-ins taking place throughout the South, they recorded the "Freedom Now Suite," a musical journey through Black history and an affirmation of the protests taking place throughout the South. The album cover featured Roach and his band mates seated at a lunch counter with the title "We Insist," leaving little doubt as to the album's inspiration. In combination with mesmerizing horns and percussion, Lincoln's singing signaled a powerful turn taking place not just at lunch counters across the South but in the music and culture of the activists participating in the movement. Whether as artists, activists, or both, they lent their talents to the struggle and helped to produce a body of music that remains synonymous with the movement. Like many African American entertainers associated with 1950s and 1960s Black Freedom Struggles, Lincoln and Roach used music as a means of highlighting racial injustice. In the process, they continued a long tradition of Black musicians and entertainers who sought to challenge racial inequality through their art.

Lincoln and Roach were also friends and associates of other performers like poet Maya Angelo, writer Julian Mayfield, trumpeter Miles Davis, and singer Nina Simone who participated in protests in addition to producing powerful art and music. In tone and texture, they often engaged elements of the struggle in their music. In 1967, for instance, Nina Simone converted Langston Hughes' poem "Backlash Blues" into a record highlighting the hypocrisy of the white backlash against the gains of the Civil Rights Movement.

> You give me second-class houses,
> Give me second-class schools,
> You must think us colored folks
> Are second-class fools.

Simone was friends with Hughes and was also a close friend of playwright
Lorraine Hansberry whom she first met in Harlem and whose death prompted
the songwriter to pen a tribute, "Young, Gifted, and Black," that boldly affirmed
the dignity and worth of Black youth and the need for educational structures
that communicated those truths.[21]

Popular music also contributed to the movement. Protesters often took songs
and adapted the words and melodies in the service of protest. Freedom songs
and anti-war protest songs by white folk artists such as Bob Dylan and Joan
Baez became the soundtrack for a generation of young people not only committed to ending segregation but also ending the war in Vietnam. While Civil
Rights music enjoyed mass appeal among white college students and movement
allies, a more distinctly Black form of expression in the nation's teeming urban
centers offered a more Black-centered view of the issues facing them. Themes
of struggle and liberation were also evident in popular music from the period.
Sam Cooke's "A Change Gonna Come" (1964) became a movement anthem.
Artists such as Curtis Mayfield consciously penned songs like "Keep on Pushing"
(1964), "People Get Ready" (1965), and "We're a Winner" (1967) that por-
tended a victory over segregation and gained popularity—even when radio
stations refused to play them.

In Detroit, affectionately known as Motown, a musical revolution took shape.
The rise of the company that spearheaded this revolution, Motown Records,
became an American success story built on the foundations of Black Freedom
Struggles. Like much of the movement history, the company began as a local
phenomenon fertilized by the intersecting streams of the Civil Rights and Black
Power Movements. Desirous of cracking the mainstream music market, Motown
owner Barry Gordy founded the company in 1959 with roughly $800 in loans
cobbled together from family. Over the course of the next two decades, he assembled an impressive array of Black artists, producers, and musicians to produce a
unique sound that remains synonymous with the era. Although not written as a
protest song, compositions like Martha and the Vandellas' hit "Dancing in the
Streets"(1964) became popular with both mainstream audiences and activists
looking to reshape the nation's social and political landscape. As Mary Wilson, a
member of the Supremes and one of the record labels most popular acts, recalled:

> We represented a social environment that was changing . . . The experience
> we had known being black was not being bona fide citizens, not being
> able to drink out of the same water fountains, playing to segregated
> audiences. When that started to fall away, and you saw that music was one
> of the components that was helping it fall away, that's when it really felt
> like we were doing something significant.[22]

Nevertheless, as historian Suzanne Smith observes, "Motown could not avoid
becoming a contested symbol of racial progress." "Motown's music," Smith

continues, "symbolized the possibility of amicable racial integration through popular culture. But as a company Motown represented the possibilities of black economic independence, one of the most important tenets of Black Nationalism."[23] White consumers who eagerly embraced the Motown sound allowed the record company to push societal boundaries and build capital in the Black community while providing an important platform for Black artists.

Over the course of the company's successful history, artists that were carefully crafted to fit mainstream models of respectability began to explore new musical frontiers. By the close of the decade, and with growing interest in Black Power, more overtly political music found a space on the airwaves. Increasingly, Motown artists took on sensitive issues. Marvin Gaye and Stevie Wonder, in particular, used their albums as a forum to engage issues of racial, economic, and political inequalities. Marvin Gaye's LP "What's Going On" (1971), for instance, melded a powerful antiwar message with appeals for unity in the face of the poverty and violence that plagued the nation's cities. The Temptations' "Ball of Confusion" followed a genre of popular songs that highlighted the problems of the day. Stevie Wonder's "Living for the City" (1973) that powerfully documented the Six Degrees of Segregation in verse explored the life of a young man born in hard times in Mississippi who through migration and a miscarriage of justice traded the cruel immovable yoke of southern apartheid for the cold penitentiary steel of northern racism.

Other talents such as the "Godfather of Soul" James Brown and the funk group Sly and the Family Stone, reflecting the influence of Black Nationalism and Black Power, also gained in popularity. Brown's 1968 release "Say It Loud – I'm Black and I'm Proud" (1968) became synonymous with the Black Power Movement. Brown also broke new ground with songs like "King Heroin" (1972) that spoke out against drug abuse in the Black community, hinting at the drug epidemic on the horizon and calling upon the community to take action. Responding to the demand for more socially conscious material, Motown launched a new label in 1970 called Black Forum to promote the ideas of prominent African Americans. Although short-lived, it produced an important catalogue of poetry, music, art, and social commentary that helped to articulate the philosophy and ideas behind the various Black Freedom Movements in the period.

Revolutionary Art

The cultural symbols of Black Freedom Struggles were also communicated through art. Across the country visual artists documented the Black experience and produced drawings and other artwork that promoted the cause of revolution and unity. One prominent example of such an artist was Emory Douglas, who served as Minister of Culture for the Black Panther Party. The Panthers were acutely aware of the importance of language and culture as tools for communicating their message and Douglas' artwork became a visible representation of the revolutionary world the Panthers imagined. Douglas first encountered the BPP in March of 1967 during a meeting by Bay area activists. He was on hand to discuss a visit by Malcolm X's widow, Betty Shabazz, for whom the Panthers were to provide security. At the time, Douglas was creating props for one of Amiri Baraka's theater workshops. Like many young artists, he was enamored with the Black Arts Movement and longed to take his activism to a different level. Impressed with BPP founders Huey Newton and Bobby Seale, Douglas ended up joining the party and participating in the Panther armed patrols of police. When the Panthers decided to launch a newspaper, Douglas, who had taken commercial art classes at the City College of San Francisco, volunteered to help with the newspaper's design. Like the Panther's Minister of Information Eldridge Cleaver, Douglas recognized that the party needed powerful imagery to connect with people in poor urban communities where literacy rates were low. Using his training, Douglas assisted in creating a compelling newspaper; his artwork featured prominently in each issue. Douglas's creations were designed to instill a sense of Black pride while depicting the enemies of the Black community, most notably the police, as "pigs." Douglas often depicted Black men, women, and children fighting back against the police in acts of revolutionary violence. The BPP's ideology and art not only captured the attention of people in the community but also of local, state, and federal law enforcement agencies. In the 1970s, the Panther newspaper and Douglas artwork became an important part of a Congressional Investigation into the origins and reach of the Black Panther Party.[24]

Black Film

While Emory Douglas and Amiri Baraka imagined a world in which revolutionary music and art inspired people to take up arms for liberation, movie producers saw a market for films geared primarily toward Black audiences. Going back to the NAACP's boycott of *Birth of a Nation* (1915), film emerged as one of the arenas where Black people sought not only positive portrayals but also increased opportunities for industry-wide employment. Inspired by the Black Power Movement in the 1970s, a new genre of Blaxploitation films seemed to answer the call for Black-centered films replacing weak and stereotypical Black characters with Black leading roles. These movies offered Black artists a chance to be involved in every aspect of the film-making process. Blaxploitation films were primarily action movies featuring strong Black protagonists who challenged the white power structure usually in an orgy of violence. The genre grew out of the emerging sociopolitical consciousness of the Black Power movement as well important changes in Hollywood itself including the relaxation of the film social code as well as the end of the Hollywood studio system. These developments allowed a new crop of young filmmakers to gain access.[25] In 1971, Black filmmaker Melvin Van Peebles' *Sweetback's Baadasssss Song* debuted. Financed on a shoestring budget, the movie touched a chord with Black Panther co-founder Huey Newton who ordered all Panther members to see it. Black Panther Billy "X" Jennings vividly recalled Newton's response to the movie. "Finally" he remembered Newton explaining, "there was a movie out that had some consciousness in it, and had all the elements for a possible revolutionary movie . . . He was also excited about the fact that there was a brother in the movie, a guy who made the movie, who directed it, and starred in it too. He thought that was a beautiful thing."[26] Newton even commissioned a special issue of the Black Panther Party newspaper devoted to the film that included an essay he wrote extolling the film's virtues as a revolutionary training tool.

Most Civil Rights groups did not share Newton's enthusiasm. While *Sweetback's Baadasssss Song* did advance a more revolutionary agenda, it also contained many of the elements of a new genre of film that exploited Black-buying power by capitalizing on the iconic style and expressions of the Black Power Movement. The films enjoyed targeted box office success in the Black community but they also came under fire for their violent, misogynistic, hyper-masculine, and overly sexualized depictions of Black ghetto life that was almost universally depicted as a den of prostitution, killing, and vice. Another source of criticism stemmed from the fact that such movies depended on the support of white studio owners—owners that reaped huge profits. Beverly Hills/Hollywood NAACP chapter president Junius Griffin codified these critiques in 1972 by combining the words "black" and "exploitation," "Blaxploitation," in an effort to highlight the problematic nature of such films. That same year the NAACP teamed up with the SCLC and CORE to form the Coalition Against Blaxploitation (CAB). Utilizing tried and true methods such as boycotts and negotiations with the major studios, CAB sought to use its influence to move Hollywood toward producing works that painted an affirmative view of African American life and culture.

While the films stirred controversy, the musical soundtracks that accompanied them earned critical acclaim, informing a new musical landscape also deeply influenced by the Black Arts and Black Power Movements. Artists such as Curtis Mayfield used music to address serious social issues within the African American community with songs like "Freddie's Dead" (1972), a powerful anti-drug song that was part of the soundtrack for the 1972 movie *Super Fly*. Black artists adopted a new Afrocentric aesthetic to express pride in their African heritage and music that celebrated that heritage. Soul singer Isaac Hayes, for example, appeared as "Jesus in Shades" on the cover of his 1971 "Black Moses," projecting a strong, even if still hyper-sexualized image of Black masculinity. At Motown, Steve Wonder's 1976 double album, "Songs in the Key of Life," spoke to the hopes and frustrations of a new generation of Black Americans. His "Pastime Paradise" called out those forces attempting to push the clock back on the gains of the Civil Rights Movement. The same album included a song, "Black Man," that highlighted Black figures in history with young children calling out historical facts about leaders such as Marcus Garvey over a driving rhythm.

Television

In television and in mainstream movies, Africans remained mostly invisible with a few notable exceptions. By 1970, actor Sidney Poitier had built up an impressive resume that brought dignity to Black men on the big screen. Talents such as Harry Belafonte, Dorothy Dandridge (who died in 1965), Sammy Davis, Jr., and later James Earl Jones joined him. As television ownership became more widespread, the small screen also offered opportunities for Black actors and entertainers to challenge inequality. At first African American roles were limited to stereotypical ones. As the 1960s progressed, however, new opportunities inspired by the Civil Rights and Black Power Movement gave African Americans an opportunity to share their talents. Gene Rodenberry's 1966 television space odyssey "Star Trek" (1966–9), for instance, featured a multiracial cast with actor Nichelle Nichols in the role of Lt. Uhura, her surname a derivative of the Swahili word for freedom. Uhura's place among the leadership team of the fictitious *Star Ship Enterprise* forecast an optimistic hope for the future of interracial and international cooperation. The show also tested taboos by featuring television's first interracial kiss between Nichols's character and the captain of the *Enterprise*. In 1968, Diahann Carroll debuted as the title character in the show "Julia" (1968–71). Carroll played a widowed nurse raising a young son. The show broke new ground for its portrayal of a Black woman outside the role of domestic but came under sharp criticism from some who saw it as an unrealistic portrait of Black life at the time. In yet another popular show from that era, actor Eartha Kitt played the recurring role of Cat Woman on the television series "Batman" (1966–8). Her success however did not protect her from government intrusion. Like many other outspoken artists and entertainers, the FBI monitored Kitt for her Civil Rights and antiwar activism. In her case, the surveillance had no direct outward impact. Others would not be so fortunate.

In spite of the success of Nichols, Carroll, and Kitt, for the most part, television remained segregated with few Black shows and actors. That changed in the 1970s when producer Norman Lear scored a number of hits with shows like "Good Times" (1974–9) and "The Jeffersons" (1975–85) that featured prominent Black actors but were also set around stereotypical roles and scenarios. The impact of the both movements was evident in many of the storylines and character development of both shows; nevertheless the caricaturing of issues of poverty and inequality depicted in both left some critics less than enthused.

The most significant television program of the era was the adaptation of author Alex Haley's 1976 novel *Roots: The Saga of an American Family*. Haley, who had collaborated with Malcolm X on his autobiography, shaped his own family history into a story of the African American experience. The miniseries, which appeared on ABC in 1977, made television history in regards to viewership and subject. The journey of one family from slavery to freedom captivated audiences.

Public access television allowed for the growth of local TV shows and markets. Shows like "Soul," a weekly talk and variety show produced by Ellis Haizlip from 1967 to 1973 and Don Cornelius's dance and music showcase "Soul Train" (1971–2006) also helped to expose the nation to Black culture.

The Birth of Hip Hop

"Soul Train" provided a powerful vehicle for debuting Black fashion and culture; it was instrumental in exposing the world to a new form of social expression that emerged on the streets of New York City in the late 1970s. Heavily inspired by the poetry of Black Arts luminaries such as Gil Scott-Heron and the Last Poets as well as Sonia Sanchez and Nikki Giovanni, hip-hop music merged the Black rhetorical tradition and heavily syncopated rhythms with an urban view of racism, and economic inequality. Hip-hop developed from what historian Jeff Chang calls the politics of abandonment. Left politically and economically isolated and vulnerable by deindustrialization hip-hop became an important form of both political and cultural expression.[27] This became especially important as inner-city spaces became more restrictive due to draconian drug laws and invasive police practices. As Chang notes, "the politics of abandonment would turn toward the politics of containment," explaining in part the rise of the carceral state. In September of 1989, President George H. W. Bush articulated the turn in what became known as his "crack speech." In order to combat the problems posed by drugs he explained, "We need more prisons, more jails, more courts, more prosecutors."[28] Hip-hop was one of the cultural responses. The Bronx, one of New York's five boroughs, was ground zero for this musical revolution. In the predominately Black and Hispanic communities hardest hit by deindustrialization and economic blight, music remained one of the few avenues left for expression. High unemployment, coupled with significant budget cuts and a loss of business left streets heavily impoverished and crime-ridden. "The Message" (1982) by Grandmaster Flash and the Furious Five with its memorable refrain, "It's like jungle sometime it makes me wonder how I keep from going on," broadcast a bleak urban reality, where poverty, drugs, and urban neglect left inhabitants to fend for themselves. Artists harkened back to the Civil Rights and Black Power Movements, making Black history and culture the focus of their music.

In New York City in the early 1980s, artists like Kurtis Blow and Run-DMC helped to transform rap into a commercial success. By the 1990s, new school hip-hop featured groups like the Jungle Brothers, Public Enemy, and A Tribe Called Quest that became staples of the Golden Age of hip-hop. Sampling, which involved reproducing segments of several records and blending them together to make new music, resurrected the music of James Brown and Jazz greats in a blend of music, style, and culture that celebrated the Black experience in song and dance. Adopting the militant style of the Black Panther Party, Public Enemy, a Black Power-inspired conscious rap group who borrowed aesthetically and philosophically from the Nation of Islam and the Black Panthers and whose early albums included reading lists, regularly sampled the words of Martin Luther King, Malcolm X, and other Black leaders in songs infused with the Black pride reminiscent of the spirit of the Black Power Movement.[29]

By the 2000s, hip-hop had not only developed into a genre of music but a distinct culture owing in great part to the legacy of Black Freedom Struggles, the traditions of truth telling and speaking truth to power through music and culture on full display. When the trial of four police officers accused of the beating of Black motorist Rodney King—a beating caught on camera—resulted in their acquittal, days of civil unrest erupted in Los Angeles, California. Public Enemy front man Chuck D could rightfully declare that hip-hop was the CNN of the streets, regularly broadcasting the urban realities of Black life and culture.

Toward the close of the century, efforts to win greater representation for African Americans in movies and on television bore fruit in a number of programs informed by the Black Freedom Movement. Director Spike Lee's 1989 film *Do the Right Thing* (1989) carried the message of both movements forward in the form of a story framed by a dichotomized choice between the paths of Malcolm and Martin. Set against the backdrop of numerous real life instances of police brutality and interracial conflict in New York City, the film reached its climax after rioters destroy a neighborhood pizzeria in retaliation for an incident of police brutality. Public Enemy performed the film's title track. That song, "Fight the Power," became a rallying cry for a new generation of activists seeking to influence the political process and fight against inequality in New York and beyond.

With an increase in Black box office success and buying power, African American filmmakers were able to bring new perspectives to the big screen. In 1992, Spike Lee released the film *Malcolm X*. The 1995 Mario Van Peebles film *Panther* followed it. Financed, for the most part, through fundraising efforts outside the framework of large studios, both films were notable not only for their subject matter but for their display of Black economic power. With a boom in hip-hop and the emergence of mega television personalities like talk show host Oprah Winfrey who broke down further barriers by the late 2000s, other films that ostensibly dealt with the Civil Rights and Black Power Movements came to the big screen. Director Taylor Tate's *The Help* (2011) and Lee Daniels' *The Butler* (2013) presented portraits of the movement told through strong Black characters. Once stereotypical roles, the characters in these films demonstrated a broader range of resistance to oppression more akin to the history of the 1950s and 1960s Black Freedom Struggles. Brian Helgeland's biopic *42* (2013) likewise told the story of Jackie Robinson, and one of the most important and transformational moments in American history, through Robinson's own eyes.

Conclusion

The Civil Rights and Black Power Movements helped to transform American society and culture. In addition to wiping away Jim Crow Segregation, these freedom struggles helped to create new avenues for Black expression and exposed the world to music, art, dance, and other forms of culture associated with the African American community. As in earlier periods such as the Harlem Renaissance, the struggle for racial justice greatly influenced the works of art produced during this period. In every aspect of American life and culture from music to poetry a new Black aesthetic challenged notions of Black inferiority while reimagining the meaning of Blackness. The enduring legacy of these movements is widespread in music, art, film, and even material culture. In this way, they continue to speak to Americans across time not only about the impact of that historical moment but the road ahead.

Notes

1 Morehouse College in 1969.
2 W.E.B. Du Bois, "Criteria of Negro Art," *The Crisis* (October 1926): 290–7.
3 Cesar Chavez, "What the Future Holds for Farm Workers and Hispanics," Speech at the Commonwealth Club, San Francisco, November 9, 1984.
4 Robin D.G. Kelley, *Africa Speaks, America Answers: Modern Jazz in Revolutionary Times* (Cambridge, MA: Harvard University Press, 2012); Ingrid Monson, *Freedom Sounds: Civil Rights Call out to Jazz and Africa* (New York: Oxford University Press, 2006); Rhonda Y. Williams, *Concrete Demands: The Search for Black Power in the 20th Century* (New York: Taylor & Francis, 2015); Peniel Joseph, *Waiting 'Til the Midnight Hour: A Narrative History of Black Power in America* (New York: Macmillan, 2007); Penny Von Eschen, *Satchmo Blows Up the World: Jazz Ambassadors Play the Cold War* (Cambridge, MA: Harvard University Press, 2004); Ruth Feldstein, *How It Feels to Be Free: Black Women Entertainers and the Civil Rights Movement* (New York: Oxford University Press, 2013); Suzanne E. Smith, *Dancing in the Street: Motown and the Cultural Politics of Detroit* (Cambridge, MA: Harvard University Press, 1999); Brian Ward, *Just My Soul Responding: Rhythm and Blues, Black Consciousness, and Race Relations* (Berkeley: University of California Press, 1998).
5 Du Bois, "Criteria of Negro Art."
6 *A Hubert Harrison Reader*, edited with introduction and notes by Jeffrey B. Perry (Middletown: Wesleyan University Press, 2001), 98.
7 On Carter G. Woodson, Jacqueline Goggin, *Carter G. Woodson: A Life in Black History* (Baton Rouge: Louisiana University Press, 1993); V.P. Franklin and Bettye Collier-Thomas, "Biography, Race Vindication, and African American Intellectuals,"

The Journal of African American History (2002): 160–74; Pero Gaglo Dagbovie, "Making Black History Practical and Popular: Carter G. Woodson, the Proto Black Studies Movement and the Struggle for Black Liberation," *Western Journal of Black Studies* 27, no. 4 (2003).

8   Louis Armstrong, quoted in Monson, *Freedom Sounds*, 1. See also Von Eschen, *Satchmo Blows Up the World*; Eric Porter, *What Is This Thing Called Jazz? African American Musicians as Artists, Critics, and Activists* (Berkeley: University of California Press, 2002); Craig Werner, *Higher Ground: Stevie Wonder, Aretha Franklin, Curtis Mayfield, and the Rise and Fall of American Soul* (New York: Crown Publishers, 2004); Monson, *Freedom Sounds*; Penny Von Eschen, "Rethinking Politics and Culture in a Dynamic Decade," *OAH Magazine of History* 26, no. 4 (2012): 9.

9   Jenny Woodley, *Art for Equality: The NAACP's Cultural Campaign for Civil Rights* (Lexington: University Press of Kentucky, 2014), 2.

10   Ibid., 2.

11   On the Lumumba Protest see Williams, *Concrete Demands*, 70; Peniel Joseph, "Malcolm X's Harlem and Black Power Activism," in Peniel Joseph, ed., *Neighborhood Rebels: Black Power at the Local Level* (New York: Palgrave Macmillan, 2009), 33. On Harlem in this period see Joseph, *Waiting 'Til the Midnight Hour*, 14–15, 40–41; Ruth Feldstein, "'I Don't Trust You Anymore': Nina Simone, Culture, and Black Activism in the 1960s," *The Journal of American History* 91, no. 4 (March 2005): 1349–79; Ward, *Just My Soul Responding*; Kelley, *Africa Speaks, America Answers*; Rebeccah Welch, "Black Art and Activism in Postwar New York, 1950–1965," Ph.D. diss., New York University, 2002; Peniel Joseph, ed., *The Black Power Movement: Rethinking the Civil Rights–Black Power Era* (New York: Routledge, 2006).

12   Larry Neal, "The Black Arts Movement," *Drama Review* 12 (Summer 1968): 29–39, in James Cone, *Black Theology and Black Power* (New York: Seabury Press, 1969).

13   C. Eric Lincoln, "The Black Revolution in Cultural Perspective," *Union Seminary Quarterly Review* 23, no. 3 (Spring 1968): 221.

14   Phyl Garland, "Is the Afro on Its Way Out?" *Ebony Magazine* 28, no. 4 (1973): 128.

15   Abbey Lincoln quoted in Monson, *Freedom Sounds*.

16   Shane White and Graham White, *Stylin': African American Expressive Culture from its Beginnings to the Zoot Suit* (Ithaca: Cornell University Press, 1998).

17   See Jeffrey O.G. Ogbar, *Black Power: Radical Politics and African American Identity* (Baltimore: Johns Hopkins University Press, 2004), 116–119; Yohuru Williams, "'They've lynched our savior, Lumumba in the old fashion Southern style': The Conscious Internationalism of American Black Nationalism," in Nico Slate, ed., *Black Beyond Borders* (New York: Palgrave Macmillan, 2012).

18   See Wayne Glasker, *Black Students in the Ivory Tower: African American Student Activism at the University of Pennsylvania, 1967–1990* (Amherst: University of Massachusetts Press, 2002); Joy Ann Williamson, *Black Power on Campus: The University of Illinois, 1965–1975* (Urbana: University of Illinois Press, 2003); Fabio Rijoas's sociological study, *From Black Power to Black Studies: How a Radical Social Movement Became an Academic Discipline* (Baltimore: Johns Hopkins Press, 2007); Delores Aldridge and Carlene Young, eds., *Out of the Revolution: The Development of Africana Studies* (Lanham: Lexington Books, 2000); William Nelson, Jr., ed., *Black Studies: From Pyramids to Pan-Africanism* (New York: McGraw Hill, 2001).

19   George C. Bond and St. Clair Drake, "A Social Portrait of John Gibbs St. Clair Drake," *American Ethnologist* 15, no. 4 (1988): 762–81, 775.

20 Faye V. Harrison, "The Du Boisian Legacy in Anthropology," *Critique of Anthropology* 12, no. 3 (1992): 246.

21 Feldstein, *How It Feels to Be Free*, 26–7.

22 Mary Wilson quoted in Alan Light, "Motown's Link to Civil Rights Movement on Display," *New York Times*, March 19, 2014. Accessed March 13, 2015, at www.nytimes.com/2014/03/20/arts/artsspecial/motowns-link-to-civil-rights-movement-on-display.html.

23 Suzanne E. Smith, *Dancing in the Street: Motown and the Cultural Politics of Detroit* (Cambridge, MA: Harvard University Press, 1999), 18.

24 Maurice Berger, *For All the World to See: Visual Culture and the Struggle for Civil Rights* (New Haven: Yale University Press, 2010), 176; James Smethurst, *The Black Arts Movement: Literary Nationalism in the 1960s and 1970s* (Chapel Hill: University of North Carolina Press, 2005); Erika Doss, "'Revolutionary art is a tool for liberation': Emory Douglas and Protest Aesthetics at the Black Panther," *New Political Science* 21, no. 2 (1999): 245–59; Erika Doss, "Imaging the Panthers: Representing Black Power and Masculinity, 1960s–1990s," *Prospects* 23 (1998): 483–516; Erika Doss, "Revolutionary Art Is a Tool for Liberation," in Kathleen Cleaver and George N. Katsiaficas, eds., *Liberation, Imagination, and the Black Panther Party: A New Look at the Panthers and Their Legacy* (New York: Routledge, 2001), 183.

25 On Blaxploitation see Ed Guerrero, "The Rise and Fall of Blaxploitation," in Ed Guerrero, *Framing Blackness: The African American Image in Film* (Philadelphia: Temple University Press, 1993); Donald Bogle, *Toms, Coons, Mulattoes, Mammies and Bucks* (New York: Continuum, 2001); Yvonne D. Sims, *Women of Blaxploitation: How the Black Action-Film Heroine Changed American* (New York: McFarland, 2006); Valerie Smith, ed., *Representing Blackness: Issues in Film and Video* (New Brunswick: Rutgers University Press, 1997); Thomas Cripps, *Slow Fade to Black: The Negro in American Film, 1900–1942* (New York: Oxford University Press, 1977); bell hooks, *Reel to Real: Race, Sex, and Class at the Movies* (New York: Routledge, 1996); Daniel Leab, *From Sambo to Superspade: The Black Experience in Motion Pictures* (Boston: Houghton Mifflin, 1975); Craig Watkins, *Representing: Hip Hop Culture and the Production of Black Cinema* (Chicago: University of Chicago Press, 1998).

26 Billy "X" Jennings quoted in "Melvin Van Peebles and the Black Panthers." Melvin Van Peebles and the Black Panthers. Web. March 13, 2015. http://www.mvpmovie.com/?BlackPanthers, accessed July 2 2015.

27 Jeff Chang, *Can't Stop, Won't Stop: A History of the Hip-Hop Generation* (New York: St. Martin's, 2005).

28 George H.W. Bush, *Speaking of Freedom: The Collected Speeches* (New York: Scribner, 2009), 84.

29 On hip-hop see Chang, *Can't Stop, Won't Stop*; Jim Fricke and Charlie Ahearn, *Yes Yes Y'all: The Experience Music Project Oral History of Hip-Hop's First Decade* (Cambridge, MA: Da Capo Press, 2002); Murray Forman and Mark Anthony Neal, eds., *That's the Joint! The Hip-Hop Studies Reader* (New York: Routledge, 2004).

5

"A LARGER FREEDOM"

The Strengths, Weaknesses, and Legacies of the Civil Rights and Black Power Movements

> Even if segregation is gone, we will still need to be free; we will still have to see that everyone has a job. Even if we can all vote, but if people are still hungry, we will not be free ... Singing alone is not enough; we need schools and learning ... Remember, we are not fighting for the freedom of the Negro alone, but for the freedom of the human spirit, a larger freedom that encompasses all of mankind.
>
> Ella Baker[1]

As with all great social movements, the Black Freedom Struggles of the 1950s and 1960s left an indelible legacy. In wiping away the legal barriers to equality, the Civil Rights Movement eradicated significant obstacles to inclusiveness. Jim Crow laws and disfranchisement, alongside custom, had relegated Black people to the humiliation of "separate but equal," involuntary residential segregation, non-citizenship status, and economic and political subordination. In rejecting the notion of Black inferiority and celebrating the importance of Black history and culture, the Black Power Movement awakened a new sense of Black pride and Black unity aimed at uplifting people of African descent social, politically, economically, and culturally.

Law and public policy had checked the Six Degrees of Segregation that once rigidly regulated Black life. African Americans now enjoyed, in theory, the privileges and immunities of citizenship, as well as secured pathways to political empowerment. Indeed, African Americans have seen the greatest gains in electoral politics—including the election of the nation's first African American president, Barack Obama, in 2008. Milestones like Obama's election and his subsequent appointment of a Black attorney general, Eric Holder, led to widespread and premature media pronouncements of a new "post-racial" America.

However, while this may have helped to bridle the overtly racist practices and political chicanery that once dominated society, it did not eliminate exclusion as much as morph into less subtle if equally restrictive forms of marginalization and disfranchisement.

Throughout the 1990s and 2000s, several symbolic gestures aimed at racial healing overshadowed growing inequality. In 1995, for instance, the state of Mississippi finally ratified the 13th Amendment, 130 years after it became part of the Constitution. It still took the state *another* 18 years for the vote to be formally delivered and counted. In 1998 President Bill Clinton expressed regret for the African Slave Trade, but stopped short of delivering an outright apology for slavery. In 2001, a resolution acknowledging the victims of lynching and their descendants passed in the U.S. Senate, but significantly, no monetary considerations or reparations accompanied these apologies.

Along with these public signs indicating reconciliation, politicians and pundits pointed to marked expansion of the Black middle class and the influence of Black artists and entertainers as further signs of equality. Racial progress, they maintained, permeated the stories of successful Black businesspersons, community leaders, and entrepreneurs who enjoyed widespread attention and popularity. Talk show host and entrepreneur Oprah Winfrey, for instance, consistently ranked among the world's wealthiest, most influential celebrities. In 2012, Winfrey was just one of an assortment of Black people to make *Forbes* magazine's list of richest African Americans. Black entrepreneurs such as BET co-founders Robert Johnson and Sheila Johnson and real estate tycoon R. Donahue Peebles highlighted Black business acumen. Still others, such as basketball star LeBron James, enjoy global recognition—becoming the face of many brands.[2]

Percolating beneath these ostensible signs of progress were the bitter vestiges of Jim Crow and newfangled systems, whether recuperated or created out of transformed political and economic conditions to reproduce and maintain inequities. Black incarceration rates rose, as did voting irregularities. Zip code apartheid continued. African Americans and Latinos remained hyper-segregated in largely urban, deindustrialized cities; access to affordable housing, decent schools, and opportunities for employment remained woefully inadequate. These inequalities dramatically surfaced in August of 2005 when a Category Five hurricane struck the Mississippi Gulf, and the levees that protected the city of New Orleans failed. The high winds and floodwaters from the storm left a huge swath of destruction, obliterating hundreds of homes and businesses and forcing the evacuation of millions of people from the region. In the storm's aftermath, the national spotlight fixed on the New Orleans Superdome where thousands of people, mostly poor African Americans, remained trapped. Concentrated in low-lying areas, the city's poor Black districts sustained the most severe flooding. The residents in these neighborhoods were also the least equipped to escape. They lacked, in many cases, access to transportation, the funds necessary for evacuation, and the financial resources to secure safe shelter in the storm's wake.[3]

Slow federal and state relief efforts exacerbated the tragedy prompting a popular Black recording artist, Kanye West, to complain during a nationally televised benefit that then President George Bush "doesn't care about black people." West also pointed to the unfair and highly racialized reporting of the behavior of the survivors of the hurricane as evidence of media bias. "You see a black family," he observed, "it says, 'They're looting.' You see a white family, it says, 'They're looking for food.'"[4] While the charges that the relief effort dragged due to racial bias were later determined to be unfounded, numerous studies and reports confirmed that the media bias persisted. Black survivors of the flood were continually referred to as "refugees"— a term more often associated with immigrants seeking asylum than U.S. citizens. Most importantly, the whole episode illustrated just how deeply race and poverty remained intertwined in American society.

While there has been significant progress in each of the areas represented by the Six Degrees of Segregation, the gains were not universal, benefiting only a small portion of African Americans. More importantly, the gains have not proved lasting. In the arena of housing, for instance, a combination of federal programs, better income, and fair housing legislation led to a pronounced jump in Black homeownership from just 35 percent in 1950 to 46.8 percent in 2005. While this percentage remained far below the 70.7 percent of white ownership documented the same year, it was still measurable growth. However, due to a variety of circumstances, these gains proved largely transitory. Black homebuyers, for instance, were more likely to encounter unethical banking practices such as predatory lending that saddled them with high interest rates and debt that made homeownership more precarious. During the recession of 2008, for example, African American homeowners were disproportionately the victims of home foreclosures.

Rising Black unemployment exacerbated the housing crisis. Unhampered by discriminatory laws and in some cases aided by affirmative action in the decades after the Civil Rights and Black Power Movements, millions of Black people took advantage of new avenues and opportunities for employment. Consistent with these gains, the median Black income rose. By the 1990s, African Americans continued to narrow the income gap, but still lagged behind white families in the actual accumulation of wealth. Again, these gains were not general. A Bureau of Labor Statistics report determined that in the 42-year period after it began tracking unemployment numbers by race, Black unemployment numbers averaged two-thirds higher than white unemployment rates. Prior to 2009, the greatest gap was in February 1989, when the Black unemployment rate was almost triple, (11.9 percent) that of whites (4.3 percent). By 2011, however, Black unemployment reached a staggering 16 percent.[5] Chronic unemployment and underemployment remained rampant in communities of color and many families lived at or below the poverty line.

In spite of the persistence of these problems, opponents of the extension of social welfare programs aimed at alleviating some of these conditions chose to focus on areas of growth, particularly in the realm of electoral politics. To be sure, the Civil Rights and Black Power Movements helped pave the way for important electoral gains at the state and local level. Between 1974 and 1980, for instance the number of Black elected officials nearly doubled from 1,593 to 2,455. From the late 1970s through the 2000s, Black candidates won notable mayoral elections in Cleveland, Atlanta, Chicago, Washington, DC, Philadelphia, and Los Angeles.

African American candidates also ran for, and won, election to national office. Since the majority of these won election from urban districts and states with large Black majorities utilizing the organizing strategies and appeals to Black unity that characterized the Civil Rights and Black Power Movements.

In 1972, New York Congresswoman Shirley Chisholm became the first African American woman to seek the nomination for president. While she finished a distant but respectable fourth at the 1972 Democratic Convention, garnering 152 or 5.04 percent of the votes, her campaign proved the viability of a Black candidate for the highest elective office. Less than a decade later in the 1980s, Movement veteran Jesse Jackson made two unsuccessful but note-worthy campaigns for the presidency, garnering 6.9 million votes and winning seven primaries, in states with large Black majorities including Mississippi, Alabama, and Georgia, as well as the District of Columbia. The precedent set by Chisholm's daring and Jackson's success enabled a Chicago community organizer and Harvard-trained lawyer named Barack Obama to seek the Democratic Party's nomination for the presidency in 2008.

Obama, however, had hard lessons to learn in the city of Chicago first. In the wake of the Civil Rights and Black Power Movements, Chicago remained a center of widespread political organizing and protest. In 1983, these forces converged, paving the way for the election of the city's first African American mayor, Harold Washington—a crowning achievement for Civil Rights as well as a demonstration of Black Power. Years later, in 2000 Obama squared off in a Congressional Race against incumbent Representative and former Black Panther organizer Bobby Rush for a Congressional Seat in the city's over-whelmingly Black, Democratic and working-class South Side. Rush won the election, but the experience helped Obama to appreciate the need for the cultivation of a "Rainbow Coalition"—a term Jesse Jackson coined in his own pursuit of national political office during the 1980s; he sought to build a campaign based on broad coalition building. Rather than attempting to reconcile outstanding differences and issues, Jackson presented himself as the bridge between two at times oppositional strategies—interracial coalition building and the push for Black Power in an arena where the former traditionally diluted the later. Jackson learned early on the difficulty of maintaining such a coalition. As part of his Rainbow Coalition and appeal to Black voters, Jackson embraced the avowedly separatist Nation of Islam and welcomed members of the group to serve in his security detail. Louis Farrakhan, who had taken over the reigns of the NOI in 1978 decided to set aside the NOI's long-standing policy of eschewing mainstream politics to endorse Jesse Jackson's presidential campaign. When a newspaper report surfaced of Jackson making anti-Semitic remarks, Farrakhan sprung to Jackson's defense and complicated matters by framing the issue as one of Blacks versus Jews. Farrakhan's own anti-Semitic diatribes forced Jackson to distance himself from the NOI and its leader in hopes of repairing a long-standing alliance between the Black and Jewish communities central to the Civil Rights Movement and raising the question could interracial coalition building and a deeply rooted philosophy of Black Power peaceably co-exist. In his 2008 presidential campaign Obama however mastered the art of projecting himself as a blue screen upon which various constituents could project their own hopes and aspirations.

For a time this strategy worked, yet race and racial unity remained a societal and political fault line especially after excerpts of sermons by the Reverend Jeremiah Wright—Senator Obama's former pastor—surfaced condemning the United States for its racist history. Rev. Wright's fiery rhetoric invoked memories of Malcolm X and his bruising critiques of the United States. Revered Wright's bitter condemnation of the United States pointed to the successes and unfinished business of the Civil Rights and Black Power era. His comments also illustrated the complexity of a people who at various times found merits in the programs and ideologies of both movements.

Obama's relationship with Rev. Wright quickly became an issue. Critics tried to use the Reverend's words to brand Obama as "disloyal." Obama, however, successfully weathered the storm by countering with strident appeals to pluralism. In a widely viewed televised speech entitled "A More Perfect Union," Obama argued that Rev. Wright's Trinity Church was similar to other Black churches and institutions; it reflected the wide diversity of opinion in the Black community that he categorized as "the kindness and cruelty, the fierce intelligence and the shocking ignorance, the struggles and successes, the love and yes, the bitterness and bias that make up the black experience in America."[6] In November of 2008, Obama soundly defeated the Republican candidate Senator John McCain and took up residence in the White House.

Race-based critiques of Obama, however, did not end with his election. Despite the fact that his administration reflected a more neoliberal ideology that promoted deregulation, outsourcing, privatization, and free trade, the president faced tremendous opposition from Conservatives and a new splinter group, the Tea Party. They challenged his fitness for public office in thinly veiled attacks on his race and status as a citizen.

At the same Obama also faced criticism from several prominent Black public intellectuals. Despite high polling numbers among African Americans and key legislative enactments such as the Affordable Health Care Act that made health care accessible to millions of uninsured Americans, author Cornel West and Black Entertainment Television talk show host Tavis Smiley expressed dissatisfaction with the policies and programs pursued by his administration, including Obama's penchant for bypassing the leadership of established Civil Rights organizations and speaking as the voice of the Black community. Obama, in the meantime, continued to frame his electoral victories as important social movement milestones. In his second inaugural address in 2012, he consciously engaged the history and legacy of three important moments, Seneca Falls, (Women Rights), Selma (Civil Rights), and Stono (Gay Liberation) to speak to challenges like gender inequality left to conquer. In so doing, he highlighted the ultimate legacy of the 1950s and 1960s Black Freedom Struggles to reimagine a more just democracy and put pressure on Americans to live up to its democratic ideals.

Bending Toward Justice

Taken collectively, Black Freedom Struggles fueled the American imagination inspiring oppressed peoples to reimagine a context in which they shared in the American dream or better still were invited to share alternative visions of an America anchored in the quest for social justice. In 1967, the Reverend Dr. Martin Luther King boldly declared:

> The black revolution is much more than a struggle for the rights of Negroes. It is forcing America to face all its interrelated flaws—racism, poverty, militarism, and materialism. It is exposing evils that are rooted deeply in the whole structure of our society ... and suggests that radical reconstruction of society is the real issue to be faced.[7]

In many ways, Black Freedom Struggles of the 1950s and 1960s lived up to King's and others' aspirations—even if the radical reconstruction of society they hoped for never took place. By the time of King's death in April of 1968, for instance, both movements had branched out in numerous directions to tackle a wide variety of social justice issues. Activists within Black Freedom Struggles inserted their powerful voices wherever they involved themselves. Activists involved in a burgeoning prisoners' rights movement found inspiration and support in the discourse of Black Freedom Struggles. By the 1970s, for instance, the NAACP focused on several key cases involving prisoners' rights including the 8th Amendment's provision against cruel and unusual punishment. Black Power era activists such as Angela Davis also connected the struggle for Civil Rights and Black Power to prison reform efforts and a burgeoning prisoners' rights movement. Inspired by the writings of people like Malcolm X, George Jackson, Angela Davis, and Eldrige Cleaver, inmates in the meantime fashioned a grassroots movement built on the same movement organizing models and language of social justice. From inmate writ writers and attorneys who pursued a legal strategy to those engaged in acts of direct action protest, the deep influence of the 1950s and 1960s era Black Freedom Struggles was clear.

Black activists also played an integral role in the Women's Liberation Movement. In the process, they complicated and deepened the discourse over gender equality by consistently pushing the agenda to address broader social justice concerns. The widespread popularity of Black Freedom Struggles, especially among young people on college campuses, provided a fertile breeding ground for political theorizing. At the same time, the work of grassroots organizers like Ella Baker and Fannie Lou Hamer provided concrete examples of how to go about organizing the masses. Many prominent leaders in Black Freedom Struggles doubled as leaders of the Anti-War Movement. Stokely Carmichael was one of the first Civil Rights activists to come out against the war in Vietnam. Martin Luther King's 1967 Riverside Church address, in which he too came out against the war, made him one of the most significant and powerful voices in the Anti-War Movement as well. Grassroots organizing and coalition building remained essential to this work.

The Gay Rights Movement that preceded the LBTGQ movement also drew inspiration from Black Freedom Struggles. Many prominent Civil Rights leaders including King's closest advisor Bayard Rustin were in fact pioneers in addressing not only the inequalities but also intimidations that faced those of different sexualities.

Black Freedom Struggles also fueled other movements by similarly situated groups including Asians and Latinos. In many cases, individuals and organizations associated with these efforts fashioned their identity and politics around Civil Rights and Black Power Organizations. For example, Maggie Kuhn formed a group called the Gray Panthers to address issues associated with the elderly that borrowed the confrontational politics and style of the Black Panther Party. Even as Black Freedom Struggles informed all these movements, substantive issues of inequality continued to plague American society. Deep economic disparities impeded the path to full equality for the vast majority of people of color in America.

Not surprisingly many contemporary struggles to address issues such as gun violence, de facto school segregation, and police brutality continue to be framed in the same spirit of 1950s and 1960s Black Freedom Struggles with which they share many of the same overlapping goals and values and an emphasis on social justice. While not always in agreement in terms of strategies and tactics the overarching concerns continue to connect these struggles. This has become particularly important over the last decade, as more and more people of color have attained positions of wealth and influence, leading to the problematic assertion that the United States is now a post-racial society in which all persons have a fair and equal shot at success.

Despite efforts to portray the United States as a post-racial society, poverty and racial inequality remained significant problems. The Black unemployment rate for instance, persisted; at percentages more than double that for whites. Poor sanitation, inadequate health care, and crime predominated. Government responses tended to treat the inhabitants as the problem rather than the deep structural inequalities that produced them. Nearly 50 years after Huey Newton complained that the police patrolled America's Black ghettoes like an army, a range of policing tactics today continued the practice in none too subtle ways. Policies such as stop and frisk have resulted in the criminalization of urban space, where police, increasingly equipped with military hardware, resemble more of an occupying army than peace officers committed to serve and protect.

Problematically one of the legacies of Black Freedom Struggles is manifested in efforts at political and economic retrenchment. By the close of the 1970s, the white backlash that emerged against both movements focused attention on stopping programs like Affirmative Action aimed at remedying age-old discrimination. Opponents identified such programs as a form of reverse discrimination. In 1978, for example, Allan Bakke sued the University of California after he was denied admission into their medical program presumably because of a racial set-aside program. While the court upheld Affirmative Action in that case, it has been the subject of numerous subsequent challenges.

The administration of President Ronald Reagan (1981–9) likewise did much to turn back the clock on the gains made by the movement. Scaled-back government subsidized housing programs disproportionately affected people of color, leaving them vulnerable to homelessness. By reducing federal assistance to the poor and using tax policies to favor the wealthy, the economic policies pursued under the Reagan administration increased the Black poverty rate to 34 percent, more than three times that of whites. Reagan also sought to limit the powers of the Equal Employment Opportunities Commission and the Civil Rights Commission, revived tax exemptions for segregated private schools, moved to arrest court-ordered school busing, and gutted efforts to protect Black voting rights.

During his administration, Reagan's successor George H. W. Bush (1989–93) continued to chip away at movement gains. Significantly, Bush replaced Thurgood Marshall, the architect of the *Brown* decision and the first African American to serve on the United States Supreme Court with Clarence Thomas, a Black conservative. Thomas opposed much of the Civil Rights agenda and joined a right-leaning block of justices intent on rolling back so-called entitlement programs such as Affirmative Action. Despite deriving benefits from many of these programs during his career and once serving as head of the Equal

Employment Opportunities Commission, Thomas radiated hostility on the topic. He was not alone. By the late 1980s, a number of Black Conservatives such as Shelby Steele and Stephen Carter sought to repurpose the rhetoric of Dr. King and the Civil Rights Movement in particular to argue against such programs.

Even Democrats seemed less inclined to champion issues related to Civil Rights and actually cut key programs to address poverty. During his two terms in office, and despite the wide support he received from African Americans, President Bill Clinton (1993–2001) ushered in welfare reform that severely restricted benefits to the poor. Consistent with the aims of the Black Power Movement Black separatist organizations such as the Nation of Islam, headed by Louis Farrakhan, continued to promote self-help and racial solidarity as the key to Black economic and political survival. In 1995, Farrakhan made a strong comeback from the scandal associated with Jesse Jackson's 1984 bid for the presidency, when he launched plans to lead a Million Man March on Washington, DC. Also billed as a day of atonement, the march took place on October 16, with some 400,000 from around the nation in attendance. The march took a decidedly more conservative and Black Power approach of demanding leadership from Black men and community accountability rather than government action to address racial inequality.

The Million Man March followed on the heels of what proved to be one of the costliest riots in U.S. history. Urban rebellions, which have become less frequent, share with their predecessors in the 1960s a connection to incidents of police brutality and vigilante violence. In 1981, for instance, Miami, Florida erupted in racial violence after an incident of police brutality. Three years before the Million Man March in April of 1992, South Central Los Angeles also exploded in violence after an all-white jury failed to indict four officers accused in the beating of Black motorist Rodney King. In March of the previous year, a resident captured the brutal beating administered to King by the officers on videotape. The footage of the incident along with widely circulated photographs of King's injuries confirmed for many the stories of racially fueled police misconduct. King's traffic stop came during a national debate over the controversial practice of racial profiling. The riot, which resulted in 53 fatalities and over a billion dollars in property damage, focused attention on police brutality and the criminalization of Black and Brown bodies in urban spaces.[8]

The acquittals of the officers involved in the King beating, for instance, came less than two weeks before a Korean storeowner, Soon Ja Du, received a 10-year suspended sentence for the killing of Latasha Harlins, a 15-year-old African American girl. In the encounter captured on a store surveillance camera, Du shot Harlins in the back of the head after accusing her of stealing a bottle of juice. Harlins' case was in some ways lost in the shadow of the King beating, but nonetheless central in the rioting that followed.[9]

Los Angeles was not the only site where simmering frustrations erupted into violence. In April 2001, rioting occurred in Cincinnati, Ohio after a patrol officer shot 19-year-old Timothy Thomas. A jury later acquitted the officer involved in the fatal shooting. Several high profile killings of Black people by police from 2005 to 2015, most notably in New York City, also drew attention to police brutality. In November of 2006, five New York City police officers shot Sean Bell 50 times after an incident outside a nightclub. In April of 2008, amid calls for citywide protests, a jury acquitted the three officers indicted in the killing on all counts. In January of 2009, an Oakland, California transit officer shot Oscar Grant in the back after detaining him for his alleged involvement in an altercation on a subway car. Grant died seven hours later. His killing spawned protests both in the Bay area and beyond demanding an end to police violence against young men of color.

The killing of 17-year-old Trayvon Martin in Sanford, Florida in February of 2012 reignited the debate over violence against African American youth. Martin's killer, George Zimmerman, a self-proclaimed neighborhood watch captain, confronted the teen while he was returning to the home of his father and stepmother in a gated community. He admitted to following the youth because he deemed him suspicious and continued to do so even after a police dispatcher told him to stop. A predominately white jury nevertheless acquitted him of any wrongdoing. Two years later, in July of 2014, cell phone camera footage surfaced of a Staten Island police officer administering a choke hold that ended the life of 44-year-old Eric Garner as he repeatedly gasped, "I can't breathe." In the month following Garner's death, the shooting of Ferguson, Missouri teen Michael Brown for jaywalking heightened racial tensions and led to a nationwide awareness campaign called Black Lives Matter. Although conducted largely on social media, the campaign also included mass demonstrations in New York, Missouri, and Washington, DC after grand juries in both cases failed to return indictments against the officers involved. A few violent altercations between police and protesters flared but, for the most part, demonstrators remained nonviolent. There was a clear effort on the part of some demonstrators to distance themselves from contemporary Civil Rights leaders such as the Reverend Al Sharpton who they felt did not properly reflect their voice or issues. At the two large rallies, in New York and Washington, DC in December of 2014, veteran Civil Rights leaders contended with a new generation of activists inspired by but not constrained by the history of the movement or obedient to the leadership of the past.

In addition to racial profiling and other controversial policing practices a federal crackdown on drugs in the 1970s culminated in a national war on drugs also under Ronald Reagan, resulting in stiffer punishments for drug-related offenses that greatly contributed to rapid expansion of the nation's prison population disproportionately affecting young men of color. Over 60 percent of those incarcerated in the United States are racial and ethnic minorities, the greatest percentage of which is African American males; the incarceration rate for African Americans was approximately 3,074 per 100,000, an astonishing six times the national average.[10]

Increases in federal funding for state and local law enforcement agencies that pursued vigorous drug arrests incentivized policies like stop and frisk and racial profiling that targeted mostly young people of color. The fruits of these policies produced a 13-fold increase in those confined for drug law violations over the past 25 years. As a result, more African Americans endure some form of supervisory control, in jails, or prisons, on probation or parole than were enslaved in 1850. The problem remained especially acute in large urban centers. In certain cities, over half of working-age African American men faced some form of legalized discrimination due to encounters with the criminal justice system.

Millions of Black youth, particularly from poor and urban communities, have been taken into custody for minor nonviolent offenses. Even after leaving prison, they remained trapped by the system. Denied many of the basic rights, including the right to vote and the right to serve on juries, they existed primarily as second-class citizens. As convicted felons, they faced difficulties in securing employment and legal restrictions preventing them from receiving public assistance and access to education programs that might help facilitate the successful transition back to society. Even as Black voting power grew, especially in urban areas, Black elected officials made little impact as deindustrialization left city budgets in shambles.

Poverty and a lack of education played a critical role. Despite the optimism engendered by *Brown* v. *Board of Education*, the landmark decision produced very little desegregation. A decade after the court's ruling, schools remained highly segregated. As mechanisms to achieve racial balance such as busing reached northern cities, a massive white backlash and exodus out of the cities left schools understaffed, underfunded, and, predominately, Black. Even within integrated districts, the large percentage of Black students classified as "special education" or "emotionally disturbed" produced de facto segregation. Census data also continued to document significant dropout rates among Hispanic and Black men, at 14.7 percent and 9.6 percent, respectively. Access to higher education had also been a challenge. In 2011, a record 16.6 million students attended college—the largest number ever. However, the participation rates for African Americans and Latinos also remained below those of whites and Asians. A Pew Charitable Trusts study found that 40 percent of Black men between the ages of 20 and 35 did not complete high school and were more likely to end up in prison than employed. The school to prison pipeline has also had a destabilizing impact on Black families. With care partners and financial contributors removed from homes, in most cases dependent on more than one income, families fell deeper into poverty, further compromising already disrupted communities. Extensive poverty and unemployment, especially in the nation's cities, contributed to rampant urban gang violence fueled by the sale of narcotics that fed a Black homicide rate that far exceeded the national average.[11]

Conclusion

The legacy of 1950s and 1960s Black Freedom Struggles can be measured in changes to the political structure that guaranteed African Americans for the first time since Reconstruction the right to exercise their rights with the full support of the federal government. The social, economic, and political gains that accompanied these struggles profoundly affected African Americans and the nation. The passage of the Civil Rights Act of 1964, as the Voting Rights Act of 1965 and the 24th Amendment to the Constitution that eliminated the poll tax, solidified into law the hard-won battles waged in the name of racial equality. In the meantime, efforts to achieve racial balance in the schools demonstrated an early commitment to implement these changes through concrete political action. Needed correctives to address centuries of political and economic inequality emerged in government set-asides and affirmative action programs to aid women and African Americans in the job market.

The Black Power and Black Arts Movements, in the meantime, highlighted the need for pride and unity. The legacy of Black Power also found expression in college students' call for Black Studies programs, in revolutionary movements like the Black Panther Party for Self Defense, and a renewed interest in Black Nationalism. Black Power also posed a challenge to the next generation of leaders to find a way to reconcile its message of Black unity with King's message of racial integration, a struggle they continued to wrestle with.

The cultural production of both movements was also profound. The music that accompanied the Black Freedom Struggle of the 1950s and 1960s came to define the era. Music, art, drama, and painting both in support of and celebrating the movement have been significant. The popularity of spoken word poetry, for instance, can be traced to the pioneering work of the Black Arts Movement and poets like Amiri Baraka, the Last Poets, Sonia Sanchez, and Gill Scott-Heron.

Black Freedom Struggles have become the subjects of interpretation in movies and on television. An early wave of films such as *Mississippi Burning* (1988) rarely put Black people at the center of the struggle. That began to change in the 1990s with movies like Spike Lee's *Malcolm X* (1992) that made the fiery Muslim minister the centerpiece of his own story. In January of 2015 on the 50th anniversary of the Selma Movement, the movie *Selma* opened up in theaters across the United States. The film dramatized the campaign around the passage of the Voting Rights Act of 1965 and earned critical acclaim. Such praise was tempered by the reality of the critical blow to the legislation, which once served as the most important tool to protect Black voting rights.

In the case of *Shelby County* v. *Holder*, a five-member majority declared unconstitutional Section 4 of the VRA that determined the states and jurisdictions required to submit changes in their voting laws for pre-approval to the Justice Department. The decision surprised some. In 2006, Congress voted by a large margin (390 to 33) in the House and unanimously (98 to 0) in the Senate to reauthorize the Voting Rights Act of 1965 for an additional 25 years. Nearly every prominent Republican at the time endorsed the reauthorization as necessary and President George W. Bush invited key Civil Rights leaders to attend a ceremonial signing. Without "the continuation of the Voting Rights Act of 1965 protections," federal lawmakers concluded in 2006, "racial and language minority citizens will be deprived of the opportunity to exercise their right to vote, or will have their votes diluted, undermining the significant gains made by minorities in the last forty years."

But the election of Barack Obama in 2008 proved a critical turning point in the consensus achieved. After the 2010 midterm elections, Republican Party officials in dozens of states pushed through laws to restrict the right to vote by a number of means, including disfranchising ex-felons, requiring proof of citizenship, curtailing early voting, and mandating government-issued photo IDs to cast a ballot. All of the laws and rules disproportionately affected the very "racial and language minority citizens" Congress pledged to protect by reauthorizing the VRA. It was perhaps not surprising that the states that adopted many of these measures were also the ones covered by Section 5 that Attorney General Eric Holder called the "keystone of our voting rights." NAACP President Benjamin Jealous even more forcefully declared the efforts to repeal Section 5 as "the greatest attack(s) on voting rights since segregation." By 2012, however, the bipartisan consensus that had successfully sustained the Voting Rights Act for almost five decades buckled. Conservatives working furiously to have the Act declared unconstitutional. Three days after the 2012 presidential election in which voter suppression was widely reported, the Supreme Court agreed to hear a challenge to Section 5 of the Act, which compelled parts or all of 16 states with a history of racial discrimination in voting to clear election-related changes with the federal government.[12]

Writing for the majority, Chief Justice John Roberts insisted that racial discrimination in voting had been eliminated because of the Voting Rights Act. Citing statistics from the increased number of minority office holders, voter turnout and registration rates in preclearance districts, Roberts concluded, "Blatantly discriminatory evasions of federal decrees are rare." The court's ruling did not sit well with former Civil Rights activists such as Georgia Congressman and Movement veteran John Lewis. "These men that voted to strip the Voting Rights Act of its power, they never stood in unmovable lines," Lewis told MSNBC's Andrea Mitchell. "They never had to pass a so-called literacy test. It took us almost 100 years to get where we are today. So will it take another 100 years to fix it, to change it?"[13]

In March of 2015, the Justice Department released its final report on Ferguson, Missouri. While declining to press for federal charges in the case of a white police officer who shot and killed Michael Brown the report nevertheless cited significant instances of police brutality and violations of the Constitution in the treatment of African Americans more reminiscent of 1961 than 2015. The fact that the population of Ferguson was 65 percent Black and yet the police force was 95 percent white was just the tip of the iceberg in terms of signs of racial inequality and racialized policing documented by the report. Coming on the heels of the 50th anniversary of the Selma Campaign, it offered the strongest rebuke to Justice John Roberts' declaration of an America that had moved past the racial divisions and inequalities of the Civil Rights and Black Power eras.[14]

Using the Reverend Dr. King's 1967 comments about the goals of the Black revolution as a measure the 50th anniversary of the Selma Campaign also offered the opportunity for sober reflection on the progress made in the last half century. In spite of substantial gains, the nation seemed a long way from triumph over "racism, poverty, militarism, and materialism." Although visible signs of progress clearly manifested the nation's triumph over more overt forms of inequality tackled by the Civil Rights Movement, the underlying philosophical arguments that informed some of its most powerful spokespersons remain unaddressed. In spite of this, many Americans remain hopeful and optimistic that the nation will one day triumph over these issues, believing, as the Reverend Dr. Martin Luther King once observed, that "The arc of the moral universe is long, but it bends towards justice."[15]

Notes

1   Ella Baker quoted in Francis Shor, "Utopian Aspirations in the Black Freedom Movement: SNCC and the Struggle for Civil Rights, 1960–1965," *Utopian Studies* (2004): 176; see also Howard Zinn, *SNCC: The New Abolitionists* (Cambridge, MA: South End, 2002), 103.
2   For statistics on Black business gains see Kevin Brown, "This is a Time for Hope and Change," *Indiana Law Journal* 87 (2012): 431.
3   James R. Elliott and Jeremy Pais, "Race, Class, and Hurricane Katrina: Social Differences in Human Responses to Disaster," *Social Science Research* 35, no. 2 (2006): 295–321. Frank Rich, *The Greatest Story Ever Sold: The Decline and Fall of Truth From 9/11 to Katrina* (New York: Penguin Press, 2004); Douglas Brinkley and Kyf Brewer, *The Great Deluge: Hurricane Katrina, New Orleans, and the Mississippi Gulf Coast* (New York: Morrow, 2006); Raymond J. Burby, "Hurricane Katrina and the Paradoxes of Government Disaster Policy: Bringing about Wise Governmental Decisions for Hazardous Areas," *The Annals of the American Academy of Political and Social Science* 604, no. 1 (2006): 171–91; Michael Eric Dyson, *Come Hell or High Water: Hurricane Katrina and the Color of Disaster* (New York: Basic Books, 2006).
4   Kanye West's comments reported in Amy Alexander, *Uncovering Race: A Black Journalist's Story of Reporting and Reinvention* (Boston: Beacon Press, 2011), 136.

5   CNNMoney, "Black Unemployment: Highest In 27 Years," September 2, 2011. May 6, 2015.

6   Accessed March 18, 2015, at http://constitutioncenter.org/amoreperfectunion/docs/Race_Speech_Transcript.pdf.

7   Martin Luther King quoted in J. Selig, "America's Selective Remembering and Collective Forgetting of Martin Luther King, Jr.," *Spring: A Journal of Archetype and Culture* 78 (2007): 219–41.

8   Nicole Maurantonio, "Remembering Rodney King: Myth, Racial Reconciliation, and Civil Rights History," *Journalism & Mass Communication Quarterly* 91, no. 4 (2014): 740–55. *America: History and Life with Full Text*, EBSCO*host* (accessed May 6, 2015); Cassandra Chaney and Ray V. Robertson, "'Can We All Get Along?' Blacks' Historical and Contemporary (In) Justice With Law Enforcement," *Western Journal of Black Studies* 38, no. 2 (2014): 108–22.

9   Brenda Stevenson, *The Contested Murder of Latasha Harlins: Justice, Gender, and the Origins of the LA Riots* (New York: Oxford University Press, 2013).

10   See Heather Thompson, "Why Mass Incarceration Matters: Rethinking Crisis, Decline, and Transformation in Postwar American History," *Journal of American History* (December 2010); Michelle Alexander, *The New Jim Crow: Mass Incarceration In The Age Of Colorblindness* (New York: The New Press, 2012.)

11   Christian Henrichson and Ruth Delaney, "The Price of Prisons: What Incarceration Costs Taxpayers," *Federal Sentencing Reporter* 25, no. 1 (2012): 68–80; "Collateral Costs: Incarceration's Effect on Economic Mobility," Pew Charitable Trusts, 2010.

12   Adam Liptak, "Supreme Court Invalidates Key Part of Voting Rights Act," *New York Times*, June 25, 2013.

13   Erin Delmore, "John Lewis: SCOTUS 'stabbed' civil rights law 'in its very heart'" (msnbc.com), http://www.msnbc.com/andrea-mitchell/john-lewis-scotus-stabbed-civil-rights-law.

14   Deona Hooper, "Ferguson Proves the United States Justice System is Not Broken, but Working Perfectly as Designed," *Critical and Radical Social Work* 3, no. 1 (2015): 141–7.

15   Martin Luther King, Jr., "Love, Law, and Civil Disobedience," *New South* 16 (1961): 3–11.

BIBLIOGRAPHY

Books

Aldridge, Delores and Carlene Young. Eds. *Out of the Revolution: The Development of Africana Studies*. Lanham: Lexington Books, 2000.

Alexander, Amy. *Uncovering Race: A Black Journalist's Story of Reporting and Reinvention*. Boston: Beacon Press, 2011.

Alexander, Michelle. *The New Jim Crow: Mass Incarceration in the Age of Colorblindness*. New York: The New Press, 2012.

Ambrose, Stephen E. *Citizens Soldiers: The U.S. Army From the Normandy Beaches to the Bulge to the Surrender of Germany*. New York: Simon & Schuster, 1998.

Anderson, Jervis. *A. Philip Randolph: A Biographical Portrait*. Berkeley: University of California Press, 1986.

Bass, Paul and Douglas Rae. *Murder in a Model City*. New York: Basic Books, 2006.

Baum, Howell S. *Brown in Baltimore: School Desegregation and the Limits of Liberalism*. Ithaca: Cornell University Press, 2010.

Berger, Maurice. *For All the World to See: Visual Culture and the Struggle for Civil Rights*. New Haven: Yale University Press, 2010.

Biondi, Martha. *The Black Revolution on Campus*. Berkeley: University of California Press, 2012.

Biondi, Martha. *To Stand and Fight: The Struggle for Civil Rights in New York City*. Cambridge, MA: Harvard University Press, 2003.

Bogle, Donald. *Toms, Coons, Mulattoes, Mammies and Bucks*. New York: Continuum, 2001.

Boyd, Alamilla Nan and Horacio N. Roque Ramirez. Eds. *Bodies of Evidence: The Practice of Queer Oral History*. New York: Oxford University Press, 2012.

Bradley, Stefan M. *Harlem vs. Columbia University: Black Student Power in the Late 1960s*. Urbana: University of Illinois Press, 2009.

Branch, Taylor. *At Canaan's Edge: America in the King Years, 1965–68*. New York: Simon & Schuster, 2007.

Branch, Taylor. *Parting the Waters: America in the King Years 1954–63*. New York: Simon & Schuster, 2007.

Branch, Taylor. *Pillar of Fire: America in the King Years 1963–65*. New York: Simon & Schuster, 2007.

Breitman, George. Ed. *Malcolm X Speaks: Selected Speeches and Statements*. New York: Merit Publishers, 1965.

Brinkley, Douglas and Kyf Brewer. *The Great Deluge: Hurricane Katrina, New Orleans, and the Mississippi Gulf Coast*. New York: Morrow, 2006.

Broderick, Francis L. *Negro Leader in a Time of Crisis*. Palo Alto: Stanford University Press, 1959.

Brown, Scot. *Fighting for U.S.: Maulana Karenga, the US Organization, and Black Cultural Nationalism*. New York: New York University Press, 2003.

Brown, Scot. *The King Years: Historic Moments in the Civil Rights Movement*. New York: Simon & Schuster, 2013.

Brown-Nagin, Tomiko. *Courage to Dissent: Atlanta and the long History of the Civil Rights Movement*. New York: Oxford University Press, 2011.

Burns, Stewart. *Daybreak of Freedom: The Montgomery Bus Boycott*. Chapel Hill: University of North Carolina Press, 1997.

Bush, George H.W. *Speaking of Freedom: The Collected Speeches*. New York: Scribner, 2009.

Bush, Rod. *We Are Not What We Seem: Black Nationalism and Class Struggle in the American Century*. New York: New York University Press, 1999.

Bynum, Cornelius L. *A Phillip Randolph and the Struggle for Civil Rights*. Urbana: University of Illinois Press, 2010.

Cable, George Washington. *The Silent South, Together with the Freedman's Case in Equity and the Convict Lease System*. New York: C. Scribner's Sons, 1899.

Carmichael, Stokely. *Black Power: The Politics of Liberation in America*. New York: Random House, 1967.

Carmichael, Stokely. *Ready For Revolution: The Life and Struggles of Stokely Carmichael (Kwame Ture)*. New York: Simon & Schuster, 2003.

Carmichael, Stokely. *Stokely Speaks: From Black Power Back to Pan-Africanism*. New York: Vintage, 1971.

Carmichael, Stokely. *What We Want*. Santa Clara County Friends of SNCC, 1966.

Carson, Clayborne. Ed. *The Autobiography of Martin Luther King, Jr.* New York: Time Warner, 1998.

Carson, Clayborne. *The Eyes on the Prize Civil Rights Leader*. New York: Penguin Books, 1991.

Carter, David C. *The Music Has Gone out of the Movement: Civil Rights and the Johnson Administration, 1965–1968*. Chapel Hill: University of North Carolina Press, 2009.

Chang, Jeff. *Can't Stop, Won't Stop: A History of the Hip-Hop Generation*. New York: St. Martin's, 2005.

Churchill, Ward and Jim Vander Wall. *Agents of Repression – The FBI's Secret Wars Against the Black Panther Party and the American Indian Movement*. Boston: South End Press, 1990.

Cleaver, Eldridge. *Eldridge Cleaver: Post-Prison Writings and Speeches*. New York: Random House, 1969.

Cleaver, Eldridge. *Soul on Ice*. New York: Ramparts Press Inc., 1968.

Cobb Jr., Charles E. *This Nonviolent Stuff'll Get You Killed: How Guns Made the Civil Rights Movement Possible*. New York: Basic Books, 2014.

Cohen, Adam and Elizabeth Taylor. *American Pharaoh: Mayor Richard J. Daley-His Battle for Chicago and the Nation*. Boston: Little, Brown, 2000.

Collier, Bettye-Thomas and V.P. Franklin. Eds. *Sisters in the Struggle: African American Women in The Civil Rights—Black Power Movement*. New York: New York University Press, 2001.

Colston, Freddie C. *Dr. Benjamin E. Mays Speaks: Representative Speeches of a Great American Orator*. Lanham: University Press of America, 2002.

Conyers, James L. and Andrew P. Smallwood. Eds. *Malcolm X: A Historical Reader*. Durham, NC: Carolina Academic Press, 2008.

Countryman, Matthew J. *Up South: Civil Rights and Black Power in Philadelphia*. Philadelphia: University of Pennsylvania Press, 2005.

Craig, Tom and Robert Shogan. *The Detroit Race Riot of 1967*. Michigan: University of Michigan Press, 1989.

Cripps, Thomas. *Slow Fade to Black: The Negro in American Film, 1900–1942*. New York: Oxford University Press, 1977.

Crosby, Emilye J. *A Little Taste of Freedom: The Black Freedom Struggle in Claiborne County, Mississippi*. Chapel Hill: University of North Carolina Press, 2005.

Daley, Richard J. *His Battle for Chicago and the Nation*. Boston: Little, Brown, 2000.

Davis, Angela. *Angela Davis: An Autobiography*. New York: International Publishers, 1974.

Deburg, William Van L. *New Day in Babylon: The Black Power Movement and American Culture, 1965–1975*. Chicago: University of Chicago Press, 1992.

Dittmer, John. *The Good Doctors: The Medical Committee for Human Rights and the Struggle for Social Justice in Health Care*. New York: Bloomsbury Publishing USA, 2009.

Dittmer, John. *Local People: The Struggle for Civil Rights in Mississippi*. Chicago: University of Illinois Press, 1995.

Donner, Frank J. *The Age of Surveillance: The Aims and Methods of America's Political Intelligence System*. New York: Alfred Knopf.

Douglas, Davidson M. *Jim Crow Moves North: The Battle over Northern School Segregation, 1865–1964*. New York: Cambridge University Press, 2005.

Dyson, Michael Eric. *Come Hell or High Water: Hurricane Katrina and the Color of Disaster*. New York: Basic Books, 2006.

Enke, Anne. *Finding the Movement: Sexuality, Contested Space, and Feminist Activism*. Durham, NC: Duke University Press, 2007.

Erenrich, Susie. Ed. *Freedom Is a Constant Struggle: An Anthology of the Mississippi Civil Rights Movement*. Montgomery: Black Belt Press, 1999.

Eschen, Penny Von. *Satchmo Blows Up the World: Jazz Ambassadors Play the Cold War*. Cambridge, MA: Harvard University Press, 2004.

Eskew, Glenn T. *But for Birmingham: The Local and National Movements in the Civil Rights Struggle*. Chapel Hill: University of North Carolina Press, 1997.

Essien-Udom, E.U. *Black Nationalism: A Search for Identity in America*. Chicago: University of Chicago

Fairclough, Adam. *To Redeem the Soul of America: The Southern Christian Leadership Conference and Martin Luther King, Jr.* Athens, GA: University of Georgia Press, 1987.

Fairclough, Adam. *Race and Democracy: The Civil Rights Struggle in Louisiana, 1915–1972*. Athens: University of Georgia Press, 1995.

Fine, Sidney. *Violence in the Model City: The Cavanagh Administration, Race Relations, and the Detroit Riot of 1967*. Michigan: University of Michigan Press, 1989.

Feldstein, Ruth. *How it Feels to Be Free: Black Women Entertainers and the Civil Rights Movement*. New York: Oxford University Press, 2013.

Forman, Murray and Mark Anthony Neal. Eds. *That's the Joint! The Hip- Hop Studies Reader*. New York: Routledge, 2004.

Fricke, Jim and Charlie Ahearn. *Yes Yes Y'all: The Experience Music Project Oral History of Hip-Hop's First Decade*. Cambridge, MA: Da Capo Press, 2002.

Garrow, David J. *Bearing the Cross: Martin Luther King Jr., and the Southern Christian Leadership Conference*. New York: Vintage Books, 1988.

Garrow, David J. *The FBI and Martin Luther King Jr.: From "Solo" to Memphis*. New York: W.W. Norton & Company, 1981.

Garrow, David J. *Protest at Selma*. New Haven: Yale University Press, 1978.

Gilmore, Glenda. *Defying Dixie: The Radical Roots of Civil Rights, 1919–1950*. New York: W.W. Norton, 2008.

Gilmore, Ruth Wilson. *Golden Gulag: Prisons, Surplus, Crisis, and Opposition in Globalizing California*. Berkeley: University of California Press, 2007.

Glasker, Wayne. *Black Students in the Ivory Tower: African American Student Activism at the University of Pennsylvania, 1967–1990*. Amherst: University of Massachusetts Press, 2002.

Greenberg, Cheryl. *To Ask for an Equal Chance: African Americans in the Great Depression*. Lanham: Rowman & Littlefield, 2009.

Gregory, James. *The Southern Diaspora: How the Great Migration of Black and White Southerners Transformed America*. Chapel Hill: University of North Carolina Press, 2006.

Guerrero, E. Ed. *Framing Blackness: The African American Image in Film*. Philadelphia: Temple University Press, 1993.

Hall, Raymond. *Meet The Press*. Washington, DC: Merkle Press, 1966.

Hampton, Henry and Steve Fayer. *Voices of Freedom: An Oral History of the Civil Rights Movement from the 1950's through the 1980's*. New York: Bantam Books, 1991.

Harrington, Michael. *The Other America*. New York: Simon & Schuster, 1997.

Hedges, Chris. *Death of the Liberal Class*. New York: Nation Books, 2010.

Hernandez, Kelly Lytle. *MIGRA! A History of the U.S. Border Patrol*. Berkeley: University of California Press, 2010.

Hill, Lance Edward. *The Deacons for Defense: Armed Resistance and the Civil Rights Movement*. Chapel Hill: University of North Carolina Press, 2004.

Hine, Darlene Clark. *Hine Sight: Black Women and the Reconstruction of American History*. Bloomington: Indiana University Press, 1997.

hooks, bell. *Reel to Real: Race, Sex, and Class at the Movies*. New York: Routledge, 1996.

Hoose, Phillip and Claudette Colvin. *Twice toward Justice*. New York: Farrar, Straus and Giroux, 2009.

Horne, Gerald. *Black and Red. W.E.B. Du Bois and the Afro-American Response to the Cold War, 1944 1963*. Albany: State University of New York Press, 1985.

Horne, Gerald. *Fire This Time: The Watts Uprising and the 1960s*. Charlottesville: University of Virginia Press, 1995.

Houck, Davis W. and David E. Dixon. Eds. *Women and the Civil Rights Movement, 1954–1965*. Jackson: University Press of Mississippi, 2009.

Jackson, George. *Soledad Brother: The Prison Letters of George Jackson*. Chicago: Chicago Review Press, 1970.

Jackson, Mandi. *Model City Blues*. Philadelphia: Temple University Press, 2008.

James, Winston. *The Struggles of John Brown Russwurm: The Life and Writings of Pan-Africanist Pioneer, 1799–1851*. New York: New York University Press, 2010.

James Jr., Rawn. *The Double V: How Wars, Protest and Harry Truman Desegregated America's Military*. New York: Bloomsbury Publishing USA, 2013.

Jeffries, Hasan Kwame. *Bloody Lowndes: Civil Rights and Black Power in Alabama's Black Belt*. New York: New York University Press, 2009.

Jones, Patrick. *The Selma of the North: Civil Rights Insurgency in Milwaukee*. Cambridge, MA: Harvard University Press, 2010.

Joseph, Peniel E. Ed. *The Black Power Movement: Rethinking the Civil Rights–Black Power Era*. New York: Routledge, 2006.

Joseph, Peniel E. *Stokely: A Life*. New York: Basic Civitas, 2014.

Joseph, Peniel E. *Stokely Carmichael*. New York: Perseus Books Group, 2014.

Joseph, Peniel E. *Waiting 'Til the Midnight Hour: A Narrative History of Black Power in America*. New York: Macmillan, 2007.

Kahrl, Andrew W. *The Land Was Ours; African American Beaches from Jim Crow to the Sunbelt South*. Cambridge, MA: Harvard University Press, 2012.

Kelly, Blair L.M. *Right to Ride: Streetcar Boycotts and African American Citizenship in the Era of Plessy v. Ferguson*. Chapel Hill: University of North Carolina Press, 2010.

Kelley, Robin D.G. *Africa Speaks, America Answers: Modern Jazz in Revolutionary Times*. Cambridge, MA: Harvard University Press, 2012.

King Jr., Martin Luther. *Chicago and the Civil Right Movement*. Cambridge, MA: Harvard University Press, 1993.

King Jr., Martin Luther. *Where Do We Go From Here: Chaos or Community?* Boston: Beacon Press, 2010.

King Jr., Martin Luther. *Why We Can't Wait*. New York: Penguin Books, 2000.

Klinkner, Philip A. and Rogers M. Smith. *The Unsteady March: The Rise and Decline of Racial Equality in America*. Chicago: University of Chicago Press, 1999.

Kluger, Richard. *Simple Justice: The History of Brown v. Board of Education and Black America's Struggle for Equality*. New York: Vintage, 2004.

Kohl, Herbert. *She Would Not Be Moved: How We Tell the Story of Rosa Parks and the Montgomery Bus Boycott*. New York: The New Press, 2005.

Kornbluh, Felicia. *The Battle for Welfare Rights: Politics and Poverty in Modern America*. Philadelphia: University of Pennsylvania Press, 2007.

Kostad, Robert. *Civil Rights Unionism*. Chapel Hill: University of North Carolina Press, 2003.

Kruse, Kevin M. and Stephen Tuck. Eds. *The Fog of War: The Second World War and the Civil Rights Movement*. New York: Oxford University Press, 2012.

Kruse, Kevin M. and Stephen Tuck. *White Flight: Atlanta and the Making of Modern Conservatism*. Princeton: Princeton University Press, 2002.

Leab, Daniel. *From Sambo to Superdpade: The Black Experience in Motion Pictures*. Boston: Houghton Mifflin, 1975

Lesher, Stephan. *George Wallace: American Populist*. New York: Addison Wesley Publishing, 1994.

Levine, Daniel and Bayard Rustin. *The Civil Rights Movement*. New Jersey: Rutgers University Press, 2000.

Levin, Lawrence. *Black Culture and Black Consciousness*. New York: Oxford University Press, 1977.

Levy, Peter. *Civil War on Race Street: The Civil Rights Movement in Cambridge, Maryland*. Gainesville: University Press of Florida, 2003.

Lewis, David Levering. *W.E.B. Du Bois: The Fight for Equality and the American Century, 1919–1963*. New York: Henry Holt, 2000.

Lin, Peter and Sharon Monteith. Eds. *Gender and the Civil Rights Movement*. New Brunswick: Rutgers University Press, 2004.

Lokos, Lionel. *House Divided*. New Rochelle: Arlington House, 1968.

Makalani, Minkah. *In the Cause of Freedom: Radical Internationalism from Harlem to London, 1917–1939*. Chapel Hill: University of North Carolina Press, 2011.

Malcolm X. *The Autobiography of Malcolm X*. New York: Grove Press, 1966.

Manis, Andrew. *A Fire You Can't Put Out: The Civil Rights Life of Birmingham's Reverend Fred Shuttlesworth*. Tuscaloosa: University of Alabama Press, 1999.

May, Gary. *Bending Toward Justice: The Voting Rights Act and the Transformation of American Democracy*. New York: Basic Books, 2013.

McAdam, Doug. *Freedom Summer*. New York and Oxford: Oxford University Press, 1988.

McDuffie, Erik S. *Sojourning for Freedom: Black Women, American Communism, and the Making of Black Left Feminism*. Durham, NC: Duke University Press, 2011.

McGuire, Danielle. *At the Dark End of the Street: Black Women, Rape and Resistance— A New History of the Civil Rights Movement From Rosa Parks to the Rise of Black Power*. New York: Knopf, 2010.

McWhorter, Diane. *Carry Me Home: Birmingham, Alabama, the Climactic Battle of the Civil Rights Revolution*. New York: Simon & Schuster, 2001.

Meir, August, Elliot Rudwick, and John H. Bracey. Eds. *Black Protest In the Sixties*. New York: Marches Wimer, 1991.

Meyer, Stephen Grant. *As Long As They Don't Move Next Door: Segregation and Racial Conflict in American Neighborhoods*. Boston: Rowman & Littlefield, 2000.

Monson, Ingrid. *Freedom Sounds: Civil Rights Call Out to Jazz and Africa*. New York: Oxford University Press, 2006.

Morris, Aldon D. *The Origins of the Civil Rights Movement: Black Communities Organizing for Change*. New York: The Free Press, 1984.

Moses, Wilson Jeremiah. Ed. *Classical Black Nationalism: From the American Revolution to Marcus Garvey*. New York: New York University Press, 1996.

Moye, Todd J. *Freedom Flyers: The Tuskegee Airmen of World War II*. Cambridge: Oxford University Press, 2010.

Muhammad, Khalil. *The Condemnation of Blackness: Ideas about Race and Crime in the Making of Modern Urban America*. Cambridge, MA: Harvard University Press, 2010.

Mumford, Kevin. *Newark: A History of Race, Rights and Riots in America*. New York: New York University Press, 2007.

Murch, Donna Jean. *Living for the City; Christian Parenti, Lockdown America; Police and Prisons in the Age of Crisis*. New York: Verso, 1999.

Murch, Donna Jean. *Living for the City: Migration, Education, and the Rise of the Black Panther Party in Oakland, California*. Chapel Hill: University of North Carolina Press, 2010.

Myrdal, Gunnar. *An American Dilemma: The Negro Problem and the American Democracy*. New York: Harper, 1944.

Neal, Marc Anthony. *What the Music Said: Black Popular Music and Black Public Culture*. New York: Routledge, 1999.

Nelson, Alondra. *Body and Soul: The Black Panther Party and the Fight against Medical Discrimination*. Minneapolis: University of Minnesota Press, 2011.

Nelson, Lichtenstein. *A Contest of Ideas: Capital, Politics, and Labor*. Urbana: University of Illinois Press, 2014.

Nelson Jr., William. Ed. *Black Studies: From Pyramids to Pan-Africanism*. New York: McGraw Hill, 2001.

Norrell, Robert J. *Reaping the Whirlwind: The Civil Rights Movements in Tuskegee*. New York: Alfred A. Knopf, 1985.

Ogbar, Jeffrey O.G. *Black Power: Radical Politics and African American Identity*. Baltimore: Johns Hopkins University Press, 2004.

O'Reilly, Kenneth. *Racial Matters: The FBI's Secret File on Black America, 1960–1972*. New York: Free Press, 1989.

Payne, Charles M. *I've Got the Light of Freedom: The Organizing Tradition and the Mississippi Freedom Struggle*. Berkeley, CA: University of California Press, 1995.

Perkinson, Robert. *Texas Tough: The Rise of a Prison Empire*. New York: Metropolitan Books, 2010.

Perry, Jeffrey B. Ed. *A Hubert Harrison Reader*. Middletown: Wesleyan University Press, 2001.

Perry, Jeffrey B. *Hubert Harrison: The Voice of Harlem Radicalism, 1883–1918*. New York: Columbia University Press, 2009.

Plummer, Brenda Gayle. *In Search of Power: African Americans in the Era of Decolonization, 1956–1974*. Cambridge: Cambridge University Press, 2013.

Porter, Eric. *What Is This Thing Called Jazz? African American Musicians as Artists, Critics, and Activists*. Berkeley: University of California Press, 2002.

Ransby, Barbara. *Ella Baker and the Black Radical Tradition*. Chapel Hill: University of North Carolina Press, 2003.

Rich, Frank. *The Greatest Story Ever Sold: The Decline and Fall of Truth From 9/11 to Katrina*. New York: Penguin Press, 2004.

Roberts, Gene. *Black Protests in the Sixties,* edited by August Meir. New York: Marches Wimer, 1991: 153.

Robinson, Dean E. *Black Nationalism in American Politics and Thought*. Cambridge: Cambridge University Press, 2001.

Rogers, Ibram H. *The Black Campus Movement: Black Students and the Racial Reconstitution of Higher Education, 1965–1972*. New York: Palgrave Macmillan, 2012.

Rojas, Fabio. *From Black Power to Black Studies: How a Radical Social Movement Became an Academic Discipline*. Baltimore: Johns Hopkins University Press, 2007.

Rout, Kathleen. *Eldridge Cleaver (Book 583)*. New York: Twayne Publishing, 1991.

Rustin, Bayard. *Down the Line*. Chicago: Quadrangle Books, 1971.

Rustin, Bayard and John D'Emilio. *Lost Prophet: The Life and Times of Bayard Rustin*. New York: Free Press, 2003.

Sales, William. *From Civil Rights to Black Liberation*. Boston: South End Press, 1994

Sims, Yvonne D. *Women of Blaxploitation: How the Black Action-Film Heroine Changed American*. New York: McFarland, 2006.

Sitkoff, Harvard. *A New Deal for Blacks: The Emergence of Civil Rights as a National Issue: The Depression Decade*. New York: Oxford University Press, 1981.

Sitkoff, Harvard. *King: Pilgrimage to the Mountaintop*. New York: Macmillan, 2008.

Sitkoff, Harvard. *The Struggle for Black Equality 1954–1980*. New York: Hill & Wang, 1981.

Slate, Nico. *Black Power Beyond Borders: The Global Dimensions of the Black Power Movement*. New York: Palgrave Macmillan, 2012.

Smethurst, James E. *The Black Arts Movement: Literary Nationalism in the 1960s and 1970s*. Chapel Hill: University of North Carolina Press, 2005.

Smith, Suzanne E. *Dancing in the Street: Motown and the Cultural Politics of Detroit*. Cambridge, MA: Harvard University Press, 1999.

Smith, Valerie. Ed. *Representing Blackness: Issues in Film and Video*. New Brunswick: Rutgers University Press, 1997.

Sokol, Jason. *There Goes My Everything: White Southerners in the Age of Civil Rights, 1945–1975*. New York: Vintage, 2008

Solomon, Mark. *The Cry was Unity: Communist and African Americans, 1917–36.* Jackson: University of Mississippi Press, 1998.

Stanton, Mary. *From Selma to Sorrow: The Life and Death of Viola Liuzzo.* Athens: University of Georgia Press, 2000.

Stevenson, Brenda. *The Contested Murder of Latasha Harlins: Justice, Gender, and the Origins of the LA Riots.* New York: Oxford University Press, 2013.

Strain, Christopher. *Pure Fire: Self-Defense as Activism in the Civil Rights Era.* Athens: University of Georgia Press, 2005.

Sugrue, Thomas J. *The Origins of the Urban Crisis: Race and Inequality in Postwar Detroit.* Princeton: Princeton University Press, 2014.

Sugrue, Thomas J. *Sweet Land of Liberty. The Forgotten Struggle for Civil Rights in the North.* New York: Random House, 2008.

Sullivan, Patricia. *Days of Hope: Race and Democracy in the New Deal Era.* Chapel Hill: University of North Carolina Press, 1996.

Sullivan, Patricia. *Lift Every Voice: The NAACP and the Making of the Civil Rights Movement.* New York: The New Press, 2009.

Taylor, Clarence. *Reds at the Blackboard: Communism, Civil Rights, and the New York City Teachers' Union.* New York: Columbia University Press, 2011.

Theoharis, Jeanne. T*he Rebellious Life of Mrs. Rosa Parks.* Boston: Beacon Press, 2013.

Theoharis, Jeanne F. and Komozi Woodard. Eds. *Freedom North: Black Freedom Struggles Outside the South, 1940–1980.* New York: Palgrave Macmillan, 2003.

Theoharis, Jeanne F. and Komozi Woodard. *Groundwork: Local Black Freedom Movements In America.* New York: New York University Press, 2005.

Thompson, Heather Ann. *Whose Detroit? Politics, Labor, and Race in a Modern American City.* New York: Cornell University Press, 2004.

Tibbs, Donald F. *From Black Power to Prison Power: The Making of Jones V. North Carolina Prisoners' Labor Union.* New York: Palgrave Macmillan, 2012.

Ture, Kwame and Ekueme Michael Thelwell. *Ready For Revolution: The Life and Struggles of Stokely Carmichael (Kwame Ture).* New York: Scribner, 2003.

Tyson, Timothy B. *Radio Dixie: Robert F. Williams and the Roots of Black Power.* Chapel Hill: University of North Carolina Press, 1999.

Umoja, Akinyele Omowale. *We Will Shoot Back: Armed Resistance in the Mississippi Freedom Movement.* New York: New York University Press, 2013.

Ward, Brian. *Just My Soul Responding: Rhythm and Blues, Black Consciousness and Race Relations.* Berkeley: University of California Press, 1998.

Watkins, Craig. *Representing: Hip Hop Culture and the Production of Black Cinema.* Chicago: University of Chicago Press, 1998.

Watson, Bruce. *Freedom Summer: The Savage Season That Made Mississippi Burn and Made America a Democracy.* New York: Viking, 2010.

Wendt, Simon. *The Spirit and the Shotgun: Armed Resistance and the Struggle for Civil Rights.* Gainesville: University of Florida Press, 2007.

Werner, Craig. *Higher Ground: Stevie Wonder, Aretha Franklin, Curtis Mayfield, and the Rise and Fall of American Soul.* New York: Crown Publishers, 2004.

White, Shane and Graham White. *Stylin': African American Expressive Culture from its Beginnings to the Zoot Suit.* Ithaca: Cornell University Press, 1998.

Whitfield, Stephen J. *A Death in the Delta: The Story of Emmett Till.* Baltimore: Johns Hopkins University Press, 1988.

Wicker, Tom. *A Time To Die: The Attica Prison Revolt.* Lincoln: University of Nebraska Press, 1994.

Williams, Donnie and Wayne Greenhaw. *The Thunder of Angels: The Montgomery Bus Boycott and the People Who Broke the Back of Jim Crow*. New York: Lawrence Hill, 2005.

Williams, Rhonda Y. *Concrete Demands: The Search for Black Power in the 20th Century*. New York: Taylor & Francis, 2015.

Williams, Rhonda Y. *The Politics of Public Housing: Black Women's Struggles Against Urban Inequality*. New York: Oxford University Press, 2004.

Williams, Yohuru R. *Black Politics/White Power: Civil Rights, Black Power, and the Black Panthers in New Haven*. New York: Branywine, 2000.

Williams, Yohuru and Jama Lazerow. Eds. *Liberated Territory: Untold Local Perspectives on the Black Panther Party*. Durham, NC: Duke University Press, 2008.

Williams, Yohuru and Jama Lazerow. Eds. *In Search of the Black Panther Party: New Perspectives on a Revolutionary Movement*. Durham, NC: Duke University Press, 2006.

Williamson, Joy Ann. *Black Power on Campus, The University of Illinois, 1965–75*. Urbana: University of Illinois Press, 2003.

Wiltse, Jeff. *Contested Waters: A Social History of Swimming Pools in America*. Chapel Hill: University of North Carolina Press, 2007.

Woodard, Komozi A. *A Nation Within A Nation – Amiri Baraka (Leroi Jones) and Black Power Politics*. Chapel Hill: University of North Carolina Press, 1999.

Woodley, Jenny. *Art for Equality: The NAACP's Cultural Campaign for Civil Rights*. Lexington: University Press of Kentucky, 2014.

Woodson, Carter G. and Jacqueline Goggin. *Carter G. Woodson: A Life in Black History*. Baton Rouge: Louisiana University Press, 1993.

Woodward, C. Vann. *The Strange Career of Jim Crow: A Commemorative Edition*. New York and Oxford: Oxford University Press, 2002.

Young, Cynthia. *Soul Power: Culture, Radicalism, and the Making of a U.S. Third World Left*. Durham, NC: Duke University Press, 2006.

Zinn, Howard. *SNCC: The New Abolitionist*. Boston: Beacon Press, 2002.

Articles

Allen Jr., Ernest. "'When Japan was champion of the darker races': Satokata Takahashi and the Flowering of Black Messianic Nationalism." *The Black Scholar* (1994): 23–46.

Bond, George C. and St. Clair Drake. "A Social Portrait of John Gibbs St. Clair Drake." *American Ethnologist* 15, no. 4 (1988): 762–81.

Brooks, Justin. "How Can We Sleep While the Beds Are Burning? The Tumultuous Prison Culture of Attica Flourishes in American Prisons Twenty-Five Years Later." *Syracuse L. Rev.* 47 (1996): 159.

Brown, Kevin. "This is a Time for Hope and Change." *Indiana Law Journal* 87 (2012): 431.

Burby, Raymond J. "Hurricane Katrina and the Paradoxes of Government Disaster Policy: Bringing about Wise Governmental Decisions for Hazardous Areas." *The Annals of the American Academy of Political and Social Science* 604, no. 1 (2006): 171–91.

Carmichael, Stokely and Kwame Ture. "Power and Racism: What We Want." *The Black Scholar* (1997): 52–7.

Chambers, Bradford. "Negro Leaders Dividing." *U.S. News and World Report*, July 18, 1966, 4.

Chaney, Cassandra and Ray V. Robertson. "'Can We All Get Along?' Blacks' Historical and Contemporary (In) Justice With Law Enforcement." *Western Journal Of Black Studies* 38, no. 2 (2014): 108–22.

Cha-Jua, Suandiata Keita and Clarence Lang. "The 'Long Moment' as Vampire: Temporal and Spatial Fallacies in Recent Black Freedom Studies." *Journal of African American History* 92 (2007).

Cleaver, Kathleen Neal. "Racism, Civil Rights, and Feminism." In *Critical Race Feminism: A Reader*, edited by Adrien Katherine Wing. New York: New York University Press, 1997, 36.

CNNMoney. "Black Unemployment: Highest In 27 Years," May 6. 2015. http:// constitutioncenter.org/amoreperfectunion/docs/Race_Speech_Transcript.pdf.

Conni, Brian. "8. The Prison Writer as Ideologue: George Jackson and the Attica Rebellion." In *Prose and Cons: Essays on Prison Literature in the United States*, edited by Quentin Miller (North Carolina: McFarland and Company, 2005), 147.

Crosby, Emilye J. "You Got a Right to Defend Yourself: Self-Defense and the Claiborne County, Mississippi Civil Rights Movement." *The International Journal of Africana Studies: The Journal of the National Council for Black Studies, Inc.* (2003): 133–63.

Cunnigen, Donald. "Bringing the Revolution Down Home: The Republic of New Africa in Mississippi." *Sociological Spectrum* 19, no. 1 (1999): 63–92.

Dagbovie, Pero Gaglo. "Making Black History Practical and Popular: Carter G. Woodson, the Proto Black Studies Movement and the Struggle for Black Liberation." *Western Journal of Black Studies* 27, no. 4 (2003).

Davenport, Christian. "Understanding Covert Repressive Action: The Case of the U.S. Government Against the Republic of New Africa." *Journal of Conflict Resolution* 49, no. 1 (2005): 120–40.

Delmore, Erin. "John Lewis: SCOTUS 'stabbed' civil rights law 'in its very heart'". Accessed July 2, 2015 at http://www.msnbc.com/andrea-mitchell/john-lewis-scotus-stabbed-civil-rights-law.

Doss, Erika. "Imaging the Panthers: Representing Black Power and Masculinity, 1960s–1990s." *Prospects* 23 (1998): 483–51.

Doss, Erika. "Revolutionary Art Is a Tool for Liberation." In *Liberation, Imagination, and the Black Panther Party: A New Look at the Panthers and Their Legacy*, edited by Kathleen Cleaver and George N. Katsiaficas. New York: Routledge, 2001, 183.

Doss, Erika. "'Revolutionary art is a tool for liberation': Emory Douglas and Protest Aesthetics at the Black Panther." *New Political Science* 21, no. 2 (1999): 245–59.

Du Bois, W.E.B. "Criteria of Negro Art." *The Crisis* (October 1926): 290–7.

Elliott, James R. and Jeremy Pais, "Race, Class, and Hurricane Katrina: Social Differences in Human Responses to Disaster." *Social Science Research* 35, no. 2 (2006): 295–321.

Ernest-LeBlanc. Angela D. "'The Most Qualified Person to Handle the Job': Black Panther Party Women, '1966–1982." In *The Black Panther Party Reconsidered*, edited by Charles Earl Jones. Baltimore: Black Classic Press, 1998, 305–34.

Eschen, Penny Von. "Rethinking Politics and Culture in a Dynamic Decade." *OAH Magazine of History* 26, no. 4 (October 2012): 9.

Fairclough, Adam. "Historians and the Civil Rights Movement." *Journal of American Studies* 24, no. 3 (1990): 387–98.

Fitzgerald, Michael W. "'We Have Found a Moses': Theodore Bilbo, Black Nationalism, and The Greater Liberia Bill of 1939." *The Journal of Southern History* (1997): 203–320.

Fleming, K. "Heat on the Highway." *Time* (1966): 7.

Fleming, K. "March Meredith Began." *Newsweek* (1966): 30.

Fleming, K. "Walk in South to Conquer Old Fears." *Life* (1966): 30–5.

Forman, James. "American Civil Rights Activist and Author Former Executive Secretary of the Student Nonviolent Coordinating Committee (SNCC)." *Biography Today: Profiles of People of Interest to Young Readers* 14 (2005): 119.

Franklin, V.P. and Bettye Collier-Thomas. "Biography, Race Vindication, and African American Intellectuals." *The Journal of African American History* (2002): 160–74.

Gaines, Kevin. "The Civil Rights Movement in World Perspective." *OAH Magazine of History* 21 (October 2006): 14–18.

Garland, Phyl. "Is the Afro on Its Way Out?" *Ebony Magazine* 28, no. 4 (February 1973): 128.

Garrow, David J. "The Voting Rights Act in Historical Perspective." *The Georgia Historical Quarterly* (1990): 377–98.

Goldman, Peter. "Malcolm X: Witness for the Prosecution." In *Black Leaders of the Twentieth Century*, edited by John Hope Franklin and August Meier. Illinois: University of Illinois Press, 1982, 325.

Green, James R. and Hayden, Robert C. "A. Philip Randolph and Boston's African-American Railroad Worker." *Trotter Review* 6, no. 2 (1992).

Hall, Jacquelyn Dowd. "The Long Civil Rights Movement and the Political Uses of the Past." *Journal of American History* 91, no. 4 (March 2005).

Harrison, Faye V. "The Du Boisian Legacy in Anthropology." *Critique of Anthropology* 12, no. 3 (1992): 246.

Henrichson, Christian and Ruth Delaney. "The Price of Prisons: What Incarceration Costs Taxpayers." *Federal Sentencing Reporter* 25, no. 1 (2012): 68–80.

Higginbotham, Michael F. "Soldiers For Justice: The Role for the Tuskegee Airman in the Desegregation of the American Armed Forces." *William & Mary Bill of Rights Journal* 8, no. 2 (2000): 273.

Hooper, Deona. "Ferguson Proves the United States Justice System is Not Broken, but Working Perfectly as Designed." *Critical and Radical Social Work* 3, no. 1 (2015): 141–7.

Joseph, Peniel E. "The Black Power Movement: A State of the Field." *The Journal of American History* 96, no. 3 (2009): 775.

Joseph, Peniel E. "Dashikis and Democracy: Black Studies, Student Activism, and the Black Power Movement." *The Journal of African American History* (2003): 182–203.

Joseph, Peniel E. "Malcolm X's Harlem and Black Power Activism." In *Neighborhood Rebels*, edited by Peniel Joseph. New York: Palgrave Macmillan, 2009.

Joseph, Peniel E. "Revolution in Babylon: Stokely Carmichael and America in the 1960s 1." *Souls* 9, no. 4 (2007): 281–301.

King Jr., Martin Luther. "Crisis in the Civil Rights Leadership." *Ebony* (November 1, 1966): 30.

King Jr., Martin Luther. "Love, Law, and Civil Disobedience." *New South* 16 (1961): 3–11.

King Jr., Martin Luther. "MIA Mass Meeting at Holt Street Baptist Church." In *The Papers of Martin Luther King, Jr., Volume 2: Rediscovering Precious Values*, edited by Clayborne Carson and Peter H. Holloran. Berkeley: University of California Press, 1994, 72.

King Jr., Martin Luther. "Nonviolence: The Only Road to Freedom." *Ebony* (October 1966): 30.

King Jr., Martin Luther. "Riots, Battles, Power Marches; It's Still a Hot Summer." *U.S. News and World Report* (1966): 7.

Korstad, Robert and Nelson Lichtenstein. "Opportunities Found and Lost: Labor, Radicals and the Early Civil Rights Movement." *Journal of American History* 75 (1988): 786–811.

Lincoln, C. Eric. "The Black Revolution in Cultural Perspective." *Union Seminary Quarterly Review* 23, no. 3 (Spring 1968): 221.

Lipstiz, George. "Frantic to Join ... the Japanese ... the Asia Pacific War." In *Perilous Memories: The Asia Pacific War(s)*, edited by T. Fujitani, Geoffrey M.L. White, and Lisa Yoneyama. Durham, NC: Duke University Press, 2001, 347–77.

Liptak, Adam. "Supreme Court Invalidates Key Part of Voting Rights Act." *New York Times,* June 25, 2013.

Lopez, Robert Oscar. "The Colors of Double Exceptionalism-The Founders and African America." *Literature Compass* 5, no. 1 (2008): 20–41.

Lumumba, Chokwe. "Short History of the U.S. War on the Republic of New Africa." *Black Scholar* 12 (January–February 1981).

Mahan, Sue. "An 'Orgy of Brutality' at Attica and the 'Killing Ground' at Santa Fe: A Comparison of Prison Riots." *Prison Violence in America* 2 (1994): 92–127.

Mamo, Andrew B. "'The Dignity and Justice that Is Due to Us by Right of Our Birth': Violence and Rights in the 1971 Attica Riot." *Harvard Civil Rights-Civil Liberties Law Review* (CR-CL) 29, no. 2 (2014).

Matthews, Tracye. "No One Ever Asks, What a Man's Place in the Revolution Is: Gender and the Politics of the Black Panther Party, 1966–1971." In *The Black Panther Party Reconsidered*, edited by Charles Earl Jone. Baltimore: Black Classic Press, 1998, 270.

Maurantonio, Nicole. "Remembering Rodney King: Myth, Racial Reconciliation, and Civil Rights History." *Journalism & Mass Communication Quarterly* 91, no. 4 (2014): 740–55.

McCone, John A., and W. M. Christopher. "Violence in the City—An End or a Beginning? A Report by the Governor's Commission on the Los Angeles Riots." Los Angeles: State of California, Governor's Commission on the Los Angeles Riots, 1965.

McDuffie, Erik S. "'For full freedom of ... colored women in Africa, Asia, and these United States': Black Women Radicals and the Practice of a Black Women's International." *Palimpsest: A Journal on Women, Gender, and the Black International* 1, no. 1 (2012): 1–30.

McDuffie, Erik S. "'I wanted a Communist movement, but I wanted to have the chance to organize our people': The Diasporic Radicalism of Queen Mother Audley Moore and the Origins of Black Power." *African and Black Diaspora: An International Journal* 3, no. 2 (2010): 181–95.

Meier, August and Elliot Rudwick. "The Boycott Movement Against Jim Crow Streetcars in the South 1900–1906." *The Journal of American History* 55, no. 4 (March 1969): 756–75.

Murch, Donna Jean. "The Campus and the Street: Race, Migration, and the Origins of the Black Panther Party in Oakland, CA." *Souls* 9, no. 4 (2007): 333–45.

Murch, Donna Jean. "The Many Meanings of Watts: Black Power, Wattstax, and the Carceral State." *OAH Magazine of History* 26, no. 1 (2012): 37–40.

Nance, Susan. "Respectability and Representation: The Moorish Science Temple, Morocco, and Black Public Culture in 1920s Chicago." *American Quarterly* 54, no. 4 (2002): 623–59.

Neal, Larry. "The Black Arts Movement," Drama Review, 12: Summer 1968. In James Cone, *Black Theology and Black Power.* New York: Seabury Press, 1969.

"Negro Leaders Dividing." *U. S. News and World Report* (July 1966): 4.

Pauley, Garth E. "'John Lewis's Serious Revolution': Rhetoric, Resistance, and Revision at the March on Washington." *Quarterly Journal of Speech* 84, no. 3 (1998): 320–40.

Peltonen, Kirsi, Noora Ellonen, Helmer B. Larsen, and Karin Helweg-Larsen. "Parental Violence and Adolescent Mental Health." *European Child & Adolescent Psychiatry* 19, no. 11 (2010): 813–22.

"Report of the National Advisory Commission on Civil Disorders." *US Government Printing Office*, March 1968.

Rosenberg, Rosalind. "The Conjunction of Race and Gender." *Journal of Women's History* 13, no. 2 (2002): 68–73.

Rowan, CT. "Crisis in the Civil Rights Leadership." *Ebony* (November 1966): 30.

Rustin, Bayard. "The Watts 'Manifesto' & The McCone Report." *Commentary* 41, no. 3 (1966): 29–35.

Sachs, Ethan. "A State and Its Prison: The Attica Riot of 1971 and Untold Stories Since." Ph.D. diss., University of Michigan, 2012.

Selig J.L. "America's Selective Remembering and Collective Forgetting of Martin Luther King, Jr." *Spring: A Journal of Archetype and Culture* 78 (2007): 219–41.

Shor, Francis. "Utopian Aspirations in the Black Freedom Movement: SNCC and the Struggle for Civil Rights, 1960–1965." *Utopian Studies* (2004): 176.

Simone, Nina. "Culture, and Black Activism in the 1960s." *The Journal of American History* 91, no. 4 (March 2005): 1349–79.

"Strange March through Mississippi." *U.S. News and World Report* (1966): 48.

Strickland, William. "The Gary Convention and the Crisis of American Politics." *Black World* 21, no. 12 (1972): 18–26.

Taylor, Arnold H. "America's Second Civil War: Review of Fred Powledge. *Free At Last? The Civil Rights Movement and the People Who Made It*." *Book World* (1991).

Thompson, Heather Ann. "Why Mass Incarceration Matters; Rethinking Crisis, Decline, and Transformation in PostwarAmerican History." *Journal of American History* (December 2010): 703–34.

Thompson, Heather Ann. "Rethinking Working-Class Struggle through the Lens of the Carceral State: Toward a Labor History of Inmates and Guards." *Labor* 8, no. 3 (2011): 15–45.

Thompson, Heather Ann. "Urban Uprisings: Riots or Rebellions." In *The Columbia Guide to America in the 1960s*, edited by David Farber and Beth Bailey. New York: Columbia University Press, 2001.

Tyson, Timothy B. "Robert F. Williams, Black Power, and the Roots of the African American Freedom Struggle." *Journal of American History* (1998): 540–41.

Welch, Rebeccah. "Black Art and Activism in Postwar New York, 1950–1965." Ph.D. diss., New York University, 2002.

Wendt, Simon. "Protection or Path Toward Revolution? Black Power and Self-Defense." *Souls* 9, no. 4(2007): 320–32.

Wendt, Simon. "They Finally Found Out That We Really Are Men: Violence, Non-Violence, and Black Manhood in the Civil Rights Era." *Gender & History* 19, no. 3 (2007): 543–64.

Williams, Rhonda Y. "Black Women and Black Power." *OAH Magazine of History* 22, no. 3 (2008): 22–6.

Williams, Yohuru R. "In the Name of the Law: The 1967 Shooting of Huey Newton and Law Enforcement's Permissive Environment." *Negro History Bulletin* 61, no. 2 (1998): 6–18.

Williams, Yohuru R. "'They've lynched our savior, Lumumba in the old fashion Southern style': The Conscious Internationalism of American Black Nationalism." In *Black Beyond Borders*, edited by Nico Slate. New York: Palgrave Macmillan, 2012.

Williams, Yohuru R. "'A Red, Black and Green Liberation Jumpsuit': Roy Wilkins, the Black Panthers, and the Conundrum of Black Power." In *The Black Power Movement: Rethinking the Civil Rights Black Power Era*, edited by Peniel Joseph. New York: Routledge, 2006, 174.

Court Cases

Berea College v. *Kentucky*, 211 U.S. 45 (1908) (Supreme Court).
Brown v. *Board of Education of Topeka*, 347 U.S. 483 (1954) (Supreme Court).
Katzenbach v. *McClung*, 379 U.S. 294 (1964) (Supreme Court).
Shelley v. *Kraemer*, 334 U.S. 1 (1948) (Supreme Court).

Media

Eyes on the Prize II: America at the Racial Crossroads 1965–1985. Directed by Hampton, Henry, Judith Vecchione, Julian Bond, and Steve Fayer. Alexandria, VA: PBS Video 1989. DVD.
Kennedy, John F. "Radio and Television Report to the American People on Civil Rights." John F. Kennedy Library and Museum, 1963.
Melvin Van Peebles and the Black Panthers. Directed by Joe Angio. Web. March 13, 2015. Accessed July 2, 2015, at http://www.mvpmovie.com/?BlackPanthers.
Miles College's Lucius Pitts, Malcolm X discuss Birmingham on ABC News; 15,000 march in San Francisco (May 26, 1963). Accessed July 2, 2015, at http://blog.al.com/birmingham-newsstories/2013/05/miles_colleges_lucius_pitts_ma.html.

INDEX

Abernathy, Ralph David 21–2
actors 102
Affirmative Action 115–16
Afro hairstyle 88, 93, 94
Afro-Asian Conference, First 51
Alabama: Governors 26, 35–6, 44; *see also* Birmingham; Montgomery; Selma
Albany, Georgia (1961–2) 29–32
Ambrose, Stephen 15
Anderson, William 30, 31
Annapolis march (1942) ix–x
armed resistance 52–6
Armstrong, Louis 90
arts/cultural productions 87–8; 1950s and 1960s 91–3; Black Arts Movement xxii, 11, 76, 92, 100; Black Power 91, 92–3, 99–100; Black Studies 95–6; fashion (dress and hair) 88, 93–4; film 89, 100–2, 104–5, 119; hip-hop 103–4; music 88, 90, 92, 96–9, 101–2, 103–4; preconditions for change 88–91; religion 94–5; television 102–3

Back to Africa Movement 12
Baez, Joan 97, 98
Baker, Ella 25, 27, 29, 108, 114
Baldwin, James 74
Baltimore and Annapolis march ix–x
Baraka, Amiri 76–7, 92, 100
Barkley, L.D. 75
Bates, Daisy 38–9
Birmingham, Alabama (1963) 32–9

Birth of a Nation (film) boycott 100
Black Arts Movement xxii, 11, 76, 92, 100
Black Guerrilla Family 71, 72
Black history 89–90, 95–6
Black homeland 51, 69; Back to Africa Movement 12; Republic of New Africa (RNA) 77–8
Black Internationalism xix–xx, 55
Black Nationalism 12, 50, 53, 55, 68–9
Black Panther Party (BPP) 57, 65–7, 69, 70–1, 94, 99–100
Black Power 4, 49–52; and armed resistance 52–6; on campus 56–7; Chicago and Meredith March 60–5; and Civil Rights Movement xx–xxi; Conferences 76–9; music and arts 91, 92–3, 99–100; predecessors and origins 1–17; prisoners 70–5; and Public Enemy (rap group) 104; racial solidarity 94; and Rainbow Coalition 111–12; and urban unrest 57–60; women 50, 67–70, 72–4
Black Studies 95–6
Black Theater 92–3
Black Women's Club Movement 6–7, 8
Blackwell, Unita 42
Blaxploitation 100, 101
Broadus, Thomas ix
Brown, Elaine 68, 69
Brown, James 99, 104
Brown, Michael 117, 121
Brown v. Board of Education xi–xii, 2, 19–20, 21, 26, 27

Burroughs, Williana Jones 50
buses *see* transport segregation
Bush, George H.W. 103, 115–16
Bush, George W. 110

Cable, George Washington 5
Carmichael, Stokely 61–2, 63–5, 67–8, 76, 78, 114
Carroll, Diahann 102
Carson, Clayborne 2, 39
Carter, Alprentice "Bunchy" 66
Chang, Jeff 103
Chavez, Cesar 87
Chicago and Meredith March 60–5
citizenship: construction of 4–5; "Double V" campaign 13
Civil Rights Acts: (1875) 5; (1957–1965) 18–19, 42
Civil Rights Bill (1960s) 36, 38, 39, 40–1
Civil Rights Movement: and Black Power xx–xxi; periodization and parameters xi–xiv; predecessors and origins 1–17
Civil War 4; second 18–48
Clark, Mark 67
Clarke, John Henrik 95
Cleage, Jr., Albert 94
Cleaver, Eldridge 70–1, 114
Cleaver, Kathleen 68
Clinton, Bill 116
Collins Harvey, Claire 28
Communism/Marxism 50–1, 56, 57, 71
Congress of Racial Equality (CORE) 27, 28, 30, 37–8, 41, 63–4
Connor, Eugene "Bull" 33–4, 35
Council of Confederated Organizations (COFO) 40, 41, 42
Crosby, Emilye 53
Cultural Association for Women of African Heritage (CAWAH) 91–2
cultural productions *see* arts/cultural productions

Daley, Richard J. (Mayor of Chicago) 60–1
Davis, Allison 96
Davis, Angela 49, 72–4, 113–14
Democratic National Conventions 41–2, 111
Detroit: Motown Records 88, 98–9; riots 54, 58–60, 77
Diggs, Irene 96
Diggs, Jr., Charles C. 37, 52
Douglas, Emory 99–100
Drake, John Gibbs St. Clair 95–6

Dred Scott 4, 5–6
dress 93–4
Drew, Timothy (Prophet Noble Drew Ali) 11–12
drug-related offenses 117–18
Du Bois, W.E.B. 7, 8, 9, 10, 11, 55, 87, 88–9, 91, 95, 96
Duke Ellington 89
Dylan, Bob 97, 98

education 26–7, 118–19, 121; Affirmative Action 115; Black Panthers 67; Black Power 56–7; Black Studies 95–6; Freedom training/schools 40, 41; higher xxi–xxii, 6, 8–9, 36; school segregation (*Brown v. Board of Education*) xi–xii, 2, 19–20, 21, 26, 27
elected officials/politicians 111–12
employment/unemployment 110–11; Equal Employment Opportunities Commission 115–16; Fair Employment Practices Commission (FEPC) 13–14
Evers, Medgar 37, 52

Farmer, James 27–8, 38
Farrakhan, Louis 112, 116
fashion (dress and hair) 88, 93–4
Federal Bureau of Investigation (FBI) 67, 74, 78, 102
Feldstein, Ruth 52
Ferguson, Missouri: shooting of Michael Brown 117, 121
film 89, 100–2, 104–5, 119
Fortune, T. Thomas 6
Freedom Rides (1960–5) 27–9, 38

Garland, Phyl 93
Garner, Eric 117
Garvey, Amy Jacques 53
Garvey, Marcus 7, 11, 12, 50, 53, 55, 96
Gary Convention 78–9
Gay Rights Movement 114
Gaye, Marvin 99
Goldman, Peter 62
Gordon, Mittie Maud Lena 12
Grandmaster Flash and the Furious Five 103
Gray, Victoria 42
Great Depression 12–13
Great Migration 10
Great Society programs 60

Haarlem Renaissance ("New Negro Movement") 10–11, 50, 89

Haley, Alex 102–3
Hall, Jacqueline Dowd 19
Hamer, Fannie Lou 42, 114
Hampton, Fred 67
Hansberry, Lorraine 98
Harlan, Justice John Marshall 9
Harlem Writers Guild 91
Harrington, Michael 58
Harrison, Hubert 50, 89, 91
Herndon, Angelo 50–1
hip-hop 103–4
Holloway, Lucius 29–30
homeownership 110
Hoover, J. Edgar 67
House of Un-American Activities
  Committee 51
Huggins, Ericka 67, 71
Huggins, Jon 66, 67
Hughes, Langston 89, 97–8
Hutton, Bobby 66

internationalism *see* Black Internationalism;
  Pan-Africanism

Jackson, Cager 43
Jackson, George 71–2, 74–5, 114
Jackson, Jesse 61, 78–9, 111–12, 116
Jackson, Mahilia 96–7
jazz 90, 97
Johnson, Lyndon B./administration 39, 41,
  42, 43, 44, 45, 60
Joseph, Peniel 50, 55, 91
justice, bending towards 113–19

Karenga, Maulana 76–7, 94
Kennedy, John F./administration 29, 32,
  34–7, 39
King, Reverend Martin Luther xiv, 3–4,
  18–19, 20, 121; Albany 31–2; on
  American society 113; Anti-War
  Movement 114; assassination 2, 26, 66;
  biblical texts 94; Birmingham 33–4, 35;
  and Black Power 54, 56, 62, 63, 65–6,
  67; Chicago 60–1; "I Have a Dream"
  speech 38; imprisonment 31–4; March
  on Washington 36–7, 38; Mississippi 41;
  Montgomery 23, 24–5, 26, 44–5; Nobel
  Peace Prize 42; and President Johnson
  41, 44; self-defense vs nonviolence 54,
  56; Selma 43; Watts rebellion 58
King, Rodney 104, 116, 121
Kitt, Eartha 102
Korstad, Robert 2

Krenn, Michael 34
Ku Klux Klan 4, 35, 45

leaders and organizations xiv–xvi
Lee, Herbert 40
Lee, Reverend George 40
Lee, Spike 104, 119
legacies 108–21
Lewis, John 1, 2, 38, 43–4, 62, 120
Lewis, Rufus 22–3
Lincoln, C. Eric 92
Liuzzo, Viola 45
lynching 10, 21

McKay, Claude 11, 89
Malcolm X xv, 35, 37, 42, 50; and Black
  Internationalism 55; film 104, 119;
  influence 57, 62, 67, 70, 77, 114; music
  and arts 91; speeches 53, 55–6
March on Washington 13–14, 36–7, 38–9,
  96–7
Martin, Trayvon 117
Marxism/Communism 50–1, 56, 57, 71
Maryland: Annapolis march (1942) ix–x;
  local movement 37–8
Mathews, Tracye 69, 70
Mays, Reverend Benjamin 26
Meredith, James 61, 63–4
Meredith March 60–5
military service 10, 14–15
Million Man March 116
Mississippi: Freedom Summer (1964)
  39–42; violent deaths 37, 40, 41, 52
Mississippi Freedom Democratic Party
  (MFDP) 40, 41–2
Montgomery, Alabama (1955–6): bus
  incident and boycott 3, 20, 21–7
Montgomery Improvement Association
  (MIA) 21–6
Moore, Audley Eloise (Queen Mother)
  68–9
Moore, William 52
Moorish Science Temple 11–12, 96
Morris, Aldon 2
Moses, Robert 39–40, 41
Motown Records 88, 98–9
Muhammad, Elijah 12
music 88, 90, 92, 96–9, 101–2, 103–4

Nation of Islam (NOI) 8, 12, 51, 94–5, 112
National Association for the Advancement
  of Colored People (NAACP) ix, x, 8,
  9–10, 14, 20, 21, 25; and film 100, 101;

Freedom Rides 27; legislative victories 45; murders of activists 37, 40; music and art 90–1; self-defense vs nonviolence 54; and SNCC 30; women 38–9
Neal, Larry 92
New Deal 13, 21
"New Negro Movement" (Harlem Renaissance) 10–11, 50, 89
New Orleans hurricane 109–10
Newton, Huey 49, 57, 65–6, 71, 100, 101
Niagara Movement 8, 9
Nichols, Nichell 102
non-violent direct action 18–21, 24–5, 26–7, 38, 45; police responses 30–1, 32, 33–4, 43–4; *vs* self-defense/armed resistance 52–6; *see also* Student Non Violence Coordination Committee (SNCC)
Northern states: migration and segregation xviii–xix

Obadele, Imari Abubakari 77, 78
Obama, Barack 108, 111, 112–13, 120, 121

Pan-Africanism 11, 55, 95–6; *see also* Black Internationalism
Parks, Rosa 3, 21, 22, 25
Patterson, John (Alabama Governor) 26
Payne, Charles 18, 39
Plessy v. Ferguson 6, 8–9
poets/writers 11, 91, 92
police: and Black Panthers 66–7; FBI 67, 78, 102; practices 116–18, 121; responses to non-violent direct action 30–1, 32, 33–4, 43–4; *see also* riots
politicians/elected officials 111–12
poverty and racial inequality 115–16, 118–19
Powledge, Fred 24
prisoners: Black Power 70–5; drug-related offenses 117–18; Martin Luther King 31–4; rights xxii–xxiii, 113–14
Public Enemy 104

racial inequality 115–16, 118–19
racial solidarity 94
Rainbow Coalition 111–12
Randolph, A. Philip 1, 10, 13–14, 36–7, 91
Reagan, Ronald 115, 117–18
Reagon, Bernice 97
Reagon, Cordell 30, 97
Reconstruction 1, 2, 12

Reeb, James 44
religion 94–5
repatriation 12
Republic of New Africa (RNA) 77–8
Revolutionary Action Movement (RAM) 57
Richardson, Gloria 37–8
riots: Detroit 54, 58–60, 77; Red Summer 10, 11; response to police practices 116–18; Springfield 9; Watts (1965) 57–8, 59–60
Roach, Max 97
Robeson, Paul 51
Robinson, Dean 50
Robinson, Jackie 3, 14, 105
Robinson, Jo Ann 22–3
Roosevelt, F.D. 12–13, 14
Roots: The Saga of an American Family (Haley) 102–3
Ross, Diana 88, 92
Rush, Bobby 111
Rustin, Bayard xvii, 21, 25, 59–60, 64–5, 114

sampling 103–4
Seale, Bobby 57, 65–6, 71, 100
segregation 6, 8–10; contemporary 109–10; Northern states xviii–xix; school (*Brown v. Board of Education*) xi–xii, 2, 19–20, 21, 26, 27; Six Degrees of xiii, 51, 53, 54, 108; *see also* transport segregation
self-defense, armed resistance as 52–6
Selma, Alabama (1965) 43–5, 105, 119, 121
separate but equal doctrine 7–8
Shelby County v. Holder 1
Sherrod, Charles 30
Shuttlesworth, Fred 33, 35
Simone, Nina 52, 87, 88, 97–8
Sitkoff, Harvard 19–20
Six Degrees of Segregation xiii, 51, 53, 54, 108
Smiley, Reverend Glenn 25
Smith, Ruby Doris 67–8
Smith, Suzanne 98–9
Soledad Brothers 71, 74
Southern Christian Leadership Conference (SCLC) 18; Albany 31–2; Birmingham 32–3, 34; March on Washington 36–7; and SNCC 25, 27, 43, 60–5
"Star Trek" (TV series) 102
student direct action campaigns 26–7, 29, 61–2

Student Non Violence Coordination Committee (SNCC) 28, 29–30, 31, 37–8; Mississippi 39–40; as "New Abolitionists" 19; and SCLC 25, 27, 43, 60–5; sexism 73
Supremes 88, 92, 98
Sweetback's Baadasssss Song (film) 101

Taylor, Arnold 19, 21
television 102–3
Terrell, Mary Church 7, 8
Thomas, Clarence 115–16
Thomas, Timothy 117
Till, Emmett 21
transport segregation 5, 6, 8; Albany, Georgia 29–32; Freedom Rides (1960-5) 27–9, 38; Montgomery, Alabama 3, 20, 21–7
Turner, Henry McNeal 5–6

Umoja, Emilye Crosby Akinyele 53–4, 94
unemployment *see* employment/ unemployment
Universal Negro Improvement Association (UNIA) 7–8, 11, 12, 50, 96
universities/colleges *see* education; *entries beginning* student
urban unrest: and Black Power 57–60; *see also* riots
U.S. Constitutional Amendments 4–6
U.S. Supreme Court 4–6

Van Deburg, William 49 50, 64
Van Peebles, Melvin 101, 104
Vietnam War 44, 60, 61, 98, 114
violence *see* armed resistance; lynching; non-violent direct action; police; riots

voting: registration 28, 29, 30, 40–1, 43; rights 1, 9, 42
Voting Rights Act (1965) 1, 18, 45, 119–20

Wallace, George (Alabama Governor) 35–6, 44
Ward, Stephen 70
Warden, Donald 57
Washington, Booker T. 7–8
Washington, March on 13–14, 36–7, 38–9, 96–7
Watts rebellion (1965) 57–8, 59–60
Wells-Barnett, Ida B. 6
West, Kanye 110
white responses xviii, 62–3
Wilkins, Roy 64–5
Williams, Rhonda Y. x–xi, 50, 51, 67, 68
Williams, Robert F. 54–5, 56, 57, 62, 68, 69
Wilson, Mary 98
Womanpower Unlimited 28
women: Black Power 50, 67–70, 72–4; Black Women's Club Movement 6–7, 8; Cultural Association for Women of African Heritage (CAWAH) 91–2; gender, and sexuality xvi–xvii; Liberation Movement critique 70, 114; NAACP 38–9; Political Council (WPC), Montgomery 23
Wonder, Stevie 99, 101–2
Woodley, Jen 90–1
Woodson, Carter 95, 96
Woodward, C. Van 6
World War I 10–11, 14
World War II 13–15
Wright, Nathan 77
Wright, Reverend Jeremiah 112
writers/poets 11, 91, 92

Zinn, Howard 19